IRISH LAW TEXTS

CONTRACT

GW00471903

AUSTRALIA

The Law Book Company Ltd.
Sydney : Melbourne : Brisbane

CANADA AND U.S.A.

The Carswell Company Ltd.
Agincourt, Ontario

INDIA

N. M. Tripathi Private Ltd.
Bombay
and
Eastern Law House Private Ltd.
Calcutta and Delhi
M.P.P. House
Bangalore

ISRAEL

Steimatzky's Agency Ltd.
Jerusalem : Tel Aviv : Haifa

MALAYSIA : SINGAPORE : BRUNEI

Malayan Law Journal (Pte.) Ltd.
Singapore

NEW ZEALAND

Sweet & Maxwell (N.Z.) Ltd.
Auckland

PAKISTAN

Pakistan Law House
Karachi

IRISH LAW TEXTS

CONTRACT

by

ROBERT CLARK, B.A., LL.M. (LOND.)

Lecturer in Law, Faculty of Law,
University College, Dublin

LONDON
SWEET & MAXWELL
1982

Published in 1982 by
Sweet & Maxwell Ltd. of
11 New Fetter Lane, London
Photoset by Promenade Graphics Ltd., Cheltenham
Printed in Scotland

Second Impression 1983

British Library Cataloguing in Publication Data

Clark, Robert
   Contract.—(Irish law texts)
   1. Contracts—Ireland—Law.
   I. Title II. Series
   344.1706′2   KDK 370

   ISBN 0–421–28540–0

All rights reserved.
No part of this publication may be
reproduced or transmitted, in any form
or by any means, electronic, mechanical, photocopying,
recording or otherwise, or stored in any retrieval
system of any nature, without the written permission
of the copyright holder and the publisher, application
for which shall be made to the publisher.

©
Sweet & Maxwell
1982

Introduction

Both Irish jurisdictions have long suffered from the problems associated with the lack of a developed local legal literature. This lack of development has been particularly acute in the Republic of Ireland, where it is only in the last few years that any works at all have appeared in the main fields of law and where many gaps still remain. The combination of the small market for law books in the Republic and a considerable lag between the achievement of political independence and the emergence of a corpus of indigenous law deterred the production of legal literature. For many years law students and the legal profession made do with the older editions of English textbooks or else did without. In Northern Ireland, the problems were never so acute since the local law generally kept pace with changes in Britain. Nevertheless, there are also significant differences between the available works on English law and procedure and the law taught and practised in that jurisdiction.

Over the last two decades a variety of factors has brought about change. In the first place there is a much greater output of local law both in legislation and through court decisions. The number of students in the universities and other third level colleges who are studying law has increased enormously. There has also been a proportionate increase in the numbers engaged in the full-time teaching of law with correspondingly a greater number of academic lawyers available to undertake research and writing. The size of the legal profession has doubled in both jurisdictions in the last decade.

One happy result of the new circumstances has been the coincidence of acute concern about the dearth of works devoted to Irish law and sufficient local demands to encourage authors to write and publishers to publish. It was in these circumstances that *Irish Law Texts* was conceived. Modelled on Sweet & Maxwell's *Concise College Texts*, it is the first series devoted exclusively to Irish law. The series aims to produce reasonably priced short works on the main fields of Irish law to meet the needs of the broadest student population. The first two titles, *Contract* and *Business Law*, have been written therefore not only with university students in mind, but also students of law, business and related subjects in the regional technical colleges, the National Institutes of Higher Education, and the professional schools. Since these two titles are the first books to be written on these areas of Irish law, the practising lawyer and other professions will also find them of considerable value.

Books in the series will be concerned primarily with the law of the Republic of Ireland, which is the larger Irish jurisdiction and the one which has seen the greatest changes in legal principles and statute law from Britain. However, wherever possible, reference will be made to the law of Northern Ireland, particularly the decisions of the courts. *Irish Law Texts* therefore hopes to make a contribution to the needs of students and the professions in both parts of the island.

Other titles in the series are planned, including a book on Irish Company Law.

Kevin Boyle
University College Galway

Preface

In this book I have endeavoured to concisely and accurately state the rules and principles which comprise and shape the Law of Contract in Ireland. These rules and principles do not in the main radically differ from those developed by the English judiciary and in the absence of wholesale legislative changes since 1922, cynics may question the validity of a work constructed upon the premise that there is an Irish Law of Contract. There are several responses to such an observation. The Irish Judiciary even before 1922 occasionally differed from their English brethren on important issues of policy; Irish case law on unconscionability, improvident contract and undue influence, for instance is unusually rich and instructive. Contemporary Irish developments that are of essential importance to students and practitioners include the subject to contract controversy and the sweeping changes initiated by the 1980 legislation on the sale of goods and supply of services. The effects of the 1937 Constitution on common law contract rules are also of importance. I have been especially concerned to identify and explain judicial decisions from both parts of Ireland in the hope that Irish lawyers and judges will follow Irish decisions where they are in point. I have also used several Commonwealth authorities particularly where they seem to produce a result which is more desirable than the prevailing Irish and English rules.

I wish to thank the **Arthur Cox Foundation** for providing financial assistance to me while I researched this book. Professor Kevin Boyle and the staff of Sweet and Maxwell provided encouragement and advice at crucial stages. Anna Sforza and Bernadette Bradley transformed my handwritten notes into quite splendid typed manuscript in record time. My colleagues Paul O'Connor and Tony Kerr helped me to obtain essential material, particularly copies of unreported judgments.

The need to preserve domestic harmony no doubt explains why many academics acknowledge, in prefaces, the assistance given by their spouses. In this case my wife, Alice provided immeasurable help by condoning repeated acts of desertion as well as my failure to contribute substantially to the first six months of our son's development.

Robert Clark

January 1982

To Alice and Robbie

For Alice and Kolore

Contents

Table of Cases

Table of Statutes

Irish Statutes

(iii) *Acts of the Oireachtas*

Other Jurisdictions

Northern Ireland

United Kingdom

United Kingdom—cont.

Table of References to Irish Constitution

Table of Abbreviations

Irish Reports and Journals

Alc. & Nap.	Alcock and Napier, King's Bench reports, 1831–33
Alc. Reg. Cas.	Alcock, Registry Cases, 1832–41
Arm. Mac. & Og.	Armstrong, Macartney and Ogle, **Nisi Prius** Reports, 1840–42
Ba. & B.	Ball and Beatty, Chancery Reports, 1802–9
Batty	Batty, King's Bench Reports, 1825–26
Beat.	Beaty, Chancery Reports, 1813–30
Con. & L.	Connor and Lawson, Chancery Reports, 1841–43
Cr. & Dix.	Crawford and Dix, Cases on the Circuits, 1839–46
Cr. & Dix, Abr. Cas.	Crawford and Dix, bridged Notes on Cases, 1837–46
Dru. *emp*. Nap.	Drury, Select Cases during the time of Lord Napier, 1858–59
Dru. *temp* Sug.	Drury, Report of Cases during the time of Chancellor Sugden, 1843–44
Dr. & Wal.	Drury and Walsh, Chancery Reports during the time of Lord Plunket, 1837–40
Dr. & War.	Drury and Warren, Chancery Reports during the time of Lord Sugden, 1841–43
D.U.L.J.	Dublin University Law Journal 1966– (current)
Fl. & K.	Flanagan and Kelly, Chancery (Rolls) eports, 1840–42
Hayes	Hayes, Exchequer Reports, 1830–32
Ir.Ch.R.	Irish Chancery Reports, 1850–66
Ir.Cir.Rep.	Irish Circuit reports (Cases on the Six Circuits), 1841–43
I.C.L.R.	Irish Common Law Reports, 1849¾466
Ir.Eq.R.	Irish Equity Reports, 1838–51
Ir. Jur.	Irish Jurist 1935–65
Ir. Jr. (N.S.)	Irish Jurist (N.S.) 1966– (current)
Ir.Jur.(os.)	Irish Jurist Reports (Old Series), 1849–55
Ir.Jur.(N.S.)	Irish Jurist Reports (New Series), 1855–66
Ir.Jur.Rep.	Irish Jurist Reports, 1935–65
Ir.L.R.	Irish law Reports, Common Law, 1838–50
I.L.R.M.	Irish Law Reports Monthly 1981– (current)
I.L.T.R.	Irish Law Times Reports, 1867–(1980). (*Note*: notes or digests only of cases in the Irish law Times and Solicitors Journal are signified by the reference "I.L.T. or "I.L.T.S.J."").
I.R.	Irish Reports, 1894–(current)
I.R.C.L.	Irish Reports, Common Law, 1867–77
I.R.Eq.	Irish reports, Equity, 1866–77
Ir. Term Rep.	Irish term Reports (Ridgeway, lapp and Schoales), 1793–95
Jebb & B.	Jebb and Bourke, Queen's Bench reports, 1842–42
Jebb & Sym.	Jebb and Symes, Queen's Bench Reports, 1838–41
Jo. & Lat.	Jones and Latouche, Chancery Reports, 1844–46
Jon.	Jones, Exchequer Reports, 1834–38
L.R.(Ir.)	Law Reports, (Ireland), 1878–93

Moll.	Molley, Chancery Reports, 1827–31
N.I.J.R.	New Irish Jurist Reports, 1900–5
N.I.	Northern Ireland Law Reports, 1925–(current)
N.I.L.Q. (N.S.)	Northern Ireland Legal Quarterly (New Series) Vol. 1 1960– (current)
Ridgw.P.C.	Ridgeway, Parliamentary Reports, 1784–96
Sch. & Lef.	Schoales and Lefroy, Chancery Reports, 1802–6
Sm. & Bat.	Smith and Batty, King's Bench Reports, 1824–25
Vern. & Scriv.	Vernon and Scriven, Irish Reports, 1786 88

Court References

C.A.N.I.	Court of Appeal Northern Ireland
C.C.	Circuit Court
Ch.D.N.I.	Chancery Division Northern Ireland
Co. Ct.	County Court
E.A.T.(Eng.)	Employment Appeals Tribunal, England
E.A.T.(Itl.)	Employment Appeals Tribunal, Ireland
E.C.A.	English Court of Appeal
E.Ch.D.	English Chancery Division
E.C.P.	English Common Places
E.Ec.	English Exchequer
E.Ex.Ch.	English Exchequer Chambers
E.K.B.	English Kings Bench
E.Q.B.	English Queens Bench
E. Rolls C.	English Rolls Court
H.C.	High Court
H.L.	House of Lords
Ir.C.A.	Irish Court of Appeal
Ir.Ch.D.	Irish Chancery Division
Ir.C. of Ch.	Irish Court of Chancery
Ir.C.P.	Irish Common Pleas
Ir.Ex.	Irish Court of Exchequer
Ir.Ex.Ch.	Irish Exchequer Chamber
Ir.K.B.	Irish Kings Bench
Ir.Q.B.	Irish Queens Bench
Ir. Rolls C.	Irish Rolls Court
K.B.N.I.	Kings Bench Northern Ireland
N.P.	Nisi Privs
P.C.	Privy Council
S.C.	Supreme Court

Part 1

Formation of a Binding Contract

1   The Rules of Offer and Acceptance

The primary characteristic of a binding contract is one of bargain. Generally, the common law rules on the enforceability of promises entitle members of society to expect that a promise will be enforced by the courts or made the subject of monetary compensation because the promise was made in the context of an exchange relationship. In other words, the common law does not normally make a promise binding as a contract simply because the promise was made. By the same token once a promise is made in return for another promise or some requested action it is generally unnecessary for the promise to be made or evidenced in writing.

As a result it has become necessary to create rules on the formation of contract that enable judges to view everyday incidents and actions as having legal consequences. The rules of offer and acceptance for example are designed to determine whether the parties have reached agreement on the subject-matter, price and other material terms or whether the parties remain locked in negotiation, still edging their way towards agreement.

Many contractual relationships are forged almost instantaneously. By stepping on a bus or buying a newspaper for example we enter into a contract and in this context it seems artificial to isolate these transactions into separate stages. Lord Wilberforce, a senior English judge remarked during a complex dispute where it seemed obvious to him that a bargain should be enforced that the only problem was to make the facts amenable to the rules on formation. "It is only the precise analysis of this complex of relations into the classical offer and acceptance with identifiable consideration that seems to present difficulty, but this same difficulty exists in many situations of daily life, *e.g.* sales at auction, supermarket purchases; boarding an omnibus; purchasing a train ticket, tenders for the supply of goods; offers of rewards; acceptance by post. . . . These are all examples which show that English law, having committed itself to a rather technical and schematic doctrine of contract, in application takes a practical approach, often at the cost of forcing the facts to fit

3

uneasily into the marked slots of offer, acceptance and consideration:" *The Eurymedon* (1974).

This observation can also be applied to the rules of offer and acceptance applied by the Irish courts for they are in substance the same.

Offer

An offer may be defined as a clear and unambiguous statement of the terms upon which the offeror is willing to contract, should the person or persons to whom the offer is addressed decide to accept. It is important to distinguish an offer from a statement made without intending that a contract result if the person to whom it is made indicates his assent to those terms. Such statements are often called "an invitation to treat." In such a case the courts often view the response itself to be an offer which can in turn be accepted or rejected. The distinction is not always easy to draw but litigation has produced a series of prime facie rules which are approximate guides to the student.

(i) Auction sales. Under section 58(2) of the Sale of Goods Act 1893 a sale by auction is complete when the auctioneer announces its completion, normally by the fall of the hammer. It is clear then that it is the bidder who makes the offer and that the offer is accepted or rejected by the auctioneer. The auctioneer who announces that a sale will take place at a certain time does not make an offer to sell goods which will be accepted by arriving at the salesroom. The auctioneer then cannot be liable in contract if the sale does not take place: *Harris* v. *Nickerson* (1873). On the other hand an announcement by an auctioneer that a sale will take place "without reserve" may give rise to liability if bidding commences but the auctioneer refuses to sell to the highest bidder.

By announcing that he will sell to the highest bidder the auctioneer is said to make an offer which is accepted by attending the sale and bidding, although the person making the highest bid at the time of refusal to sell is said to be the only person entitled to recover damages: see *Tully* v. *Irish Land Commission* (1961). Therefore the statement that goods will be sold "without reserve" has two consequences; it invites persons to make offers to purchase the property or the goods in question and constitutes an offer made by the auctioneer for which he will be liable in damages should he refuse to knock down the goods after bidding has started. Of course if the auctioneer has been authorised to sell "without reserve" and the refusal to sell is the result of the owner's change of mind the auctioneer should be indemnified by the owner for any damages he has had to pay.

(ii) Display of goods. In the case of *Minister for Industry and Commerce* v. *Pim* (1966) a coat was displayed in a shop window with a notice declaring the cash price and indicating that credit terms were available. It was an offence to offer for sale goods on credit terms without specifically setting out those terms and the shopkeeper was prosecuted. The prosecution failed. It was held that to display goods with a price tag is not to offer them for sale. This display constitutes an invitation to treat, an action tantamount to inviting offers from members of the public. This rule is said to protect shopkeepers who would otherwise be obliged to sell goods to anyone who saw them in the window and came into the shop demanding that they can be purchased. If this represented the law a shopkeeper who had already sold the goods to another person would by obliged to sell them a second time, making him liable in contract or tort to the first seller.

On the other hand, if I camp outside a department store for three days waiting for the January Sale to commence in the hope of purchasing a furniture suite displayed in the window with a sale tag of £5 attached, it would be monstrous if the salesman could lawfully refuse to sell it to me when the sale began. Remember that these are only prime facie rules and in such a case the display would be regarded as an offer. See the American case of *Lefkowitz* v. *Gt. Minneapolis Surplus Store* (1957). In the leading English case of *Pharmaceutical Society* v. *Boots Cash Chemists* (1953) the Court of Appeal held that when a shopper takes goods from a shelf he does not accept an offer made by the storekeeper when he displays the goods. The acts of appropriation and approaching the cash desk constitute an offer by the prospective purchaser which is accepted by the cashier.

Many of these cases are not contract cases at all but are criminal prosecutions for misleading advertising. Some statutes make it an offence to "expose for the purpose of sale" which would catch acts of display; see *Minister for Industry* v. *Commerce* v. *Pim* (1966).

(iii) Advertisements. In most cases an advertisement is considered to be an invitation to treat so if an advertisement for goods appears in a newspaper a person writing to order those goods cannot sue in contract if the vendor replies that he is out of stock and cannot meet the order. The rationale behind this rule is the same as that mentioned in relation to display of goods cases.

An advertisement will however be considered to be an offer if the court is convinced that it is seriously intended to be binding should persons come forward prepared to act on it. Such contracts are known as *unilateral* contracts. In normal cases where a contract exists both parties are bound. These contracts are called *bilateral contracts*. An advertisement may bind the party issuing the advertisement without creating any concurrent obligation upon any other person. The leading English case of *Carlill* v. *Carbolic Smoke Ball* (1893) is an example of a unilateral contract in which an advertisement was declared to be an offer. The defendants manufactured a proprietary medicine that was advertised to be so efficient that should anyone catch influenza after purchasing and using it they would be entitled to £100. As a mark of the manufacturers sincerity, the advertisement continued, £1,000 was deposited with a bank to meet any claims. Mrs. Carlill read the advertisement, used the medicine but caught influenza nevertheless. The advertisement was held to be an offer and Mrs. Carlill entitled to £100.

On the other hand in *Wilson* v. *Belfast Corporation* (1921) an unauthorised newspaper report which indicated that the council would pay half wages to any employee who enlisted during the Great War was held incapable of being an offer. An advertisement in similar terms, posted by the employer on his own premises, was held in *Billings* v. *Arnott* (1945) to be an offer, accepted by his employees when they enlisted.

(iv) Tenders. When a manufacturer or a local authority issues advertisements soliciting tenders, whether it be to supply goods or build a school for example, the advertisement is an invitation to treat. The tender setting at the terms upon which the supplier or builder is prepared to contract constitutes an offer. There is no obligation upon the offeree to accept any of the tenders unless he has promised in the statement inviting tenders to accept the lowest figure.

Contracts for the sale of land are not subject to a special rule

Given that contracts for the sale of land are often negotiated over a prolonged period of time and given that conveyancing practice is often complicated and protracted it is often said that there is a presumption against mere agreement on price constituting a binding contract. *Harvey* v. *Facey* (1893) is the case most often cited in this respect. The appellants telegraphed "will you sell us Bumper Hall Pen Telegram lowest cash price." The respondents telegrammed "Lowest cash price for Bumper Hall Pen £900." The appellants replied that they would pay that price. The appellants action failed. The Privy Council held that the respondents telegram was only a statement of the price they would be prepared to accept should they decide later to sell. If the correspondence is clear and unequivocal however there is no reason why the courts will not hold an agreement to have been made although enforceability will depend on compliance with the Statute of Frauds (Ireland) 1695.

The action in *Harvey* v. *Facey* failed because there was no indication that the sellers wanted to assent to a sale of their property. The negotiations were still in their early stages. In the leading Irish case of *Boyers & Co.* v. *Duke* (1905) the plaintiff wrote asking for the lowest quotation the defendants could make for 3,000 yards of canvas. The defendants wrote that the lowest price was 4⅝d. per yard. The plaintiffs replied that they would accept this "offer." The defendants then realised that they had underestimated the price and refused to make up the fabric at the price quoted. O'Brien, L.C.J., following *Harvey* v. *Facey*, said of the plaintiffs second letter that "it is not the acceptance of an offer because the letter to which it was a reply was a quotation and not an offer." It should be noted that the purported letter of acceptance itself recognised that no binding contract was concluded by it because the plaintiffs gave the names of referees who would vouch for their commercial reliability.

Acceptance

Acceptance may be defined as a final and unequivocal expression of agreement to the terms of an offer. To acknowledge that an offer has been received is not to accept the offer. In one English case an offer to build a freight terminal was made by tender. The offeror who quoted two prices in the alternative, was told that his offer had been accepted. The "acceptor" however did not indicate which price he was prepared to accept. It was held that the acceptance was invalid: *Lind* v. *Mersey Docks & Harbour Board* (1972).

Acceptance is divided into two constituent parts.

(1) *The fact of acceptance* by performance.

It is particularly obvious that acceptance may take place by performing a stipulated or requested action if the offer is a unilateral contract. So in *Billings* v. *Arnott* the offer to pay half of any employees wages who joined the defence forces was accepted by Billings when he performed the action requested. In commercial life offers are often accepted, not by stating "I agree" or "I accept" but by performance. An offeror who posts a letter asking for goods to be supplied will often find his offer has been accepted when the delivery van arrives to transfer the goods themselves. As a general rule acceptance may often take place by the offeree acting in response to the offer in the manner stipulated: see the recent English case of *Howard Marine Dredging* v. *A. Ogden* (1978) and the old Irish case of *Saunders* v. *Cramer* (1842). If the response by the offeree is not a clear and unconditional acceptance of the offer the response itself may be described as a counter-offer which in turn may be accepted or ignored by the person to whom it is addressed. In *Swan* v. *Miller* (1919) the defendants offered to sell their interest in a lease for £4,750 plus ground rent of £50. The plaintiffs replied that they would pay £4,450. This response to the defendants offer was a counter-offer and as such was not itself capable of producing a binding contract.

The rules on counter-offers have another consequence. If an offer is met with a counter-offer then this response has the same effect as a rejection of the first offer. If the counter-offer is in turn refused the initial offer cannot now be accepted. If A offers to sell iron to B for £100 and B replies with an offer to purchase for £90 which A refuses, B cannot now hold A to his offer to sell for £100.

Of course it becomes particularly difficult to tell when an offer or counter-offer has been made when negotiations consist of each party sending printed forms back and forth. This problem has been discussed recently by the English Court of Appeal in *Butler Machine Tool Co.* v. *Ex-Cell-O Corp.* (1979).

(2) *Communication of acceptance*

Once it is established that the offeree intends to accept the offer he generally has to go further and communicate his acceptance to the offeror. The offeror may stipulate that it will be enough to communicate acceptance to an agent or he may dispense with, or "waive," the need for communication. This is impliedly the case when the offer is an offer to enter into a unilateral contract. Mrs. Carlill did not have to inform the Carbolic Smoke Ball Company that she intended to purchase and use their medicine; the employee in *Billings* v. *Arnott* (1945) did not have to inform his employer that he intended to enlist. In these cases the act of acceptance and performance are one and the same.

It should be noted that the offeror can only waive the need for acceptance to be communicated to him; he cannot oblige the offeree to respond to the offer by stipulating that failure to communicate rejection of the offer shall be deemed consent. This is illustrated by the facts of *Russell & Baird* v. *Hoban* (1922). The defendant in Castlebar negotiated with the plaintiffs to purchase oatmeal. He asked the plaintiff's manager if they could supply a fixed amount. The plaintiff's manager, on his return to Dublin sent a note indicating that they could supply that amount. The note provided that "if this sale note be retained beyond three days after this date, it will be held to have been accepted by the buyer." The Court of Appeal for Southern Ireland held that there was no contract. Ronan L.J., observed: "[n]o man can impose such conditions upon another. The document is conclusive evidence against the parties who sent it, that it was an offer which required acceptance." Because the defendant decided not to respond there was no contract.

So the practice of inertia-selling, that is, posting unsolicited goods to members of the public and obliging them to return them within a certain period of time, or, in default, pay the price is both a dubious commercial practice and is outside established principles of law. In the Republic s. 47 of The Sale of Goods and Supply of Services Act 1980 deems such a delivery a gift in certain cases. In Northern Ireland The Unsolicited Goods and Services Act 1971 is in force (S.I. 1976 No. 57(N.I.1)).

For acceptance to be effective the general rule is that the offeror is bound when he (or his agent for the purpose of receipt of acceptance) learns from the offeree of his acceptance. At that moment a contract springs into existence. This general rule was once illustrated by Lord Denning by two hypothetical examples. A is in communication with B, both parties standing on opposite banks of a river. A shouts an offer to B. B shouts his reply but this is drowned out either by an airplane flying overhead or by the sound of rushing water. B must repeat his reply before any contract can result. The second example extends this rule into modern means of communication. A telephones an offer to B. B replies but the line goes dead. If B intends to accept he must repeat his words of acceptance, the contract being concluded when A hears them. The point is not as metaphysical as it sounds because important jurisdictional questions may depend on where a contract is concluded. In the leading English case of *Entores Ltd.* v. *Miles Far East Corporation* (1955) an offer sent by telex from the plaintiffs offices in London to the defendants in Amsterdam was accepted by telex. The only problem concerned where the contract came into existence. The Court of Appeal held the contract was concluded in London when notice of acceptance was received there.

Acceptance by Post   ~~Postal acceptance Rule.~~

The general rule which determines that a contract comes into being when the offeror learns of acceptance does not apply where the parties intend that acceptance is to be communicated by post, neither party stipulating that acceptance is only to be valid when the offeror receives notification thereof. The so-called "postal rule" indicates that a contract is concluded when the offeree posts the letter of acceptance. This rule, which was established in England as early as 1818 has not found universal acceptance; German law for example holds acceptance to be effective when brought to the place of business of the offeror. The Irish courts however have followed the English rule. In *Sanderson* v. *Cunningham* (1919) the plaintiff, through a Dublin insurance broker sent in a proposal for an insurance policy. This constitutes an offer by the prospective insured. The defendant company in London decided to issue a policy which they posted to the plaintiffs agent. The plaintiff read the policy and indicated his assent by signing it. The plaintiff, who wished to sue the defendants in Ireland could only commence proceedings if the contract was concluded in Ireland. The claim failed. The Court of Appeal in Ireland held that the contract was concluded by posting it in London; see also *Dooley* v. *Egan* (1938).

The postal rule has been heavily criticised as leading to injustice. The well known English case of *Household Fire Insurance* v. *Grant* (1879) illustrates this point graphically. Grant issued an offer to take an insurance policy. The company posted acceptance. The letter never arrived. Grant was held liable to pay the premiums.

The rule has been said to rest upon the unsatisfactory theory that a letter handed to the postal authorities amounts to communication to an agent. This of course ignores the fact that the "agent" is unaware of what the letter contains. Even if the postal agency knows that the letter contains a reply to an offer the agency presumably has not opened the letter to discover its contents.

In truth the rule is one of convenience. It is said to be convenient for two reasons. The now obsolete practice of recording the date of issue of letters in office ledgers indicated to the nineteenth century judges that a letter had at least been posted. The fact of posting was easier to verify than arrival of the letter. Secondly, the postal rule, while it seems to unduly favour the offeree, is rational enough for if another rule applied the offeree could not rely on his act of acceptance. He would have to contact the offeror to ensure that his letter had actually arrived before he could safely assume that a contract had resulted, and act accordingly. Indeed, it has been argued that the rule does not in fact unduly favour the offeree. In *Household Fire Insurance* v. *Grant* it was pointed out that the offeror can stipulate for receipt of the acceptance, thereby protecting himself from the perils of an inefficient postal service. This was successfully achieved by the defendant in *Holwell Securities* v. *Hughes* (1974) when the contract provided that if the plaintiff wished to exercise an option to purchase a house owned by the defendant this had to be done "by notice in writing" within six months. Shortly before the time elapsed the plaintiff posted a letter which did not arrive. The English Court of Appeal held that while the parties intended the postal service to be the means of communication the agreement indicated that the defendant was only bound when the letter arrived. The postal rule was displaced and it mattered not that the defendant had been told by his solicitor who had received a copy of the letter of acceptance that the plaintiff was about to exercise the option. Lawton L.J. in the English Court of Appeal stated that not only will the rule not apply where the offeror specifies that acceptance must reach him "it probably does not operate if its application would produce manifest inconvenience and absurdity." The implications of this dictum have yet to be explored.

The courts may decide not to apply the postal rule for reasons other than a desire to avoid injustice between the parties. In *Apicella* v. *Scala* (1931) the plaintiffs in England sued the defendant who had purchased Irish sweepstake tickets as part of an alleged partnership arrangement. One of the tickets drew first prize. Meredith, J. considered whether the worldwide distribution of tickets could be considered an offer, accepted when the counterfoils are posted back to the organisers of the sweepstake. The learned judge concluded that "the ticket is not an offer. It, with that attached counterfoil, is more like a proposal form, and an offer is first made by forwarding the counterfoil with the price of the ticket, the ticket being retained by the purchaser. If the offer is accepted the price of the ticket is retained and an official receipt is forwarded, the contract is thus concluded." In rejecting the postal rule in this context, Meredith, J. was concerned to permit the organisers the freedom to regulate the number of tickets included in the draw, and more importantly, to ensure that the organisers did not envisage breaches of the domestic law of other states in which lotteries are illegal; "if the transmission of the counterfoils was illegal in a particular country, and if the encouragement of breaches of the law of that country were resented, the Management Committee might decide to refuse all counterfoils transmitted from that country." In short, the postal rule will not be allowed to operate so as to breach principles of international law such as the rule relating to comity of nations: contrast the approach taken in *Stanhope* v. *Hospitals Trust (No.2)* (1936).

No Irish court has considered whether a letter of acceptance which has been posted can be rendered ineffective if the offeree changes his mind before the letter arrives. If this issue arises in the near future Lawton L.J.'s dictum quoted above may help allow the offeree to retract for unless there is proof of loss to the offeror no hardship would be produced by such a result: (*see* C. F. Fried, *Contract as Promise*, p. 52–3.)

Termination of an Offer

An offer may be incapable of producing a contract for a variety of reasons.

(1) *Revocation*

It is established that an offer can be revoked or withdrawn at any time before it is validly accepted. In cases where the offer is to enter into a bilateral contract, that is, a contract to which both parties are bound, it should be remembered that acceptance has two elements; (i) the intention to accept and (ii) communication of acceptance. In the case of *The Navan Union* v. *McLoughlin* (1855) the defendant submitted a tender to the plaintiffs, a Poor Law authority. The guardians met amongst themselves and agreed to accept the defendants tender but before acceptance was communicated to McLoughlin he revoked his offer. Because the plaintiffs had not validly accepted the defendants offer, he was held to be entitled to withdraw it.

For revocation to be effective the offeror need only show that at the time of purported acceptance the offeree knows that the subject-matter is no longer available to the offeree. This follows from the much criticised English case of *Dickinson* v. *Dodds* (1876). Dodds offered to sell his house to Dickinson for an agreed sum. The offer was to remain open "until Friday, June 12th 9:00 a.m." On the Thursday, Dickinson was told that the house may have been sold to a third party. This information was communicated to Dickinson by a man called Barry who had not been authorised by Dodds to communicate this information to Dickinson. Dickinson handed a letter of acceptance to Dodds before the deadline set. The Court of Appeal held that because Dickinson had notice of the sale, even if the informant was not the offeror or an agent, the offer then became incapable of acceptance. Dickinson could not obtain the property or damages.

It seems that Dickinson intended to purchase before he learnt of the intervening sale. Had he given even a nominal consideration then the promise to keep the offer open until Friday would have been binding. In the United States a promise to keep an offer open is described as a "firm offer" and it cannot always be revoked. The English Law Commission in a 1975 Working Paper suggested that the law be changed to make a promise such as that made by Dodds binding if it is deliberately meant and made in the course of business.

It should also be noted that a letter of revocation does not become effective by posting it. In other words, the postal rule does not apply to letters revoking an offer. That letter only becomes effective when it arrives. This is established by the English case of *Byrne* v. *Van Tienhoven* (1880).

The recent decision of Lord Lowry L.C.J. in the Northern Ireland case of *Walker* v. *Glass* (1979) provides an excellent analysis of the basic rules on offer and acceptance. Walker wished to purchase an estate owned by Glass and to this end persuaded Glass to consider selling it to him. The parties contracted solicitors to draw up a form of offer in which Glass offered to sell the estate for £400,000, a deposit of £40,000 being payable. The offer was declared to be open for acceptance until March 13, 1979. Acceptance was prescribed; Walker had to sign a form of acceptance and forward the deposit before that date. On March 1, Walker notified Glass of his intention to sell but failed to forward the deposit until March 12. In the meantime Glass on March 2, "revoked" the offer. Walker's action for specific performance failed. Despite the statement to the contrary in the offer revocation could be effective at any time before acceptance. Walker argued that the offer had been effectively accepted on March 1. By communicating acceptance before purported withdrawal on March 2, this effectively, "froze" the transaction which was concluded on payment of the deposit. Lord Lowry L.C.J. refused to accept this theory. He noted that the prescribed mode or acceptance had to be satisfied. Payment of the deposit was not a neutral act, as counsel for Walker contended, because the failure to proceed would result in any deposit paid being forfeited (see Chap. 17).

If the offer is an offer to enter into a unilateral contract then difficulties may arise in regard to revocation. If, as we said earlier, acceptance and performance are one act and if revocation is possible before it is accepted then it should follow that an offer of this nature can be revoked any time until completion, even if the offeree has started to accept by performance. If I offer a man £20 to walk from Cork to Dublin can I revoke the offer when I see him on the outskirts of Carlow?

An affirmative answer would be clearly unjust but finding a jurisprudential basis for denying the offeror the right to revoke is difficult. If the offeror revokes before the offeree starts to perform no injustice results. However, the English Court of Appeal, in dealing with the more difficult problem of revocation after performance has commenced, has decided that an offer to enter into a unilateral contract is subject to an implied obligation "that [the offeror] would not render the performance by [the offeree] of the acts necessary for acceptance impossible ... and ... that the [offeror] could not withdraw . . . once [the offeree] . . . embarked on those acts": *per* Buckley L.J. in *Daulia Ltd.* v. *Four Millbank Nominees* (1978).

(2) *Rejection of the offer*

Clearly his refusal to accept the offer will make it impossible for the offeree, in the absence of a fresh offer, to change his mind and later accept. As we have seen if a counter-offer is made by the offeree in response to an offer this has the effect of destroying the first offer. Such drastic consequences have been criticised and the courts often give the offeree's response a neutral effect by characterising it as a request for information—which does not destroy the offer—rather than a counter-offer. If this is the case then the offer can be validly accepted. The court may also describe the added term as of importance to the offeree only which he can also waive; see the decision of the House of Lords in the Irish case of *Maconchy* v. *Trawer* (1894).

(3) *Lapse of time*

If the offeree does not respond quickly to the offer he may find his tardiness will prevent him from being able to accept the offer. The offeror may expressly stipulate that the offer is for immediate acceptance only as was the case in *Dooley* v. *Egan* (1938). If the offeror is silent the courts may hold that the medium of communication used indicates that acceptance take place immediately. An offer posted by airmail or sent by telegram from Australia to Dublin could not be validly accepted by sending a reply by surface mail. In all other cases acceptance must take place within a reasonable time. The commodity in question will be an important factor here because acceptance of an offer to purchase perishable goods or a commodity that fluctuates wildly in price such as oil or shares may have to take place earlier than a similar offer to purchase land.

(4) *Death*

There are no Irish cases which decide or discuss whether an offeror's death before acceptance can make it impossible to accept the offer, so as to hold the estate of the deceased liable. Even the English cases are unclear on this question. Death may of course terminate a contractual obligation through the doctrine of frustration but we will deal with this question later.

Ambiguous, Illusory and Uncertain Contract Terms

If the parties have concluded negotiations then they will consider agreement to have been reached. It often becomes apparent later that the parties have not reached agreement on every important issue or it may be that the contract document is unclear on certain matters. It is suggested that there are three distinct problems here.

(1) A contract term may be ambiguous, that is, capable of being interpreted in two or more ways. The courts do not readily hold that the doubts surrounding the negotiations must lead to the contract being deprived of all effect. In *E.S.B.* v. *Newman* (1933) the plaintiffs supplied electricity to a Mrs. Waddington at four different premises in Dublin. The defendant who had agreed to indemnify Mrs. Waddington, was sued by the plaintiffs for the total sum due on all four "accounts." The defendant pleaded that the contract of indemnity applied only to one of the four premises. Judge Davitt held that the word "accounts" was ambiguous because it could apply either to all four premises or the periodic accounts submitted in relation to one of them. Judge Davitt refused to hold that no contract existed; he instead admitted parol evidence to show that the indemnity was intended only to apply to one of the premises.

(2) Just as a contract term may be capable of more than one meaning so too can a contract term be devoid of any meaning. This kind of term is called an illusory promise. Here words are used which show that the "promisor" has attempted to give himself a discretion to perform by qualifying his promise so much that it has no promissory content at all. This often happens with a clause excluding or limiting liability for goods sold or services to be conferred. In the recent Australian case of *MacRobertson Miller Airlines* v. *Commissioners of State Taxation* (1975) an airline company promised to fly a passenger from X to Y but reserved for itself the power to cancel any flight, ticket or booking. This promise was held by the High Court of Australia to be illusory. The airline had given itself a discretion to perform or decline to do so. Promises "to deliver goods if I feel like it" or to supply "all the petrol you may require if I am not liable for non delivery" are also illusory. On the other hand, in the case of *O'Mullane* v. *Riordan* (1978) a purchaser of land agreed to pay £1,500 an acre or such larger sum as the purchaser felt like paying. McWilliam J. held that this promise was not illusory. The purchaser was obliged to pay a minimum of £1,500 per acre even though this sum could be increased at his absolute discretion.

If a promise lacks any substance the courts may do one of

two things: the court can look to see if the "promisee" subsequently performs and permit him to recover the remuneration "promised". So, if I ask someone to deliver a ton of coal indicating that in return "I may pay you £50" the supplier who delivers coal will be entitled to recover the sum in question. This is necessary to prevent unjust enrichment. Secondly, the court may delete or sever the illusory promise from the contract and enforce the rest of it.

(3) A vague or uncertain contract can exist in a variety of forms. In *Central Meat Products* v. *Carney* (1944) an action was brought to prevent the sale of cattle by the defendants to third parties, the plaintiff claiming that he had concluded an agreement with the defendant which provided that all the cattle the defendant acquired for canning purposes would be sold to the plaintiff. Overend J. held that there was no agreement capable of being enforced. There was no clear acceptance, nor was there agreement on important issues including price variation clauses and insurance arrangements.

If the parties agree in principle that the purchaser will pay a price the agreement is not illusory but it may be too uncertain to be capable of enforcement. If the parties agree to contract "at a price to be agreed later" the courts may not imply that the price will be a "reasonable one." However, section 8 of the Sale of Goods Act 1893 implies this term into agreements covered by the Act where the parties are silent on price. If the contract is outside the Act, a building contract or sale of land for instance, failure to agree on a price may be fatal as was the case in *Courtney Brothers* v. *Tolaini* (1975) a recent English Court of Appeal decision where a builder who had provided finance to a developer in return for a promise that he would be awarded the construction contract itself, the developer's quantity surveyor to negotiate fair and reasonable sums. The plaintiff argued that while he had not entered into a binding contract to build the defendant had broken a contract to negotiate. The theory that someone can "contract to make a contract" was rejected by the Court of Appeal, primarily because the damages to be awarded are too uncertain. Who can tell if the negotiations will be successful?

Nevertheless the view that "a contract to contract" may exist finds tentative support in the case of *Guardians of Kells Union* v. *Smith* (1917). The Guardian of a Poor Law District advertised by tender for the supply of meat, the advertisement providing that a formal contract would be signed on a fixed day. The defendant was told that he had been the successful offeror but he refused to sign the formal contract. It was held that while no contract to supply meat existed because no formal contract had been concluded the defendant had broken a contract to enter into this formal contract and he was liable. Damages were nominal. It can be argued that this "contract to contract" is designed to show that parties are obliged to negotiate in good faith: *culpa in contrahendo*.

If the parties fail to agree on important terms and they fail to appoint an arbitrator to fill in the details on behalf of them the courts will, reluctantly, hold the agreement void. It is for this reason that many contracts for the sale of land cannot be enforced. Failure to agree on the period for which a lease is to run will be fatal: *Lindsay* v. *Lynch* (1804), as will failure to agree on the date of commencement of the lease: *Kerns* v. *Manning* (1935). In commercial contracts however the courts are particularly keen on finding that an enforceable agreement exists, so if there is a history of dealing between the parties or an established trade custom on the question the parties may find that these factors—"as a matter of interpretation or construction"—will fill in the gaps. Students will find the leading English case of *Hillas* v. *Arcos* (1932) instructive. It has been said that the courts are so anxious to hold that commercial contracts are enforceable that for such an agreement to be void "indefiniteness must reach the point where construction becomes futile;" Kessler and Gilmore *Contracts* (1970) p.146.

"Subject to Contract"

Where two persons seemingly conclude negotiations for the sale of land either or both of them may wish to protect themselves by stipulating that in certain instances the agreement will not be binding. The owner may want to reserve for himself the right to accept a better offer for example; the purchaser on the other hand may want to ensure that he has the money to pay for the property and permit himself to withdraw without being liable for breach of contract. Each could stipulate that agreement is conditional on such and such an eventuality. In *O'Mullane* v. *Riordan* (1978) the purchaser agreed to buy subject to planning permission being obtained. Until planning permission is given the contract is said to exist but it is unenforceable. If planning permission is not given the purchaser is not bound to purchase but he can waive this term (if property values have risen he may do this) at which point the contract becomes enforceable.

Instead of inserting a specific stipulation into the contract, lawyers, estate agents and others may use the expression "subject to contract." This formula has been interpreted to mean that until the formal contract is signed by both parties, (the normal Irish practice) or until contracts are exchanged, (the conventional practice in England) no contract of sale exists. The English authorities are summarised by Lord Denning in the leading case thus: "the effect of the words 'subject to contract' is that the matter remains in negotiation until a formal contract is executed." *Tiverton Estates* v. *Wearwell* (1974),

The Irish courts have also ruled that if the phrase is used by the parties during negotiations then there is no contract until exchange of contracts or signature by both parties takes place. The leading Irish case is *Thompson* v. *The King* (1920). If the owner of the land offers to sell "subject to contract," "acceptance" by the offeree will simply mark a step in the march towards a binding contract. If the offeree on the other hand introduces the term "subject to contract" his response is not a counter-offer requiring the offeror to respond but of course the point is of little importance given that either party can refuse to proceed.

There are important differences between the Irish and English cases on the question of "subject to contract" agreements. Suppose the words are added by the solicitor for the purchaser in a letter "confirming" that agreement has been reached "subject to contract." Suppose also neither the vendor nor the purchaser used the words when they were discussing details of the sale. Under English law the "subject to contract" letter cannot satisfy the statute requiring a memorandum in writing evidencing the agreement. The Irish courts would permit the vendor to introduce parol evidence to show that oral agreement was reached. The letter containing the "subject to contract" phrase will not be allowed to operate because it was added after the oral agreement had been struck. This important difference between the English and Irish position is established by *O'Flaherty* v. *Arvan Property* (1976) and *Kelly* v. *Park Hall Schools* (1979). In the *O'Flaherty* case the purchasers of property were handed a receipt for the deposit which contained all the material terms adding, "subject to contract." The plaintiffs successfully argued that at the time of negotiation nothing was said about the sale being "subject to contract." McWilliam J. ordered that the sale be completed. This means that Irish solicitors, auctioneers and others cannot rely on this phrase to protect their clients if they attempt to add the "subject to contract" formula after oral negotiations between the principals have ended, the principals themselves failing to use the phrase. The courts look to see if all the terms have been settled and if so "subject to contract" added in any letter will be treated as if it were an ambiguous or meaningless phrase. In the recent Supreme Court case of *Carthy O'Neil* (1981) Henchy J. said "subject to contract" normally means that "a full contract" has yet to be agreed, which in the authors view is a mistaken interpretation of the older cases. The author favours a return to the orthodox position set out in *Tiverton* and *Mulhall* v. *Haren* (1979); see articles in (1979–80) D.U.L.J. & (1981) D.U.L.J. where this topic is discussed in greater detail.

On the other hand if the "subject to contract" formula is not used the correspondence may make it quite clear that only upon exchange of contracts in some form will a contract come into existence: *Kelly* v. *Irish Landscape Nursery* (1981). The courts will honour such an intent. The exact meaning of such a conditional statement is a matter of interpretation; see *Guardians of Kells Union* v. *Smith* (1917) discussed above, p.16. In the recent case of *Irish Mainport Holdings Ltd.* v. *Crosshaven Sailing Centre Ltd.* (1980) the words "my Board have agreed in principle," were held not to prevent a concluded agreement coming into existence. Keane, J. held these words could not be equated with the words "subject to contract," in the traditional sense of the phrase.

2 The Doctrine of Consideration

If it is clear that one party has made a promise to another person who in turn has assented to it, to the knowledge of the promisor, there is at first sight no reason why the Irish courts should refuse to enforce the promise. Yet this would make all promises enforceable and legal historians have pointed out that no legal system has enforced a promise simply upon proof that it was made.

The English common law recognised a promise to be enforceable if the promisee provided something in exchange for the promise—a *quid pro quo*—or if the promise was contained in a deed under seal. This first route to enforcement helps form the basis of the modern doctrine of consideration. The alternative, obtaining the assent of the promisor to a deed under seal is not as difficult or technical as it sounds. Once the seal is affixed (and this is done by placing a red sticker on the paper or simply drawing a circle with L.S. stamped on it) the deed takes effect on delivery. It seems that the promisor does not even have to sign the document. In *Drimmie* v. *Davies* (1899) two partners exchanged promises and recorded these promises in a deed under seal. The Irish Court of Appeal held that adopting this form made it unnecessary to decide if consideration was present. Several Lords Justices stated *obiter* that consideration was also present. In normal business practice people do not execute deeds under seal so if a promise is enforceable the promisee must show that he has provided consideration in exchange for the promise. It is through the doctrine of consideration that the common law identifies promises that are to be enforced simply because they have been made.

For example, if I promise to give my car to X the promise alone cannot lead to X successfully suing for delivery. He has provided nothing for my promise. Suppose I deliver the car to X. My action will make it difficult if not impossible for me to recover the vehicle but it is the transfer of possession allied with my gratuitous promise that makes it impossible to recover the vehicle. Even so, there is still no contract. I have made a promise but the promise is to be seen as a promise of a gift. Until delivery of the promised item the promisee has no right to performance, merely a hope or expectation which the courts will not, of itself, realise for the promisee.

Suppose however I promise to give my car to the first person to pay £5 for it. Here the promise has an entirely different quality. My promise is allied to a request: I stipulate that in return for my promise I require something to be done in exchange. On performance of the act, or when performance is promised, a bargain springs into existence. The opening sentence to this book drew attention to bargain as the primary characteristic of a contract; it is through the doctrine of consideration that the distinctive features of the common law model of contract takes shape.

The best definition of consideration is that of Sir Frederick Pollock who argued that consideration is the price a promisee pays in return for a promise. This price however must have been stipulated or requested by the promisor; the doctrine of consideration is not satisfied by a promisee showing that but for the promise he would not have performed a certain act. Consideration then does not depend on causation alone.

If we return to the first example above the point will become clearer. I promise X that on her birthday next week I will give her my car. My promise is conditional on her reaching her next birthday. However, my failure to honour the promise will not be actionable because it is simply a promise to make a gift. Suppose X now informs me that she has given away her bicycle because she expected me to honour my promise. To be sure, "the price she has paid" for my promise is loss of her bicycle; she has not however provided consideration. My own promise caused this to occur but I did not request or stipulate that before X could acquire my car she had to transfer her bicycle. Holmes would have described this as a case where "reciprocal inducement" was absent.

It may be that X will receive some limited compensation through the doctrine of estoppel but she cannot satisfy the needs of the conventional doctrine of consideration.

Historical Antecedents

The doctrine of consideration is foreign to many legal systems including that of Scotland which historically is closer to the Roman law tradition than that of the common law world. If a Scottish court is convinced that a promise is seriously meant then the fact that it was not given in the context of a bargain will not prevent enforcement of the promise. Lord Mansfield was undoubtedly the most influential figure in moulding modern English commercial law and his Scottish ancestry no doubt helps explain his attempts during the eighteenth century to uproot the doctrine of consideration. One attack mounted against the doctrine occurred in a series of cases in which Lord Mansfield argued that a promise to pay an antecedent debt, the debt itself being unenforceable, would be supported by moral consideration alone. If an infant, a discharged bankrupt or a married woman promised to pay a debt incurred during infancy, or prior to bankruptcy or coverture respectively, this promise would be void. However, Lord Mansfield argued, a subsequent promise would be enforceable for this promise, in his view, should be both morally and legal binding. The "moral consideration" theory was dismissed as alien to English law in *Eastwood* v. *Kenyon* (1840). It is also clear that the moral consideration theory at no time formed part of the jurisprudence developed by the Irish courts. In *Ferrar* v. *Costelloe* (1841) the Irish Court of Exchequer held that a married woman who promised to be jointly and severally liable upon a bill of exchange signed with her husband could not be liable upon a new promise made after her husband died and the disability of coverture ended. Brady L.C. noted that *Eastwood* v. *Kenyon* went "a great way to overrule this doctrine of moral obligation." Richards C.B. in *Bradford* v. *Roulston* (1858) also rejected the moral obligation theory.

The doctrine of consideration is not as irrational as many of its critics have argued. It is through the doctrine that the courts often satisfy themselves that a promise was in fact seriously meant. This has been described as "the deliberative function": Fuller, 41 Col. L. Rev. 799. By adopting the form of an exchange of promises this ritual should indicate to a court that each intended to be bound. Whether other forms of ritual evidencing intent should be permitted this effect, such as recording a promise in writing, is another question. Several American jurisdictions enforce promises evidenced in this fashion.

Adequacy and Sufficiency of Consideration

If the terms of the bargain are unduly favourable to one of the parties in the sense that the price paid by him is disproportionate to that which he obtains in return, the consideration may be said to be inadequate. Nevertheless, it is axiomatic that that the courts will not investigate the adequacy of the consideration. If a landowner wishes to let his property for a handful of peppercorns or give an option to purchase for £1 that is his affair. The attitude of the courts was neatly summed up by Manners, L.C. in *Grogan* v. *Cooke* (1812): "if there be a fair and bona fide consideration the court will not enter minutely into it, and see that it is full and ample." So if the bargain is an honest one it will be enforced, even if one party gets more from the bargain than the other. Disparity of consideration will however be an important factor in alerting the courts to possible fraud or unconscionability, considered later in this book.

The leading English textbook writers however indicate that while consideration need not be adequate it must be sufficient. This means that before the consideration promised can support a counter promise it must not run foul of a series of rules designed to indicate when a promise will not suffice in law. These rules are often dictated by the needs of public policy. The Irish courts have not as yet ruled conclusively on sufficiency. For the sake of completeness the English rules will be shortly stated.

First, a promise in exchange for performing a duty already imposed by the general law, such as answering a subpoena, would not be enforceable. Public agencies and citizens should perform their duties without hoping for or encouraging extra payment. The owner of a burning building who promises to pay £1,000 to a group of firemen if they save the premises could only be sued on this promise if the firemen's actions went beyond those required or expected of public service firemen.

Secondly, performance of a duty already owed *to the promisor* may constitute consideration although the limits of this doctrine have yet to be established. The older cases, *Stilk* v. *Myrick* (1809) and *Hartley* v. *Ponsonby* (1857) suggest that only if the initial executory contract is discharged can a second promise be actionable by a party who in substance performs the duty owed under the first contract. This view is supported in the Irish case of *Farrington* v. *Donoghue* (1866). More recently however it has been suggested that generally a promise to perform an existing duty is sufficient consideration for a promise: *Williams* v. *Williams* (1957). These two lines of authority have been recently discussed in *North Ocean Shipping* v. *Hyundai* (1978). Mocatta J. suggested that if the duty owed arises under *statute* then performance of that duty will be consideration for a promise. Under the Social Welfare (Consolidation) Act 1981, s.214 the mother of an illegitimate child has a statutory duty of support. Should the father promise to pay a fixed sum every week the mother would on this modern line of authority be able to recover, even though she owes a statutory duty to do that requested by the promisor. If however, the duty owed springs from *contract* it cannot provide consideration for a promise. In *North Ocean Shipping* a shipbuilding company was promised an increase in the price payable for building a vessel. Mocatta J. held the promise enforceable because on the facts additional consideration was provided for the increased price.

Thirdly, performance of a duty owed *to someone other than the promisor* may support a promise. Students will find the application of the old case of *Scotson* v. *Pegg* (1861) by the Privy Council in *The Eurymedon* (1974) instructive. Simply put, if A owes a contractual duty to marry B and a third party, (the father of B perhaps) promises to pay A £1,000 after the ceremony A can enforce this promise. While it is no longer possible to sue in the Republic of Ireland for breach of promise to marry, the cause of action having been abolished by the Family Law Act 1981, *Saunders* v. *Cramer* (1842) is an Irish authority in favour of this rule.

The Rule against Past Consideration

Because the common law recognises that contracts are enforced in order to carry into effect the expectations of the parties responsible for creating them there are instances where a contract will be held to exist where neither party has attempted to perform their respective promises. If A agrees to purchase six tons of coal from B in six months time and to pay a price of £10 a ton a contract exists as from the exchange of promises. The consideration provided is the promised act of each; in this bilateral contract the consideration is said to be executory; while neither party has performed as yet both parties are said to have provided consideration by their exchange of promises. Should *one* party perform (for example, when A forwards the price of the coal to B) the consideration by A is executed and he can of course maintain an action against B in the event of delivery.

It is well established however that if a promise is made after some gratuitous act has been performed by the promisee the subsequent promise is not supported by consideration. The benefit conferred before the promise was made cannot be said to have been made by reference to an antecedent promise. We have already seen that promises are not enforced because they satisfy a test of causation; if I promise to give my house to my brother because he paid my hospital bill during an earlier illness my promise was the result of a benefit already conferred. Nevertheless, it was not given in the context of an exchange of promises so no bargain or contract will result. Here the consideration is said to be past consideration which is no consideration at all.

The leading English case is *Roscorla* v. *Thomas* (1842). The plaintiff purchased a horse for £30 from Thomas who, following the sale, warranted the horse "free from vice." The horse bit and was therefore not as warranted. The action failed, the pleadings clearly indicated that the sale had been completed when the warranty was given. Roscorla then had provided no consideration; the promise to pay the purchase price was not given in exchange for the warranty sued upon. The courts however do not sit over the negotiations ready to time and examine the exchange of promises second by second. In *Smith* v. *Morrison* (1846) the Irish Queens Bench Division distinguished *Roscorla* v. *Thomas*. It was pleaded that the sale of a horse took place contemporaneously with the giving of the warranty. It was held that if this be so the promise will not be held to have been given for a past consideration.

The wording of the promise will no doubt provide guidance on this; the past tense will indicate that the promised act has already been performed but parol evidence is admissible to show whether the consideration is past or not. In *Bewley* v. *Whiteford* (1832) The Court of Exchequer indicated that if after hearing parol testimony the court is in doubt whether the consideration is wholly executed (past) or executory than an action on the promise will not succeed.

The leading modern Irish case is *Provincial Bank of Ireland* v. *Donnell* (1932) a decision of the Northern Ireland Court of Appeal. The bank sued the defendant on a deed (not under seal) in which she agreed to provide security for her husband's overdraft in consideration of "advances heretofore made or that might hereafter be made." The action failed. The consideration stated here was either past or illusory; the advances that had earlier been made were a past consideration while the advances that "might hereafter be made" gave the bank a total discretion whether they would provide advances or not. The promise then should have been recorded in a deed under seal in order to render them enforceable.

A promise made after the promisee has conferred a benefit upon another person may be enforceable if the court is able to bring the case within the seventeenth century English case of *Lampleigh* v. *Braithwait* (1615). This case holds that while a past consideration will not of itself provide support for an implied promise to pay it may support a subsequent express promise made by the beneficiary. The rule itself, which predates *Lampleigh* v. *Braithwait*, was applied by the Court of Exchequer in *Bradford* v. *Roulston* (1858). Roulston was employed by Bradford to find a purchaser for Bradford's boat. A third party agreed to purchase the vessel but when the bill of sale was to be completed the purchaser did not have sufficient funds to pay the purchase price. Bradford was about to withdraw from the transaction when he was asked by Roulston to sign. Bradford signed the bill of sale. After the bill of sale was signed Roulston promised in writing that he would ensure payment of the balance the following day. Roulston was sued on this promise. The consideration provided, signature of the bill of sale by Bradford, was clearly past. Pigot C.B. stated in his speech however that "where there is a past consideration, consisting of a previous act done at the request of the defendant, it will support a subsequent promise; the promise being treated as coupled with the previous request." Bradford was entitled to claim the sum promised because he had signed the bill of sale at Roulston's behest. What is important here is that when the requested act is provided, the parties must not have intended the act to be gratuitous. Evidence that the parties intended the promise to be compensable at some later date will be necessary. In fact in *Bradford v. Roulston* the defendant may well have uttered his promise to pay the plaintiff when the bill of sale was to be signed but the plaintiff chose to rely on the promise in the letter because had he relied exclusively on the earlier oral promise he may have encountered problems in relation to the Statute of Frauds (Ireland) 1695; see Chap. 4.

Consideration must Move from the Promisee

Where the contract is executory the bargain may remain to be performed yet the exchange of promises gives each party the right to seek and obtain performance or monetary compensation. If A promises to buy coal from B tomorrow, paying £100 for the goods, each is a promisor; each is a promisee. A has given his promise to pay £100 and has received B's promise to deliver and *vice versa*. The nineteenth century authorities indicate that consideration exists where the promisor, the party seeking enforcement, can point to performance of a requested detrimental act (or the promise thereof) on the part of the promisee: *Lowry* v. *Reid* (1927). Alternatively, if the promisor has received a requested benefit from the promisee consideration is present.

Take the facts of *McCoubray* v. *Thompson* (1868), AG owned land, goods and chattels worth £196 which he intended to transfer to M, and T, share and share alike. T wanted the land to himself and it was agreed that in consideration for AG transferring everything to T, T would pay M £98, half the value of the property. T defaulted and was sued by M. Clearly the defendant had made a promise; it was also addressed to both AG and M so they constituted joint promisees. Applying the rule requiring consideration to move from the promisee however it is clear that M had no cause of action in contract. He had made no promise in return for T's own promise to pay £98; the sole consideration for T's promise moved from AG. Monaghan C.J. held that where three parties join in an allegedly tripartite contract such as this the plaintiff must be able to show that *he* has provided consideration in some sense.

In *Barry* v. *Barry* (1891) a similar transaction was held to give a valid cause of action. Under the terms of his father's will the defendant was to receive the family farm if he promised to personally pay legacies to members of the family, including the plaintiff, a younger brother. If the defendant was unwilling to do this the legacy was to be payable from the land. The defendant promised to be personally liable to pay the legacies, whereupon the executors permitted him to use the farm. The promise was addressed to the executors and the plaintiff. When the defendant defaulted the plaintiff sued claiming the plaintiff was personally bound by his promise. The Court of Appeal held that consideration had moved from the promisee. The defendant by his promise led the plaintiff to give up any right to have the legacy realised out the property; by forbearing to exercise rights over the estate at the implied request of the defendant the promisee had provided consideration. The difference between this case and *McCoubray* v. *Thompson* is that McCoubray had no rights at all, however ill-defined, over the property which he could give up or refrain from exercising so consideration could not be provided from this source.

For an English case illustrating that it is not necessary in tripartite contracts for the promisor to actually receive a benefit see *Re Wyvern Developments* (1974).

Although the joint promisee should provide consideration before he can enforce this promise it has been recognised that this may be inconvenient if a joint bank account is opened but one of the parties does not intend to provide consideration by paying funds into the account. Could a bank refuse to pay him funds held in the account on the grounds that it has no contract with this person because he has not provided consideration? It seems not. See the opinions of the members of the House of Lords in *McEvoy* v. *Belfast Banking Co. Ltd.* (1935) and the controversial Australian case of *Coulls* v. *Bagot's Trustee* (1967), criticised by Coote (1978) C.L.J. 301.

We will return to this question when we examine the doctrine of privity of contract.

Compromise of a Claim

It is well established that an undertaking not to continue civil litigation or an agreement to compromise a claim will provide consideration for the promise of another. Indeed, the courts view it as in the public interest to encourage out of court settlement of civil disputes. A difficulty may arise however if the claim that one party agrees to give up subsequently turns out to have had little or no chance of success. The promisor who is sued upon this agreement to compromise may argue that the claim was so vacuous and of such doubtful validity that it cannot provide consideration for his own promise.

The courts however refuse to hold that because the earlier cause of action had no chance of success the compromise is invalid. It is the legitimacy of the compromise that much be assessed. If both parties however know that the initial claim was invalid then the compromise too will fail. This view was taken by Palles, C.B. in *O'Donnell* v. *O'Sullivan* (1913). The parties agreed to compromise a claim for £137 by the defendant paying £75. During the trial it became clear that the original debt was a gambling debt, unenforceable at law. While this fact alone did not make the compromise invalid for want of consideration the fact that both parties knew this to be so did. The Chief Baron declared "it is settled law that unless there is a reasonable claim which is bona fide intended to be pursued the settlement of that claim cannot be good consideration for a compromise."

In general, the compromise must satisfy three conditions:

1 the initial claim must have been reasonable and not vexatious or frivolous;

2 the plaintiff must have had an honest belief in the chances of its success;

3 the party contending that the compromise is valid must not have withheld or suppressed facts that would have shown the claim in a truer light.

The third condition is normally broken by a defendant who threatens an action while suppressing facts which clearly show that the claim would no doubt fail. In the case of *Leonard* v. *Leonard* (1812) a claim was compromised between two half brothers who each claimed entitlement to an estate. The plaintiff agreed to compromise his claim because he had been advised that on the facts the claim was not certain to succeed. The defendant however had withheld information from the plaintiff which suggested that the claim would indeed succeed. The compromise was held invalid because the defendant had exploited the plaintiff's ignorance of all the facts.

Forbearance—Promise and Fact

A promise to abstain from doing something will in many cases be as valuable to the promisee as a positive action. Pollock's definition of consideration refers to forbearance *or the promise thereof* as capable of supporting another promise. In the American case of *Hamer* v.

Sidway (1891) an uncle promised his nephew $5,000 if he refrained from drinking, using tobacco, swearing or gambling until 21. The nephew met these conditions and was successful in an action for the promised sum. He had a legal privilege to do these things and the acts of forbearance, requested by his uncle, provided consideration for the promise. The court was satisfied that the promise was seriously meant; it had been earnestly repeated before assembled members of the family.

Any expressly requested forbearance then will provide consideration. If I indicate I wish to leave my job and my employer promises me £100 if I remain in his employment for another six weeks this will be good consideration for although I will be performing the same tasks as before my forbearance will entitle me to claim the sum promised after performance.

The most common act of forbearance to come before the courts arises in cases where a promise is given in return for a promise not to enforce a legal remedy. In the leading English case of *Cook* v. *Wright* (1861) parish trustees threatened the occupant of a house with proceedings unless he signed promissory notes. Under a local Act of Parliament rates could be levied on owners in order to maintain local services. An action on the notes succeeded because the trustees had provided consideration by refraining to take proceedings to recover the rates due. Incidentally, the claim by the defendant that he was not the owner and therefore not liable to pay the rate failed; as we have seen it was enough for the trustees to have a reasonable belief that proceedings would have been successful.

If the promise has to be recorded in writing so as to satisfy the Statute of Frauds the courts have held that the consideration should be stated in the alleged memorandum. It is sufficient if the consideration is stated, expressly or impliedly, on the memorandum itself. In *Hibernian Gas Company* v. *Parry* (1841) a hotel business fell into receivership, one of the creditors being the plaintiff company. The plaintiffs were owed £32 for gas supplied. The receiver executed a document in favour of the company promising to pay all sums due six months hence. The consideration for this promise was not expressly stated on the memorandum (a contract of guarantee requiring a memorandum) but the Court of Exchequer unanimously held the receiver liable on his promise. Pennefather B. pointed at that the memorandum implicity recorded two requested acts:

(1) forbearance to sue for the £32 already due;
(2) continued supply of gas into the future.

When the company agreed to these terms a contract was concluded, for as Brady, C.B. observed, if the company sought to recover sums due before the six month period elapsed the action would not have succeeded. Students should contrast the terms of the promise given here with that in the earlier English case of *Wood* v. *Benson* (1831) where part of a similar guarantee was held to infringe the rule against past consideration.

The role of forbearance as part of the doctrine of consideration takes on a very controversial aspect when it is said that a promise may be supported simply upon proof that the promisor relied upon the promise. At this point the entire bargain theory of consideration begins to split at the seams. The leading English case of *Alliance Bank* v. *Broom* (1864) was applied by the House of Lords in *Fullerton* v. *Bank of Ireland* (1903). The bank wrote a letter to Colonel Stevenson, drawing his attention to the fact that his account was overdrawn. The client responded that he would provide title deeds to property as security. The Law Lords held that the consideration provided for this promise was the restraint and patience displayed by the bank in not immediately calling in the overdraft; "such forbearance in fact although there was no agreement by the bank to forbear suing Colonel Stevenson for any indefinite period was sufficient consideration to support his promise to give the security": *per* Lord Davey.

Payment of an Existing Debt

The rule in *Pinnels* case (1602) as laid down by the English Court of Common Pleas dictates that if a liquidated sum is owed by A to B a promise by B to take a lessor sum in full satisfaction of the larger debt will not bind B. After receipt he can immediately sue for the balance because the debtor has only performed part of a contractual duty already owed to the creditor. In other words, the creditor's promise is unenforceable for lack of consideration.

If however a new element is introduced into the relationship the promise will be binding; there will be both agreement (accord) and consideration (satisfaction) for the promise to release the debtor from his obligation to pay the larger debt. So, if instead of paying £10 I pay by giving a chattel this new element will suffice, regardless of the worth of the chattel. It is established that payment by cheque is not a new element. Alternatively, payment of the lesser sum before the date due or in a different place to that agreed will suffice.

Although this rule was not applied by the House of Lords until 1884 it has been accepted and (reluctantly) acted upon by the courts for centuries. In *Corporation of Droghoda* v. *Fairtlough* (1858) premises were demised in 1820 for a period of 99 years to a local clergyman. The Corporation in 1837 passed a resolution agreeing to reduce the rent as a gesture to the tenant but before this could be done the clergyman died. The Corporation decided to carry out the resolution and in 1842 the old lease was surrendered and a new lease executed for the remainder of the 99 year period, rent reduced from £11.9s.8d. per annum to £5.6s per annum. The rent was paid at the new rate until 1854 when the Corporation sued for the arrears of rent calculated at the original higher rate from 1842 until 1854. The action succeeded. Lefroy C.J. indicated that payment of a lesser sum under a parol agreement rather than one by deed cannot at common law be deemed any satisfaction of larger, liquidated sum unless some collateral advantage, however small is given. In this case there was no collateral advantage: "What is the consideration which the corporation received for this agreement? They received a less rent; but upon the other hand the tenant was allowed to keep in his pocket the balance of the greater rent." This common law decision directly confronts the modern cases on promissory estoppel but before we turn to this difficult problem two exceptions to the rule that payment of a smaller sum is not sufficient consideration should be noted.

(1) *Compositions with creditors*

Suppose X, a trader, has a large number of creditors but a small number of banknotes with which to pay them. He faces bankruptcy and the creditors run the risk of being paid little or nothing. It will be in the interest of all concerned for the creditors to agree to take less than that due. This agreement or composition is a valid way of ensuring that payment of the lesser sum will bind a creditor. So in *Morans* v. *Armstrong* (1840) a partner in the plaintiff firm agreed to take 6s.8d. in the £ on sums due the firm. When the money was tendered it was refused. An action to recover the original sum due failed.

(2) *Payment by a third party*

In *Lawder* v. *Peyton* (1877) the administrator of a creditor's estate sought execution over the property of the defendant who owed a debt of £534, £268 of which had been paid, not by the defendant but by a third party on the defendants behalf. It was held that to permit recovery of the entire sum after payment would be a fraud upon the defendant. Although both this case and *Morans* v. *Armstrong* (above) seem based on the desire to prevent fraud it is doubtful whether it is the defendant who is defrauded. In these cases it seems more likely that the third parties involved are the sole victims. This alternative reasoning has been selected to justify similar rules developed by the English judges.

Promissory or Equitable Estoppel

The doctrine of estoppel is historically a common law doctrine. In the case of *Jorden* v. *Money* (1845) the House of Lords declared the doctrine to apply only to cases where the statement made is one of existing fact. If therefore I say "X does not owe me 100" I will at common law be prevented or estopped from denying the truth of this promise. If, however I say "you owe me £11 but pay me £6; I do not intend at any time to recover the balance," estoppel will not operate. My statement is one of intention, not fact. So if we return to *Drogheda Corporation* v. *Fairtlough* above we can see that those facts fall into the second category. In the 1940 case of *Munster & Leinster Bank* v. *Croker* Black J. upheld the view that estoppel cannot operate on statements of intention.

Nevertheless it is clear that the line of equitable authority commencing with *Hughes* v. *Metropolitan Railway Co.* (1877) threatens this limited view of the estoppel doctrine. In that case it was said by Lord Cairns L.C.—an Irishman—that:

> "It is the first principle upon which all courts of equity proceed that if parties who have entered into definite and distinct terms involving certain legal results . . . afterwards by their own act . . . enter upon a course of negotiations which has the effect of leading one of the parties to suppose that the strict legal rights arising under the contract will not be enforced or will be kept in suspense . . . the person who otherwise might have these rights will not be allowed to enforce them where it would be inequitable, having regard to the dealings which have thus taken place between the parties."

This line of authority, if carried to its logical conclusion, would mean that the dicta in *Pinnels* case of 1602 would be bad law; that all promises and not merely those made in the context of a pre-existing contractual relationship are enforceable if the promise is seriously meant and the other party acts on it, even in a way not stipulated or requested by the promisor. In short, the rule in *Drogheda Corporation* v. *Fairtlough, Jorden* v. *Money* and the entire bargain doctrine of consideration would be swept aside. This movement towards making a non-bargain promise enforceable began in earnest after the judgment in *Central London Property Trust* v. *High Trees House* (1947). In that case Denning J. (as he then was) stated *obiter* (on facts substantially similar to *Drogheda Corporation* v. *Fairtlough*) that he would apply Lord Cairns principle to hold a landlord estopped from going back on a promise to reduce the rent.

In later cases the English courts have attempted to limit Lord

Cairns principle to promises made (1) to suspend and not give up a legal right; (2) to promises made to someone with whom a legal relationship already exists; (3) to cases where the promisee has acted to his detriment; (4) to cases where the promisor is seeking to resile from his promise. The equitable rule does not extend into cases where the promisee (who cannot show he has provided consideration) seeks to enforce the promise as a cause of action.

It is clear that these limitations represent an attempt to shore up the doctrine of consideration as well as the older cases on estoppel and part payment of a debt. Other judges, particularly Lord Denning reject such limitations on the *Hughes* v. *Metropolitan Railway* principle and dicta in several recent cases can be found to contradict each of the four rules stated above. Students should turn to recent English textbooks. The Irish Supreme Court has yet to consider *Hughes* v. *Metropolitan Railway* in the context of its relationship with the threatened bargain theory of consideration although Kenny J. in *Revenue Commissioners* v. *Moroney* (1972) ruled at first instance that a father who obtained his two son's signatures to a deed by promising that at no time would they have to pay the consideration stated in the document would be estopped from reneging on his promise. Because the sons had acted to their detriment the promise was binding under the *High Trees* principle. Kenny J. expressly rejected limitations (1) and (2) above, ruling that estoppel can operate in cases where the promisee was not contractually bound at the time of receipt of the promise. The Supreme Court decided the case on appeal by using conventional contract rules.

It is the present writer's view that it is a mistake to see the *High Trees* case as a problem of reconciling the authorities in such a way as to leave the bargain theory of consideration intact. Lord Denning, ((1951) 5 M.L.R. pp.9–10) once wrote "we are approaching a state of affairs which Ames regarded as desirable, namely that any act done on the faith of a promise should be regarded as sufficient consideration to make it binding." Some 28 years later Lord Denning viewed the cases on estoppel in his book *The Discipline of Law*, p.223 as abolishing "the doctrine of consideration in all but a handful of cases." While is doubtful that the present English cases go so far the implications of equitable or promissory estoppel are profound; are we not in fact returning towards Lord Mansfield's moral obligation theory?

The student may well ask, what practical importance results from this shift in jurisprudence? Let us return to the gift promise example earlier in the chapter where my promise to give a car to X caused X to give away her bicycle. We established no bargain was made so no contract resulted.

If we approach the same problem from a promissory estoppel viewpoint my promise induced the promisee to act in a way I should have foreseen as possible so even if no bargain exists I should be liable on my promise.

The estoppel theory however has repercussions beyond the rules on formation. What should I pay? Should I only compensate for the value of the bike or be obliged to pay the value of the car? What does this twentieth century theory of promissory liability mean for the nineteenth century rules on offer and acceptance? Students might like to turn to the authors note in (1980) 58 *Canadian Bar Review* 170.

3   Intention to Create Legal Relations

It is established that negotiations which meet the requirements of offer, acceptance and consideration may fail to be enforceable at common law as a contract because it is said that there was an absence of legal intent. This view has been challenged by several commentators who point out that it is only through the application of the doctrine of consideration that the common law distinguishes enforceable promises from non-enforceable promises. The need to show legal intent is said to be an interloper, of foreign extraction, which may be a legitimate requirement in civil law jurisdictions where no doctrine of consideration exists but it is quite superfluous to the needs of the common law.

Professor Williston put forward this argument very strongly when he argued that "the views of parties as to what are the requirements of a contract, as to what mutual assent means, or consideration, or what contracts are enforceable without a writing, and what are not, are wholly immaterial . . . [in this context] the law not the parties fixes the requirements of a legal obligation:" 1 Williston on Contracts, s.21 (1936).

Even though many of the legal intent cases can be argued away on alternative grounds there are several which can only be explained on the basis of lack of intent. No matter what objections may be levied against the legal intent requirement it has now taken root in English and Irish law.

Family Arrangements

In *MacKay* v. *Jones* (1959) the plaintiff's uncle promised that if the plaintiff, then a boy of 14 came to live with him and look after the farm the plaintiff would, on his death convey it to the boy by will. On the death of the promisor the property was bequeathed to a third party. Judge Deale in the Circuit Court refused to characterise the promise as absolutely binding: it was said to be an agreement to work in the expectation that the legacy would be given. This case can only be explained as one where the court refused to find that the

35

promisor intended his promise to be binding: see also *Baldwin* v. *Lett* (1971).

The leading case on family arrangements in English law is that of *Balfour* v. *Balfour* (1919). In that case, Atkin L.J. stated *obiter* that contracts between husband and wife are not intended to be attended by legal consequences. In *Courtney* v. *Courtney* (1923) an agreement made between a husband and wife who had decided to solve their matrimonial differences by living apart was upheld as legally binding. Although *Balfour* v. *Balfour* was distinguished in *Courtney* as applicable only to executory contracts it is established that where the parties have not been living together amicably any agreement made between them falls outside *Balfour* v. *Balfour*, otherwise separation agreements would not be enforceable. It has been suggested that if the parties in *Balfour* v. *Balfour* had done anything to indicate that they intended the promise to be legally enforceable, by getting a solicitor to draw up an agreement, for example, the presumption against enforcing an arrangement between husband and wife would be inapplicable. Note that in *Courtney* v. *Courtney* the promises were made with the sanction of the local priest and this seems to have indicated to the court that the arrangement was seriously meant: see also *Hamer* v. *Sidway* (1891), p.29 above.

The decision of the Supreme Court in *Rogers* v. *Smith* (1970) illustrates that when a family arrangement is made the terms agreed are often ambiguous. Members of a family do not often haggle and bargain with the intensity of dealers at a horse fair. In *Rogers* v. *Smith* a mother promised her son that the cost of supporting her would be recoverable from her estate following her death. The Supreme Court refused to hold this promise was seriously intended. It was made in the most general terms; the "promisee" also gave evidence that if the promise had not been made he would have supported the "promisor" anyway.

Commercial Agreements

If the parties are commercial men then it is to be presumed that the contract will be attended by legal intent. The leading English case on honour clauses, *Rose and Frank Co.* v. *Crompton* (1925) would no doubt be followed in Ireland. Readers should note that on the facts of *Rogers* v. *Smith* (*supra*) it might have been possible to characterise the contract as a commercial one between the plaintiff and his father; this would have pointed towards enforcement. In *Apicella* v. *Scala* (1931) an arrangement between plaintiffs and defendant designed to enable all parties to take a share in sweepstake tickets to be purchased by the defendant was described as "a conditional or revocable decision"; even though Meredith J. would have found consideration to be present the absence of any intention to conclude a bargain was fatal to the plaintiff's action in contract.

Collective Agreements

Two issues should be kept apart. First to all collective agreements may be a valid source of contractual terms if they are subsequently incorporated into individual contracts of employment; *N.C.B.* v. *Galley* (1958). So in the E.A.T. case of *Lynch & O'Brien* v. *Goodbody Ltd.* (1978) the appellants had been dismissed according to the terms of an agreement struck between union and management governing procedures for dismissal. Applying the dictum in the leading English case of *Blackman* v. *P.O.* (1973) it was held that the appellants were dismissed by reason of the union/management agreement and not because of redundancy.

The second issue is whether breach of a disputes procedure by unions or management will be a breach of contract rendering the party in breach liable in the ordinary courts.

Following the decision in *Ford* v. *AEF* (1969) the common law position in England is often said to be that a collective agreement between trade unions and employers or employers organisations is not enforceable in the courts. In *Ford* however it was held that *this particular agreement* was not intended to have legally enforceable consequences: see Hepple [1970] C.L.J. 122. Otto Kahn Freund argued that a collective agreement resembles an industrial "peace treaty" rather than a contract. The view that collective agreements are not enforceable at common law is of fairly recent origin; Kahn Freund himself argued (4 and 6 M.L.R.) that in general such agreements are contractually enforceable: contrast his later views cited in *Ford* v. *AEF* (1969).

Irish case law provides support for the view that at common law the collective agreement may be enforceable in the ordinary courts; See *McLoughlin* v. *G.S. Ry. Co.* (1944). In *Ardmore Studios* v. *Lynch* (1965) the plaintiffs, who owned a film studio entered into an agreement with a trade union that electricians would be drawn only from a "seniority list" of union electricians. The plaintiffs hired electricians not on the list. The plaintiffs sought an injunction to restrain the defendants from picketing their premises. The company argued that the agreement had been terminated before the electricians who had been the cause of the dispute had been hired. Budd J. gave the plaintiffs an interlocutory injunction, refusing to decide whether the agreement was binding. McLoughlin J. at trial of the action declared *obiter* that in his view the agreement was not binding *because of uncertainty of terms*. In other words, had the agreement been clear and specific the collective agreement would have possessed contractual effect.

In Ireland the Supreme Court have unanimously endorsed the view that collective agreements can be binding in the ordinary courts. In *Goulding Chemicals Ltd.* v. *Bolger* (1977) trade union members refused to accept the terms of a redundancy scheme agreed between their employer and the unions. Picketing commenced in breach of the agreement. While the Supreme Court advanced the view that unauthorised industrial action by the union members did not involve a breach of contract on their part, (there being no evidence that the agreement was incorporated into their contract) the agreement did bind the unions and union officials. O'Higgins C.J. said that in this situation *Edwards* v. *Skyways* (1964) indicated that the agreement was binding; Kenny J. went so far as to state that *Ford* was wrongly decided in the light of *Edwards* v. *Skyways*. Kenny J. approved Megaw J's dictum in *Edwards* that the onus of showing absence of legal intent is a heavy one. While the Supreme Court's observations on the point were delivered *obiter Ford* is clearly not good law in Ireland if it is held to be authority for the view that *all* collective agreements are unenforceable.

In general collective agreements are (often deliberately) loosely drafted and ambiguous in their terms so in practice the agreement may fail to satisfy the requirements as to certainty of terms.

The Industrial Relations Act 1946 provides for a method of enforcing certain kinds of collective agreement. Agreements relating to wages and conditions of employment, defined as an "employment agreement," can be registered and enforced by the Labour Court under the terms of section 32 of the Act.

If the agreement is vague and ambiguous the Registrar may refuse to register it. The agreement can be varied or cancelled with the consent of all parties to the "employment agreement."

4 Formal and Evidentiary Requirements

In this Chapter we will consider those contracts which can only be enforced if the contract itself is reduced into written form or if the contract (which may have been struck orally) is evidenced in writing.

(1) Contracts that must be Evidenced in Writing

Section 2 of the Statute of Frauds (Ir.) 1695 (7 Will. 3, c.12) provides in part:

> "no action shall be brought ... whereby to charge the defendant upon any special promise to answer for the debt, default or miscarriage of another person, or to charge any person upon any agreement made upon consideration of marriage, or upon any contract or sale of lands, tenements or hereditaments or any interest in or concerning them, or upon any agreement that is not to be performed within the space of one year from the making thereof, unless the agreement upon which such action shall be brought, or some memorandum or note thereof, shall be in writing, and signed by the party to be charged therewith, or some other person thereunto by him lawfully authorised."

(1) *Contracts to pay for debts of another*

Before such a contract falls within the Statute of Frauds it is essential to show that the contract is one of guarantee and not one of indemnity. The classical example of a contract of guarantee arises where A asks B to supply goods to C, a trader, adding that if C does not pay up then B, the supplier, can turn to A for payment. In such a case it can be seen that both C and A are liable to pay; C is described as the principal debtor, A the guarantor. A's promise is said to be a collateral promise, the consideration for it being B's act of supplying goods to the principal debtor; see the decision of the Court of

Common Pleas in *Bull* v. *Collier* (1842) and that of the Court of Exchequer in *Fennel* v. *Mulcahy* (1845).

On the other hand, if the promise made envisages the promisor being soley liable to pay the debt then it is said to be an original promise and not a collateral one. This is a contract of indemnity and no memorandum is necessary here; the promisor can be liable on the oral promise. In *Barnett* v. *Hyndman* (1840) the plaintiff held a bill of exchange which had been accepted by one Moore who was therefore liable on it. The bill had been dishonoured. The plaintiff was asked to relinquish his claim against Moore by the defendant who promised to give half the sum due and another note for the balance. The plaintiff agreed but payment was not made. The defendant was held liable on his promise; by dropping the claim against Moore the plaintiff provided consideration for the defendant's promise that he alone would meet the debt. It should be noted that the cause of action was the tort of deceit.

It is established that if the promise is made in the context of a larger contract, an agent's promise to pay sums due to his principal for example, that because such a promise is given in the context of the contract of agency the statute does not apply. Nor does the Statute of Frauds apply to cases where the liability arises on an implied promise or an account stated; *Wilson* v. *Marshall* (1866).

(2) *An agreement made in consideration of marriage*

This provision does not require a contract of marriage to be evidenced in writing; the old practice of members of a family agreeing to transfer property or a sum of money to an engaged couple has to be evidenced in writing before the promise can be enforced: see the judgment of Sugden L.C. in *Saunders* v. *Cramer* (1842). This part of the Statute is of little importance to-day.

(3) *Contracts for the sale of lands or an interest therein*

This very important part of section 2 has been considered by the Irish courts in a great many cases. Apart from contracts for the sale of freehold interests, contracts of assignment, leases and grants of incorporeal hereditaments, the sale of things attached to the land may also involve the sale of an interest in land and therefore fall within section 2. A conacre letting of land, that is, one under which certain grazing rights are transferred to another does not create an interest in land and as Professor Wylie argues should not be within the Statute: *Irish Conveyancing Law*, para. 9009. If, however the contract is for the sale of crops or the natural products of the land it is arguable whether, in each individual case, the contract is for the sale of goods or for the disposition of an interest in land.

(4) *Contracts not to be performed within one year*

In order to eliminate the possibility of cases being decided on the strength of oral testimony which may be deficient simply because of the interval between formation of the bargain and the litigation the Statute of Frauds required such contracts to be evidenced in writing. In *Tierney* v. *Marshall* (1857) the plaintiff alleged that it had been agreed between himself and the defendant landlord that the rent payable by the plaintiff would not be paid over to the defendant but would be set off against sums due to the plaintiff as arrears of wages earned while in the defendant's employment. The plaintiff claimed that this oral agreement made the defendant landlord's acts of distress unlawful. The rent payable was £17 per annum; sums due were in excess of £200. For the set-off to operate then the contract would run for 12 years before the arrears would be paid. It was the view of the court that the contract was intended to run for more than one year and because it was not evidenced in writing was unenforceable. Similarly, in *Naughton Limestone Land Co. Ltd.* (1952) an oral contract of employment which was to run for four years was held unenforceable without a memorandum of agreement.

It is established however that if at the time the contract is struck the parties intend it to be performed within one year the Statute does not apply. If the contract is to be performed within one year by one of the parties, as would be the case if A promised to convey Whiteacre to B next week in return for B's promise to support A for life, the Statute does not apply; *Murphy* v. *O'Sullivan* (1865). It does not suffice for there merely to exist the possibility that one party may perform within the one year period; *Farrington* v. *Donoghue* (1866). In this case the contract will be unenforceable unless there is a memorandum. If the contract is terminable at will *Dublin Corporation* v. *Blackrock Commissioners* (1882) holds the contract outside the Statute.

If however the employee performs his part of the bargain he may be entitled to reasonable remuneration by making a claim in *quantum meruit* as occurred in *Savage* v. *Canning* (1867). It is established in *Naughton* v. *Limestone Land Co.* (supra) that the courts will not sever the contract and allow an action in contract to lie for the first year of the oral contract.

(5) *Contracts for the sale of goods in excess of £10*

Section 13 of the 1695 Statute of Frauds declares that such contracts cannot be good unless the buyer: (i) accepts and receives part of the goods sold or (ii) he gives something in earnest to bind the bargain or (iii) the buyer makes part payment. In all other cases a memorandum must exist. This section was substantially repeated in section 4 of the Sale of Goods Act 1893 and although the 1893 Act did not expressly repeal section 13 of the Irish Statute of Frauds the courts seem to regard the 1893 Act as effecting an implied repeal.

The three alternatives that present a means of enforcing the contract where no memorandum exists hinge upon the conduct of the buyer. "Acceptance and receipt" was considered in *Hopton* v. *McCarthy* (1882). A coach-builder in Tipperary ordered materials from the plaintiff in England but he refused to proceed with the transaction when he learnt that the price payable was three times that indicated during negotiations. The seller sent the materials by rail. They were held in the carriers warehouse awaiting collection by the defendant. The acceptance and receipt formula did not apply here because the defendant had not actually received them: delivery into the custody of a carrier was held not to satisfy this requirement because the carrier was not authorised to accept them for the defendant.

The buyer can also be held liable if at the time of the bargain something in earnest is given. This ancient and obscure provision would be satisfied if the buyer gave his business card for example as a gesture of his good faith.

For part payment to have been made it is essential that the payment be tendered and accepted. To post a cheque which is immediately returned uncashed will not satisfy the part payment provision. It was argued in the case of *Kirwan* v. *Price* (1958) that when the buyer offered the cash price payable for a horse which he had orally agreed to buy, (the seller declining to proceed with the sale at the agreed price) this constituted "something given in earnest." The Circuit Court Judge refused to accept the argument, indicating that while the distinction between part payment and tendering of something in earnest is not clear, acceptance by the seller is essential to both. If the contract is marginal in the sense that it may be either a contract for the sale of goods or an interest in land it seems that the party arguing for enforcement may stand a greater chance of success if he argues that it is a contract for the sale of goods. The decision in *Scully* v. *Carboy* (1950) held a letting of meadowing to be a contract for the sale of goods and because there were acts of part payment the absence of a memorandum was not fatal under section 4. Had the court decided otherwise the action would have failed because payment of part of the price in a contract for the sale of an interest in land does not satisfy the doctrine of part performance; *Clinan* v. *Cooke* (1802). We will consider this doctrine later in the section devoted to equitable routes to enforcement.

The Memorandum. It is not necessary for the memorandum to have been specifically drafted as a memorandum before the Statute of Frauds can be satisfied. Letters written by solicitors, estate agents and others setting at the terms of the agreement have been held to constitute a memorandum even though the writer did not intend the document to take on the character of such an instrument. Other instruments that have been held to suffice include auctioneers sale books, cheques for a deposit, receipts, all of which were not intended to *evidence* the contract.

Contents of the memorandum. The memorandum must contain the names of both parties to the contract or describe them in such a way as to make it possible to identify them. This provision is, like other parts of the Statute, read liberally, the courts preferring to find a contract to be enforceable than unenforceable. In *Bacon & Co.* v. *Kavanagh* (1908) the words "you" and "your employment" in a contract of guarantee were held to be sufficiently clear to identify the party charged after surrounding circumstances were adverted to.

The property itself must also be identified, as must the price payable. As we saw in the opening chapter if the parties fail to agree upon a price or fail to appoint a valuer to do this for them the contract will be void for uncertainty. Unlike contracts for the sale of goods the courts will not imply that the price for a contract to purchase land will be a reasonable price. In *Lynch* v. *O'Meara* (1973) Butler J. held that it is not necessary to add whether payment will be made in cash or by cheque.

If these three material terms are set out then most contracts will be enforceable unless on the evidence it is clear that the parties intended additional provisions to be essential terms. Failure to add these material terms will result in the memorandum being defective.

Two distinct problems must be distinguished here. First of all, the parties may fail to agree on additional terms that the courts consider to be essential before a contract can be said to exist at all. Here the contract is void for uncertainty. This is to be contrasted with the case of an agreement struck on all essential terms, the parties failing to record these terms in the memorandum. Here the contract is unenforceable unless some other means of enforcement exists.

If the contract is for the sale or transfer of a leasehold interest in land it is well established that unless the parties agree on the date of commencement the contract is void; *Kerns* v. *Manning* (1935). If the contract is divisible then failure to agree may not always be fatal. In *Godley* v. *Power* (1961) a contract to sell a leasehold interest in a pub with stock in trade was held not to be void because the parties had not agreed on the price of stock-in-trade. The majority of the

Supreme Court held the contract for stock-in-trade to be a separate collateral contract.

On the other hand a memorandum that fails to record all agreed terms is not defective for only essential terms need be included. The decisions of Lord MacDermott in *Stinson* v. *Owens* (1973) and Gannon J. in *Black* v. *Kavanagh* (1974) show that only terms thought to be material by the parties are essential. The courts are prepared to indicate that, unless there is clear evidence to the contrary, it is not essential for the memorandum to state whether a deposit is payable. Nor is the closing date normally a material term. It is also unnecessary to state the nature of the interest sold if on the evidence both parties know what this is. In some cases the courts will imply terms into both the contract and the memorandum. In *Kelly* v. *Park Hall School* (1979) a failure to agree on the date for signing the contract was not fatal, the Supreme Court implying that this will take place within a reasonable time.

Signature. The memorandum should be signed by the person to be charged or his agent. "Signature" has been interpreted very loosely and it has been held that a rubber stamp, typed words or an illiterate's mark may suffice. In the recent Supreme Court decision in *Casey* v. *Irish Intercontinental Bank* (1979) a solicitor who instructed a secretary to type a letter setting out the material terms of the memorandum on headed notepaper was held to adopt the heading as his signature so even if he fails to personally sign the letter a signed memorandum will exist. On the other hand, the initials of a solicitor added as a reference were held not to constitute a signature in *Kelly* v. *Ross & Ross* (1980). It is established that if the "signature" is added as a point of information rather than a means of authenticating the document this will not be a valid signature for the purpose of the statute: see *McQuaid* v. *Lynam* (1965). If initials are included at the foot of the page where the signature is normally to be found this may satisfy the Statute.

On the complex problem of the authority of the agent to bind his principal students should examine Professor Wylies book, *Irish Conveyancing Law* pp.355-365.

Joinder of documents. It is established that a memorandum may be made up of two or more documents. If only one of the documents is signed however difficulties will arise because it is said that signature must authenticate the entire memorandum. If at the time of signature the other document does not exist it is illogical to hold the signature to refer to that document. The leading case on joinder of documents is *McQuaid* v. *Lynam* (1965).

The Irish courts have followed the English practice of requiring the signed document to expressly or impliedly refer to the other documents. In *Kelly* v. *Ross & Ross* (1980) McWilliam J. held that particulars and conditions of sale, drawings, solicitors attendance dockets, an estate agents day book and correspondence—a total of nine items in all—could not collectively or individually constitute one memorandum because the signed documents (which did not contain all material terms) did not refer to the other documents submitted in evidence.

"Subject to Contract." The English authorities show that if a document contains the hallowed phrase, "subject to contract" that document cannot constitute a memorandum because the memorandum must acknowledge that an oral contract exists. We saw at the end of Chapter 1 that "subject to contract" will be taken to mean that the parties are still negotiating and have yet to reach an agreement.

Although there is no statutory authority to support the position the modern Irish cases indicate important differences in approach to the "subject to contract" formula. If oral negotiations have been concluded without the phrase being used a solicitor who adds the "subject to contract" formula in correspondence will not prevent a court from finding that an oral contract has been struck. Furthermore, the letter written will be held to constitute a memorandum even though the "subject to contract" phrase is thought to indicate that no contract exists. This unhappy conclusion is the result of the decision of the Supreme Court in *Kelly* v. *Park Hall Schools* (1979). The parties orally agreed to contract for the sale of land. The defendants solicitor wrote "I confirm that we have agreed terms 'subject to contract' . . . ." The defendants refused to proceed and were held liable. The Supreme Court held that the letter acknowledged that an oral contract had been struck; this suggests that a memorandum cannot exist unless it acknowledges the existence of a contract. The Supreme Court however seem to have decided that over 100 years of conveyancing practice must be disregarded when the Court further held that in this context the words "subject to contract" were ambiguous and that they do not deny the existence of a contract; the words are seen as meaningless.

This decision has been critically examined by Keane J. in *Mulhall* v. *Haren* (1979) where the learned judge (who was incidentally the defendant's counsel in the *Park Hall Schools* case) went some way towards re-establishing the orthodoxy by "distinguishing" *Park Hall* as depending on its own special facts. The *Park Hall* case makes it difficult for lawyers and auctioneers to know how they can protect their client and it makes it possible for oral testimony to override written documents, something the 1695 Statute was designed to prevent.

Equitable means of enforcing an unenforceable contract.
The doctrine of part performance is the most obvious route leading to enforcement of a contract which fails to satisfy the formal requirements of the Statute of Frauds. Although the precise basis of this equitable doctrine is disputed it seems that the acts of part performance raise an equity in favour of the plaintiff, an equity which the courts should enforce. This view was recently expressed by Lord Reid in the House of Lords in *Steadman* v. *Steadman* (1974). The classic act of part performance is entry into possession of the land with the agreement or acquiesence of the defendant. In *Starling Securities* v. *Woods* (1977) entry onto the site and demolition of derelict property was held to constitute part performance. Payment of money is said to be such an equivocal act as never to be capable of satisfying the doctrine but this was doubted by members of the House of Lords in *Steadman* v. *Steadman*.

The precise limits of the doctrine of part performance remain unsettled in English law. There are suggestions in a handful of Irish cases that failure to satisfy the Statute and the doctrine of part performance may not always be fatal. Given that the 1695 Statute was designed to counteract conveyancing frauds it would be ironic if a person could shelter behind the strict letter of that Act and avoid liability for breach of contract. This irony has not escaped the judges. It has been said that the courts will not allow the Statute to be used as "an engine of fraud" and while this helps explain the doctrine of part performance the matter does not end there.

In *Doherty* v. *Gallagher* (1975) the purchaser agreed to give the vendor a reasonable time to clear the land of his, the vendors, cattle. This material term was not mentioned in the memorandum. Finlay P. awarded Specific Performance nevertheless, declaring that where there is a danger of encouraging fraud by a strict interpretation of the Statute this should be avoided if possible. Similarly, a trustee cannot plead failure to meet the strict requirements of the Statute if to do so would permit him to commit a fraud; *McGillycuddy* v. *Joy* (1959). If there is a mistake in the memorandum in circumstances where rectification is not possible an oral agreement may be enforced regardless of the memorandum's deficiencies; *Black* v. *Grealy* (1977). It is also established that if a term orally agreed is inserted into the memorandum, the term being for the benefit of one party alone, if the term cannot be realised it may be waived. In *Healy* v. *Healy* (1973) the plaintiff agreed to purchase land for £46,000. The memorandum inaccurately stated the consideration to be £40,000.

The plaintiff was able to enforce the oral contract by waiving the mistake in the memorandum and agreeing to pay the £46,000 orally agreed. Similarly, if the memorandum fails to record a material term it will be defective but enforceable through waiver; see the English case of *Martin* v. *Pyecroft* (1852) which has been cited with approval in several Irish cases.

Corporations. At common law a contract was enforceable against or by a corporation only if the contract was executed under the common seal. The rule was never absolute however. In *Donovan* v. *South Dublin Guardians* (1904) it was held that if work was ordered, carried out and accepted by a statutory corporation the work being within the scope of its objects, the absence of a contract under seal was no defence if the corporation was sued; similarly if it was the corporation that was endeavouring to sue upon the contract; *Dublin Corporation* v. *Blackrock Commissioners* (1882).

Certain contracts require special procedures to be adopted; under the Public Health (Ireland) Act 1878, s.201(1), contracts whose value exceeds £50 must be in writing and sealed by the health authorities with their common seal; see also The Dublin Fever Hospital Act 1936, s.37(2).

In other cases the position of a company is assimilated to that of a living person by s.38 of the Companies Act 1963.

(2) Contracts that are Void unless Recorded in Writing

Under the Hire Purchase Acts 1946–80 a contract which fails to meet the terms set out in section 3 of the 1946 Act will generally be void. See O'Malley, *Commercial Law*.

Part 2

Construction of a Contract

5   Express Terms

Even if both parties to a dispute agree that a contract has been concluded the court will still have to determine what obligations each party has consented to. The statements made by each of them will be of paramount importance in limiting the scope of the bargain. Not every statement made will form part of the contract however.

A distinction must be drawn between representations that do not have contractual effect from those that do. The former are called "mere representations" while the latter are often described as "warranties." In this context the word warranty is used in the neutral sense of "contractual" term rather than as a technical expression denoting a term, breach of which gives rise to a remedy in damages; See Chap. 6.

The evolution of the law on warranties and mere representations is closely linked with the law of evidence and now outdated rules of pleading. A person who claimed that he had contracted because the other party represented a state of affairs existed which subsequently turned out to be untrue could recover only if the word "warrant" or similar phrases had been used. The courts moved towards protecting a purchaser by discarding such a rule: as Lefroy B. remarked in the 1843 case of *Scales* v. *Scanlan* "to make a warranty it is not necessary that the word 'warrant' or 'warranty' should be used. There was a time in the law when it was otherwise . . . but it has been long since well settled, that words of affirmation, affirming a matter of fact, on the faith of which the party contracts, are as competent to make a warranty as any strict technical term." Nevertheless, if a person simply affirms his belief to be "such and such" in circumstances that make it apparent that he does not take any responsibility for the accuracy of it then such a statement may be held to be an affirmation rather than a warranty. To state that a car is believed to be a 1948 model when it is in fact a 1939 model may be held to be a non-contractual affirmation or representation if the seller advises the buyer to verify this statement. Indeed, the seller may not be liable in contract if the purchaser is a motor dealer who had the resources available to check the year of manufacture and the seller is an individual lacking any professional skill, honestly believing the car to be as stated: see *Oscar Chess Ltd.* v. *Williams* (1957). On the whole the Irish courts have been less troubled by the affirmation/warranty dichotomy than their English brethren. In *McGuinness* v. *Hunter* (1853) the defendant, who owned a horse told the plaintiff, a prospective purchaser, that "the horse is all right and I know nothing wrong about him." The plaintiff purchased the horse which soon afterwards died. Counsel for the plaintiff conceded that the words "is all right" amounted to a promissory statement and that if they had not been uttered the remainder of the statement would only amount to an affirmation. The statement was held to be a warranty. In *Schawel* v. *Reade* (1913) the owner of a horse informed the plaintiffs agent, who was about to inspect the animal, that "you need not look for anything; the horse is perfectly sound. If there was anything the matter with the horse I should tell you." The agent broke off his inspection, the horse was purchased and later turned out to suffer from an eye defect that made it unsuitable for the purchaser's purpose. The Court of Appeal in Ireland held the statement to be merely an affirmation; the House of Lords unanimously reversed this decision. Had *McGuinness* v. *Hunter* been cited before the Irish Court of Appeal (which it was not), it is suggested that the purchaser would have there succeeded; the statement in *Schawel* v. *Reade* seems to be a more obvious warranty than the words uttered in *McGuinness* v. *Hunter*. See also *Murphy* v. *Hennessy* (1897).

The courts often ask whether the representee acted on the faith of the truth of the statement rather than whether the representor intended the statement to be a warranty, the latter being a metaphysical test at the best of times. The modern law is admirably summarised by Kenny J. in *Bank of Ireland* v. *Smith* (1966). After discussing the older English case law he said: "The modern cases, however, show a welcome tendency to regard a representation made in connection with a sale as being a warranty unless the person who made it can show that he was innocent of fault in connection with it." Indeed, in the old case of *Cobden* v. *Bagnell* (1886) a father who stated an honest belief that his daughter was entitled to an estate under a complicated settlement was held not liable because the statement was found to be a reasonable but mistaken interpretation of the effect of the instrument. The test is not entirely new it seems.

The Parol Evidence Rule

This controversial rule of evidence is designed to deal with problems that arise from attempts to introduce testimony about the terms agreed upon where the parties have subsequently executed a written document setting out their contract. The rule was stated in absolute terms by Lord Morris in *Bank of Australasia* v. *Palmer* (1897); "parol testimony cannot be received to contradict, vary, add to or subtract from the terms of a written contract or the terms in which the parties have deliberately agreed to record any part of their contract." At first blush the rule is a harsh one for it would exclude all parol evidence which was not incorporated into the written document. It is apparent that the rule is capable of causing injustice. The rule was designed to prevent litigation from being protracted, the theory being that if parol testimony was excluded and the attention of the jury (whose task was to decide issues of fact, including contract terms) focused on the written document alone then civil trials would be shorter and less expensive. One nineteenth century English judge observed that it was "better to suffer mischief to one man than an inconvenience to many." Nevertheless, it is doubtful if litigation was shortened by the rule; indeed, the fact that the court heard the evidence and then decided whether to rule it admissible means that the rule often had the contrary effect. In any event, the decline of the institution of the jury in civil cases renders the rule out of date. The rule, however, has never been applied absolutely and we shall now consider the many exceptions to it.

(1) *To explain the circumstances surrounding an agreement*

In *Harries* v. *Hardy* (1851) a ship-repairer brought an action against B and C, who, along with A were the registered owners of the vessel under bills of sale. The action, brought to recover the cost of repairs carried out on the vessel failed because B and C were able to introduce parol evidence to show that the bills of sale were executed as mortgages. B and C were not liable as they were mortgagees, not owners. Similarly, in *Revenue Commissioners* v. *Moroney* (1972), the Supreme Court admitted parol evidence to show that an apparent sale was in fact intended to be a transfer by way of gift. See also *The Ulster Bank* v. *Synott* (1871).

(2) *To explain the subject matter of the contract*

In *Chambers* v. *Kelly* (1873) a contract was concluded for the sale of "*all the oaks* now growing on your lands called Greenmount near Enniscorthy, together with all other trees growing through the oak plantations and mixed with the said oak." The plaintiff vendor successfully contended that the parties had designated part of the plaintiffs land to be the oak plantation so that the felling of oak trees on other parts of the plaintiffs land constituted a breach of contract. A literal interpretation of the written document would produce a

different result. Furthermore, the words "all other trees" were
limited to larch trees, this being part of the oral contract.

It is said that parol evidence is only admissible if the contract
itself is ambiguous. This view was categorically rejected by
Chatterton V.C. in *The Ulster Bank* v. *Synott* (1871) but it was applied
in the Circuit Court case of *Oates* v. *Romano* (1950). A hairdresser,
employed by the plaintiff, agreed not to serve in "a like business"
when he left the plaintiff's employment. The plaintiff attempted to
adduce parol evidence that "like business" meant a specific type of
hairdressing establishment catering for the needs of the more
affluent sector of Dublin society. The clause was not intended to
prevent the defendant from working as a hairdresser in all salons.
The Circuit Court judge held the rule to be that parol evidence was
not admissible if the contract was on its face unambiguous. This
case must be regarded as wrongly decided. On the other hand, the
court will understandably be reluctant to adduce parol evidence if
this serves to render the terms of an otherwise unambiguous
contract uncertain. In *Kinlen* v. *Ennis U.D.C.* (1916) the House of
Lords refused to allow a tender to be admitted in evidence when the
contract itself was at variance with the tender. Lord Buckmaster
pointed out that preliminary documents and discussions which are
intended to be gathered up in the contract are inadmissible unless
the contract is ambiguous. There are obvious dangers in admitting
into evidence a tender which is itself ambiguous.

(3) *The consideration*

If a contract is silent on the consideration to be provided parol
evidence will be admissible to prove the price payable; *Jeffcott* v.
North British Oil Co. (1873), as well as to help the court decide
whether the price has in fact been paid: *Revenue Commisioners* v.
Moroney (1972). If one party has waived the right to payment of part
of the price, or indeed any other term, evidence of this will also be
admissible according to *Greenham* v. *Gray* (1855).

(4) *Custom*

If the parties to a contract recognise that a particular trade
custom exists then the parties will be permitted to adduce parol
testimony to bring this custom to the attention of the court. In *Wilson
Strain Ltd.* v. *Pinkerton* (1897) a bread roundsman who sold bread on
credit terms was able to adduce evidence to show that it was an
almost universal practice in the bakery industry in Belfast for the
employer to take over outstanding debts when a roundsman left
employment, rather than hold the roundsman personally liable.
Clearly the unreasonableness of the view that the employee was

himself liable influenced the court. If however the contract itself
clearly provides another rule then the custom cannot be admissible;
Malcolmson v. *Morton* (1847). Should the contract be silent the
position will be otherwise. In *Page* v. *Myer* (1861) a custom peculiar
to the grain trade was held admissible because the express terms of
the contract did not cover the point in question. In exceptional cases
it is not necessary for both parties to know of the existence of the
custom or trade practice; *King* v. *Hinde* (1883).

(5) *Where the written document is not the entire contract*

Wedderburn, in his important article in the 1959 Cambridge Law
Journal, argued that the parol evidence rule is little more than "a
self-evident tautology." If the contract document is intended to be
the entire contract parol evidence will not be admissible. If,
however, the written document is not intended to be the entire
contract but is to be supplemented by parol evidence then parol
evidence will be admissible. The rule then, provides us with a
presumption: a document that looks like a contract will be presumed
to be the entire contract unless evidence to the contrary is
forthcoming. The validity of this observation is graphically illustrated by the judgment of Wilson J. in *Howden* v. *Ulster Bank* (1924).
The plaintiffs ordered a ship to be built by a Larne shipyard which
went bankrupt shortly before the vessel was completed. The
plaintiffs sued to recover damages for wrongful detention of the
vessel by the trustee in bankruptcy who claimed that the ship
formed part of the assets of the bankrupt. The issue turned on
whether property in the vessel remained in the defendants or
whether it passed to the plaintiffs on payment of the price by
instalments. A memorandum of agreement indicated that title
remained in the defendants but Wilson J. found for the plaintiffs
after hearing oral testimony: "parol evidence of a verbal transaction
is not excluded by the fact that a writing was made concerning or
relating to it unless such writing was in fact the transaction itself and
not merely a note or memorandum of it or a portion of the
transaction." In *Clayton Love* v. *B+I Steampacket* (1966) Davitt P.
held that parol evidence of the terms of a telephone conversation
between the parties could be added to a written contract so as to
form one contract, partly written and partly oral. Although the
Supreme Court reversed Davitt P.'s judgment on another issue this
view of the limits of the parol evidence rule was undisturbed.

If there is a contradiction between a written contract and an oral
promise the courts will not enforce the oral promise, choosing
instead the terms of the written document if they have been
expressly drafted by one of the parties and agreed to. If however the

written term is on a printed, standard form document the recent English case of *Evans* v. *Merzario* (1976) suggests that the oral promise is to be given preference. It is hoped that this view will prevail in Ireland.

It should be noted that although the exceptions to the rule are so numerous and well established that it is doubtful whether any real injustice is caused by the rule, if it is applied properly, cases like *Oates* v. *Romano* (discussed above) show that judges who do not properly understand the role of the rule *as a presumption* may fall into error. The English Law Commission in a Working Paper have suggested the formal abolition of the rule.

Collateral Contracts

The partly written, partly oral contract seems to take effect as one contract. Nevertheless certain judges take the view that the strict terms of the parol evidence rule can be evaded by holding that *two* contracts may come into existence. The facts of *Webster* v. *Higgin* (1948) are instructive. The plaintiff inspected a vehicle owned by the defendants and was told by one of their employees, "if you buy the Hillman we will guarantee that its in good condition and that you will have no trouble with it." An exclusion clause attempted to nullify this promise by excluding all warranties. Lord Greene M.R. held that this promise was a *collateral* warranty which was not covered by the exclusion clause in the contract document.

Consideration must exist before this second or collateral contract can be enforced. In *Webster* v. *Higgin* consideration is provided by entering the main contract of purchase. Similarly, a landlord who promises to repair drains if the promisee signs a lease which is silent on this obligation to repair will be liable on this collateral contract. By signing the lease the promisee provides consideration for his prospective landlord's promise. In most cases it makes no difference if the promise is enforced either as a collateral warranty, *i.e.* it forms part of one contract, or if it takes effect as a separate or collateral contract. This will not always be the case. Should a contract for the sale of land be unenforceable because the memorandum is defective it may be possible to remedy the situation by holding that there are in fact two contracts. In *Godley* v. *Power* (1961) the Supreme Court held that a contract for the sale of a public house plus stock in trade was in fact two contracts. The memorandum setting out the terms of the sale of the premises did not recite the terms of the contract for sale of stock in trade. By holding that the stock was the subject of a collateral contract which, by definition, did not have to be included in the memorandum, the sale of the pub was enforceable. A similar problem may arise if a contract is void for illegality; English case law suggests that, notwithstanding this, a separate collateral contract will be valid.

The most important use to which the collateral contract— described by Roskill L.J. as "a lawyer's device"—can be put is to avoid the common law rule that a mere representation cannot lead to an award of damages. In order to avoid this rule it is increasingly common to plead that the statement made is independent or collateral to the main contract. While this practice may not now be as important, given the limited statutory reform effected in the Republic by the Sale of Goods and Supply of Services Act 1980, the collateral contract remains a useful part of a contract lawyer's armoury. We will return to this in Chapter 10.

6 Implied Terms

(1) Implied Terms at Common Law

We have already seen that not everything stated, before or at the time of agreement, will necessarily form part of the contract. In this Chapter we will consider the converse proposition: can the courts hold the bargain to include terms or obligations not expressly stated? The question is a difficult one to answer. While it is clear that additional terms may be read into the contract the circumstances in which the implication may be made are not the subject of universal agreement amongst the judiciary. Traditionally, the courts do not relish implying terms into a bargain because this results in a modification of the contract as struck by the parties. The courts shelter behind the maxim that "it is for the parties to strike a bargain; the judiciary serve merely to enforce it." On the other hand, some judges take the view that it is in the interests of justice for the courts to take a more active role. Lord Denning M.R. would support this view of the judicial function and he has argued that the courts may imply a term into a bargain simply because it is reasonable so to do. The House of Lords have rejected this view as "undesirable and way beyond sound authority:" per Lord Wilberforce in *Liverpool City Council* v. *Irwin* (1976).

(1) *The officious bystander test-obligations tacitly assumed*

It is clear that if a term is so obvious that it goes without saying that the bargain is subject to this unstated term then it will be included in the contract. This proposition is most clearly stated in an English Court of Appeal decision handed down in 1939; MacKinnon L.J. said in a famous passage: "[p]rima facie that which in any contract is left to be implied and need not be expressed is something so obvious that it goes without saying; so that, if while the parties were making their bargain, an officious bystander were to suggest some express provision for it in their agreement they would testily suppress him with a common 'oh, of course.' "

This test is extremely narrow. The court must find that *both*

58

parties had the term contended for in mind when they contracted. The facts of *Kavanagh* v. *Gilbert* (1875) may make this test clearer. The plaintiff sued an auctioneer who had agreed to sell the plaintiff's farm by auction. A bid was accepted by the auctioneer but no binding contract was concluded because the auctioneer failed to draft a memorandum of agreement. While the contract was silent on this point an officious bystander who interjected; " . . . surely the auctioneer will have to fill out a memorandum after the sale . . . " would incur the wrath of both parties in the manner predicted by McKinnon L.J. It was held that there was an implied obligation placed on the auctioneer that he would use care and skill. See also *Ward* v. *Stivack Ltd.* (1957).

The English case of *The Moorcock* (1889) is also said to be a case supporting the view that only if the court draws the conclusion that each party intended such and such a term to form part of their bargain can a term be implied. Bowen L.J., in giving judgment in that case however stated that "the law is raising an implication from the presumed intention of the parties with the object of giving the transaction such efficacy as both parties must have intended that at all events it should have." This test is extremely ambiguous. It is a wider test that the officious bystander test for it is doubtful whether the facts of the *Moorcock* would fall within McKinnon L.J.'s test. At its widest the *Moorcock* has been used to support the view that a reasonable term may be implied in the contract. Many judges have said that Bowen L.J. did not mean to go so far.

In commercial contracts the courts often present the test in *The Moorcock* in a different way: is it necessary to imply this term into the contract so as to give the contract the business efficacy both parties must have intended it to have? This business efficacy test has been considered in several Irish cases. In *O'Toole* v. *Palmer* (1943), Palmer, an auctioneer agreed with O'Toole that if O'Toole was able to find a purchaser willing to buy Vesey's land, then Palmer would agree to share the 5 per cent. commission fee so long as the fee was paid by the purchaser. O'Toole introduced a client of his to Palmer and the sale was completed. The purchaser however did not agree to pay the commission and Palmer closed the sale without the commission having being paid. O'Toole sued Palmer claiming that by closing the sale without obtaining the agreement of the purchaser to pay a commission Palmer had broken an implied term that he would not prevent the plaintiff from earning his remuneration. Gavan Duffy J. dismissed the action; "I do not think there is any necessity to imply a term for the purpose of giving the contract a business efficacy. Here the terms are clearly expressed in writing and the plaintiff has undertaken an ordinary business risk."

In *Murphy Buckley & Keogh* v. *Pye (Ireland)* (1971) the defendants engaged the plaintiffs to sell a factory in Dundrum on a sole agency basis. The defendants later sold the premises to a purchaser not introduced by the plaintiffs. The plaintiffs were unable to claim that the contract impliedly prevented the defendants from finding a purchaser; not only was such a term inconsistent with the presumed intent of the parties, the contract expressly provided that the auctioneers fee was only payable on completion of a transaction involving a purchaser introduced by the plaintiffs. The auctioneers were only entitled to recover advertising expenses. The view that the implied term doctrine has a limited scope has been recently reaffirmed by the Northern Ireland Court of Appeal in *Dept. of the Environment* v. *Watson* (1979), criticised by Dickson (1980) N.I.L.Q. 147.

(2) *Terms implied by law*

Even though the courts have not carved out for themselves a sweeping power to insert terms into a bargain simply because the judge feels it reasonable so to do, there are well established instances of legal duties being imposed upon contracting parties when it is clear that the parties themselves have not anticipated the dispute. In other words, a term will be implied at law because it is felt *necessary* so to do.

These duties often arise as incidents of well recognised legal relationships. A landlord, for example, owes the implied duty to allow the tenant quiet enjoyment of the premises. A particular difficulty arises where a contract for the sale of a house or for the lease of unfurnished premises is silent upon the condition of the property. The English common law rule provided that if a house was sold or let unfurnished and it turned out to be defective the purchaser could not recover on an implied warranty. It has been the view of many judges and commentators that Davitt P. in *Brown* v. *Norton* (1954) held this rule applicable in Ireland too. A close reading of the case discloses that Davitt P. held that on the sale of a house there is no *rule of law* that the premises will be fit for the purpose of occupation but there may still be room for an *implied term*. The Supreme Court recently held in *Siney* v. *Dublin Corporation* (1979) that when the Corporation let a new unfinished flat to the plaintiff they were liable in contract when it transpired that the flat was badly ventilated, causing damp which damaged the plaintiff's belongings.

The Supreme Court pointed out that while the case depended upon the specific fact that Dublin Corporation were under a statutory obligation as a Housing Authority, (which would not operate in private sector letting contracts) a reluctance to allow the vendor of property to continue to be immune from implied obligations may foreshadow overruling of the older case law. Indeed, if the vendor of property is also in the process of building the house there will be an implied term that the house will be built in an efficient manner and that it will be inhabitable: *Morris* v. *Redmond & Wright* (1935). In the Northern Ireland case of *McGeary* v. *Campbell* (1975) this implied term was extended to apply to work completed before and after the contract of purchase was concluded.

Lord Wilberforce, a senior member of the present House of Lords has pointed out that terms implied without reference to the intention of the parties are often implied in order to make an existing contractual relationship work efficiently. The test then is necessity, not reasonableness. A contract to let premises in a multi-storey apartment building will not be effective unless the tenant can gain access to the apartment. The letting contract will include an obligation at law obliging the lessor to do everything reasonable to maintain and repair the stairways lifts and escalators not included in the lease; *Liverpool City Council* v. *Irwin* (1976).

Contracts of employment also contain terms that are imposed by operation of law. An employer has to provide a safe system of work for his employees. He must give a reasonable period of notice to an employee he wishes to discharge. In *Carvill* v. *Irish Industrial Bank* (1968) the plaintiff served as Managing Director of the defendant company. By resolution of the Board the plaintiff was discharged from his post and from the Board of the company. He successfully contended that he had been discharged from a contract of employment in such a way as to breach the employers obligation to give a reasonable period of notice. Given the position of the plaintiff, his length of service and other factors, a reasonable period of notice was calculated at one year. Similar obligations are imposed by law on the employee. He has an obligation to faithfully serve his employer so if he "moonlights" by working for a rival concern he will break this implied term. In the Tasmanian case of *Orr* v. *University of Tasmania* (1956) a university professor who seduced a student was held to be in breach of the implied obligation to faithfully serve his employer and could be summarily dismissed. As we will see in a moment, there are also constitutional and statutory considerations which apply in employment contracts.

If a contract is silent on the method of termination then the courts will have to imply terms which will safeguard the legitimate interests of both parties. The leading authority here if the judgment of Finlay P. in *Irish Welding* v. *Philips Electrical (Ireland) Ltd.* (1976). The defendants appointed the plaintiffs to be sole agents for the sale of electrodes manufactured by the defendants. The defendants supplied electrodes to another wholesaler whereupon the plaintiffs sought an injunction to restrain the defendants. The defendants denied that this agreement prevented them from supplying electrodes to third parties and they purported to immediately terminate the agreement. Finlay P. considered the question of whether and how the contract could be terminated. The plaintiffs argued it was not terminable at all. Finlay P., after referring to the complex chain of distributors built up by the plaintiffs said it was "quite unreal to suggest that it could possibly have been within the contemplation of either party that the other should be entitled to terminate the agreement instanter and without notice." Finlay P. held that the contract should be viewed as terminable after a reasonable period of time, in this case nine months.

An obligation not to derogate from an express grant will also be implied; a vendor who agrees to sell land subject to the granting of planning permission will not be allowed to obstruct the completion of the sale by objecting to the application should there be a change of mind. In a recent English case a soccer club agreed to pay a transfer fee of £200,000 for a player, with an additional sum if he scored 20 goals. The player was transferred to another club before he had a reasonable time to score the goals. This was held to breach an implied term: *Bournemouth A.F.C.* v. *Manchester United* (1980).

(2) Terms Implied Under Statute

Several common law obligations have been codified into statutes which form part of a contractual relationship. The most important example of this is presented by the implied obligations arising under the Sale of Goods Act 1893 and the Republic's Sale of Goods and Supply of Services Act 1980. Common law obligations requiring the seller of goods to supply goods which are of merchantable quality and which are fit for the purpose for which they are intended are part of the 1893 Act, s.14. These obligations could formerly be excluded if the parties so agreed but this is no longer possible in consumer sales after the 1980 Act. This issue is too complex to be dealt with here and readers are referred to O'Malley, *Commercial Law*. Similar obligations are placed on the owner of goods under a hire purchase contract; see *Butterly* v. *UDT* (1963).

The employment contract provides another rich source of statutory implied terms. Wages are often pegged in a variety of industries by statutory bodies rather than by agreement between the parties; *e.g.* wages of agricultural labourers. The obligation on an employer to provide holiday pay stems from statute and not a contract expressly struck by the parties. There are important restrictions on the freedom of an employer to dismiss his employees without giving a *minimum* period of notice. An employee dismissed after 13 weeks of employment but before two years service is entitled to one week's notice or wages in lieu thereof. This sliding scale progresses until workers who have served for more than 15 years are entitled to eight weeks' notice. These provisions, to be found in section 4 of the Minimum Notice and Terms of Employment Act 1973, cannot be excluded by agreement. They are a *minimum* requirement and can be expanded by agreement or by circumstances. The case of *Carvill* v. *Irish Industrial Bank*, discussed above, would not be decided differently today.

Statute also provides for implied terms to exist in landlord and tenant agreements. See for example the power of a Housing Authority to pass by-laws under section 70 of the Housing Act 1966 to impose minimum standards for rented property within their functional area.

(3) Terms Implied Under the Constitution

Important differences between Irish contract law and English contract principles arise because of the operation of the 1937 Constitution which sets out certain fundamental freedoms, absent from the English common law.

Article 40.6 subsections (1)(iii) and 2° have been interpreted as conferring upon citizens the right not only to form associations and unions but an implicit right not to join—a right of disassociation; *Educational Company of Ireland Ltd.* v. *Fitzpatrick* (No.2) (1961). The Supreme Court have ruled in *Meskell* v. *C.I.E.* (1973) that this right of dissociation must be respected by an employer, even if the employer threatens to exercise his common law right of dismissal in a manner permissible at common law. Meskell was employed as a bus conductor. C.I.E. offered Meskell a new contract of employment which would oblige him to join and maintain membership of a trade union. Failure to assent would lead, after a reasonable period of notice, to termination of his employment. Meskell objected in principle and, following his refusal and dismissal, sued, alleging an actionable conspiracy by the unions and C.I.E. to infringe his constitutional right of disassociation. Walsh J., in the leading judgment, held that the fact that a person seeks to exercise a common law right in such a way as to dissuade a citizen from exercising a constitutional right "must necessarily be regarded as an abuse of the common law right because it is an infringement, and an abuse, of the constitution which is superior to the common law and which must prevail if there is a conflict between the two." In other words, if a statutory provision can override a common law right (or even an express agreement) then a right implied under the Constitution must, *a fortiori*, take priority over this common law right. Damages will also be recoverable for infringement of this constitutional right even if no other cause of action would appear to exist; per Walsh J. in *Meskell* v. *C.I.E.*

Article 40.3 has been held to require that procedures and machinery established to reach decisions which effect the rights or liabilities of citizens must be fair. These procedures must allow a party to be heard if he is accused of breach of contract. In *Glover* v. *B.L.N.* (1973), an employee was summarily dismissed for alleged misconduct. Clause 12(*c*) of the contract provided he could be so dismissed without compensation for serious misconduct. Walsh J. held that "this procedure was a breach of the implied term of the contract that the procedure should be fair, as it cannot be disputed, in the light of so much authority on the point, that failure to allow a person to meet the charges against him and afford him an adequate opportunity of answering them is a violation of an obligation to proceed fairly." See also *Garvey* v. *Ireland* (1979), discussed on p. 222.

These implied obligations are not immutable however. If the parties agree in circumstances where it is clear that each is in a position to freely negotiate and that each understands the bargain then it may be possible for a citizen to waive a constitutional right of dissociation or fair procedures. As yet no cases have been decided on the doctrine or waiver of fundamental freedoms.

(4) Custom

It is possible for terms to be implied into contracts because of the commercial or local backcloth against which a contract is to take effect. Customs within a trade or industry can become part of the contract; in *Taylor* v. *Hall* (1869) an alleged custom in the building industry was rejected as inconsistent with the evidence adduced. This question was considered in the preceding chapter. Local agricultural customs become part of the agreement as an implied term. See for example the Ulster tenant's right of sale, discussed in Vol.32 (1898) I.L.T. at page 309 and Wylie, *Irish Land Law* s. 1.44–1.45.

7 The Exemption Clause

An exemption clause is a contractual term by which one party attempts to cut down either the scope of his contractual duties or regulate the other parties right to damages for breach of contract. So in a *non-consumer* contract for the sale of goods any attempt by the seller to exclude implied obligations as to merchantability can be interpreted as effectively removing any obligation to supply merchantable goods; under the 1893 Sale of Goods Act, as amended in the Republic by the Sale of Goods and Supply of Services Act 1980 such an attempt to eliminate this obligation must be shown to be fair and reasonable; see sections 14(2) and 55(4).

One party may not attempt to eliminate the other's rights altogether but simply require any complaints about defective performance to be lodged within a set period, say within 14 days; failure to satisfy this term will result in loss of any cause of action. Alternatively, the seller may limit the damages recoverable to a fixed sum, *e.g.* £50. In *Leonard* v. *Gt. Northern Ry. Co.* (1912) plaintiff sent a consignment of turkeys by rail. On arrival, four were missing. Under the terms of the contract set out on the forwarding note the plaintiff was required to notify the carriers of loss within three days. The plaintiff failed to do this. The plaintiff's claim was dismissed because of failure to comply with the notice provision.

If the clause negatives a right to performance it is said to have *substantive* effect; if the clause regulates entitlement to damages it is *procedural;* only failure to satisfy the procedural steps laid down results in loss of the right to damages.

The exemption clause possessing substantive effect is designed to allocate risk between contracting parties: should goods stored with a bailee under a bailment contract be destroyed while in his possession the bailee may have anticipated this possibility and by contract transferred risk to the owner. In principle there is no reason why this should not be permitted where the bailee has not acted negligently or deliberately destroyed the goods. Difficulties arise when the party invoking the exemption clause is in a stronger bargaining position and has exploited this by including a draconian provision which, on its face, protects him in every situation. The courts and the legislature have dealt with such instances of abuse of freedom of contract in different ways.

Judicial Response to Exemption Clauses

Before an exemption clause (also known as an exclusion or exculpatory clause) will be permitted to take effect it must pass two tests. First of all, the provision upon which the party asserting it seeks to rely, (the proferens) must be incorporated into the contract. Secondly, as a matter of construction, the clause must cover the events that have occurred. We will deal with these issues separately.

Incorporation

(1) *Incorporation—basic rules*

The Irish courts, like their English brethren have struggled with the problem of incorporation because the tests advanced have varied from time to time. This is particularly so when it is clear that the party against whom the clause is asserted has not read the exempting provision. In one early Irish case the plaintiff was held bound by an exempting provision printed on a railway ticket which exempted the company from liability should passengers be injured. The plaintiff was bound because he was said to have had the means of discovering the clause, that is, constructive notice; *Johnson* v. *Gt. Southern & W. Ry.* (1874). Three years later the English Court of Appeal decided the leading case of *Parker* v. *S.E. Railway.* In cases where someone is given a ticket or document which sets out or refers to limiting conditions to be read elsewhere the proferens will be able to rely on the terms if he can show that the other party read them or that he, the proferens, did everything reasonable to bring the clause to the attention of the public. Several questions were set out in *Parker* v. *S.E. Railway* which the court should ask; these questions can be paraphrased in the following way:

(i) Did the party know of the conditions? If so he is bound.
(ii) Was notice given? If not the other party is not bound; *Roche* v. *Cork, Blackrock and Passage Railway Co.* (1889).
(iii) If notice was given but the other party did not know the notice contained writing he will not be bound.
(iv) If he did know there was writing on the document then the court must ask whether reasonable notice of the conditions has been given. If the other party knows the ticket contained not merely writing but conditions he will be bound even if he is unaware of the precise terms; *Taggart* v. *Northern Counties Ry.* (1898) c.f. *Miley* v. *R. & J. McKechnie* (1949).

The reasonableness test marks an improvement on the earlier *Johnson* case but there are still difficult issues of fact to be resolved. Nevertheless *Johnson* must be regarded as having been overruled by the House of Lords in *Rowntree's Case* (1894) which was in turn applied in *Ryan* v. *Gt. Southern & Western Ry.* (1898). A company which lost the plaintiff's baggage were held to be liable notwithstanding the terms of the plaintiffs ticket which referred to limiting provisions which could be inspected; the plaintiff was unaware that the ticket contained limiting conditions.

The Irish courts have not laid down exacting standards which a proferens must meet before the limiting term will be incorporated. In the case of *Early* v. *Gt. Southern Ry.* (1940) the plaintiff was given an excursion ticket which on its face referred the passenger to the company's special conditions containing the limiting provisions. The plaintiff was injured. Notwithstanding the fact that the conditions were not available for inspection at this particular booking office the defendants were held entitled to rely on this clause: see also *O'Donovan* v. *Gt. S. Ry.* (1938) and *Shea* v. *Gt. S. Ry.* (1944).

There are signs that the English courts are revising these rules on incorporation, particularly where the risk is an unusual one; see Lord Denning M.R. in *Thornton* v. *Shoe Lane Parking* (1970). Even the rules laid down in *Parker* v. *S.E. Ry.* (above) have been revised; see the author's note in (1979) 30 N.I.L.Q. 39.

If the proferens wants to be sure that the clause will be incorporated into the contract he should obtain the signature of the other party to a contract document setting at the term: *Duff* v. *Gt. Northern Railway* (1878). On signature the other party will be bound, even if the document is unread and the terms are set out in miniscule print. Again, Denning M.R. has hinted that signature may not automatically incorporate the term; *Levison* v. *Patent Steam Carpet Cleaning* (1978).

(2) The time at which notice was given

The general rule is that notice of a limiting clause, given after the contract is concluded, cannot bind the other party. In *Sproule* v. *Triumph Cycle Co.* (1927) the plaintiff approached an agent of the defendants with a view to buying a motor cycle. He did not read a catalogue which attempted to limit the defendants' obligations to replacement of defective parts for 3 months after purchase. This "guarantee" was also set out on a card attached to the bike although this was not handed to the plaintiff and read by him until after the sale had been concluded. The plaintiff was held entitled to rely on section 14(1) of the 1893 Act. Moore C.J. held the guarantee

ineffective because it was not read until after the contract had been
concluded. It should be noted that when the case does not involve a
railway ticket case the onus on the proferens is greater when he
alleges incorporation has occurred.

Two Irish cases that seem to be inconsistent with this reasoning
are *Knox* v. *Gt. Northern Railway* (1896) and *Slattery* v. *C.I.E.* (1972).
Both cases concerned contracts to transport a horse, the horse being
injured as a result of the defendant's employees' negligence. In
Slattery v. *C.I.E.* the plaintiff signed a consignment note which stated
that delivery would take place at the owners risk. This note was not
signed until after the injury to the horse had occurred and after the
journey had been completed; this was an oversight on the
defendant's part. The defendants were held to be entitled to rely on
the document as setting out the terms of the agreement. It should be
noted that in this case, as in *Knox,* the plaintiffs envisaged that the
contract document had still to be completed; as Holmes J. said in
Knox: "It is neither illegal, unreasonable nor unusual, for the terms
of a contract to be reduced to writing after the performance of the
services contracted for has been begun." If this was a case of the
proferens attempting to add an exempting clause when a written
contract had already been completed, as occurred in the English
case of *Olley* v. *Marlborough Court Hotel,* such an attempt would no
doubt fail in Ireland: *Moynihan* v. *Crowley & Warren & Co.* (1958).

(3) *Incorporation by a course of dealing*

The rules on incorporation present difficult issues of fact for the
courts because a litigant who argues that he did not read the
document cannot prove this contention very easily, and *vice versa*. If
the parties contract with each other frequently and on a regular
basis however the court has to balance the obvious injustice of
holding one party bound by a term which he did not read, (much
less assent to), against the expectations of the proferens. If the
parties contract regularly and the proferens issues documents which
transfer risk to the other party he is entitled to assume that there is
assent to the terms offered. Thus, in *Spurling* v. *Bradshaw* (1956) the
owner of goods contracted to store his property with the defendant.
These bailment contracts took place regularly. On each occasion the
bailee handed a document which limited the bailee's liability. The
plaintiff at no time read the document or the conditions. This was
not a ticket case: it was a contract freely negotiated. The English
Court of Appeal held the plaintiff bound by this limiting clause; "by
the course of business and conduct of the parties these conditions
were part of the contract."

For incorporation by course of dealing to occur the trade practice relied on by the proferens must be consistent. One or two isolated transactions do not constitute a course of dealing unless both parties are of similar bargaining strength and operate on terms which are acknowledged to be common within their industry: *British Crane Hire* (1975). The courts are less inclined to find a limiting clause incorporated if the transaction involves a large business and an individual consumer. In *Hollier* v. *Rambler Motors* (1972) the owner of a motor vehicle had left his car to be repaired with the defendants on three or four occasions over a number of years. He had then been given a receipt containing a limiting clause. On the occasion in question he left his car with the defendants again but he was not given a receipt containing the clause. The Court of Appeal held that the three or four isolated transactions between consumer and proferens did not incorporate the limiting clause into their last contract. The plaintiff was able to recover for the loss of his car when the garage burnt down.

In *Miley* v. *R. & J. McKechnie Ltd* (1949) the plaintiff left a garment to be cleaned. The defendant's employee gave her a receipt, marked "important" which set out in on the face "All orders accepted without guarantee" and directed the attention of holders to conditions printed on the back. Miss Miley had contracted with the defendants regularly and had always been given such a receipt. She claimed that she at no time read the conditions but did know that the writing contained conditions. Judge Shannon held that display of conditions, the invariable practice of handing a ticket were sufficient to exempt the defendants from liability. The fact that Miss Miley had not read the conditions and that the ticket was given after the contract concluded was unimportant given the course of dealing between the parties. See also *Bates* v. *O'Connor* (1932). *Miley* would be decided differently under the 1980 Act; s.40 requires a limiting clause to be specifically brought to the attention of the consumer.

Construction of the Exempting Clause

While it is no doubt paradoxical to adopt less than demanding rules on incorporation while at the same time requiring the proferens to draft the clause with great precision Lord O'Hagan defended this position when he said in *McNally* v. *Lancs & York Railway* (1880); "[t]here can be no hardship imposed by requiring companies to be clear and explicit in the framing of conditions designed for their own security. The humble and ignorant dealers who enter into transactions are at a disadvantage and at least they should be held strictly to the terms of the contracts deliberately prepared by their skilled advisors."

In viewing an exemption clause restrictively the courts have developed several important rules or maxims of construction.

(1) *The contra proferentum rule*

If the exempting provision is ambiguous and capable of more than one interpretation then the courts will read the clause against the party seeking to rely on it. In consumer transactions this will be an important rule, of benefit to the consumer, because it will generally be the seller who asserts that he is entitled to rely on the clause. In *Sproule* v. *Triumph Cycle Co.* (1927) the seller of a motor bike tried to rely on a limiting clause excluding liability for breach of warranty: the purchaser argued that because section 14 of the Sale of Goods Act 1893 implies a condition this word "warranty" should be given its narrower meaning under that Act. The point was not decided by the Court of Appeal for Northern Ireland. See *Webster* v. *Higgin*, discussed in Chapter 5.

The *contra proferentum* rule is only one of interpretation and can be overcome by intelligent drafting. A court may find that the proferens has employed a lawyer who has designed a clause so as to eliminate all liability for "breach of all conditions and warranties express or implied under statute or common law, and all collateral warranties." In such a case the usefulness of this rule comes to an end.

(2) *The risk covered*

Another approach advanced by the courts is to hold the words of an exempting clause inapplicable to certain eventualities. The words of the clause may not be viewed as excluding liability in several extreme cases. In *Ronan* v. *Midland Railway Co.* (1883) the plaintiff agreed to ship his cattle with the defendants and he was given a receipt which said that the cattle were to travel "at owners risk." The cattle were wilfully damaged and mutilated by the defendants employees. The phrase "at owners risk" was held not to exclude liability for deliberate acts of destruction.

The courts are reluctant to permit a proferens to exclude liability for the negligence of himself or his agents or employees but if the clause is specific enough then this will be permitted: *Millar* v. *Midland Gt. W. Ry.* (1905). If this happens the proferens will only be liable for wilful default. The judgment of Lord Morton in *Canada Steamship Lines* v. *The King* (1952) provides the best summary of the rules a court should follow where a cause of action in negligence is at issue:

(1) If the clause expressly exempts the proferens from liability for his own negligence the clause must be given effect.

(2) If the clause does not expressly refer to negligence the question is whether the words, given their ordinary meaning, cover negligence. The *contra proferentum* rule comes into play here. Phrases that do exclude liability for negligence include "liability for all loss, *howsoever caused* is excluded" and "cars are driven at owner's sole risk" if the only liability possible is negligence: *Rutter* v. *Palmer* (1922).

(3) If the ordinary words are wide enough to exclude liability for negligence the court has to consider whether some other basis of liability—statutory or contractual for example—can exist. If so, the proferens will be taken to have intended only to exclude liability for actions other than negligence. So in *White* v. *Warrick* (1953) the hirer of a bicycle was injured when the saddle slipped while he was riding the machine. The limiting clause was held to exclude strict liability in contract while leaving the owner liable in negligence.

At one time the view was expressed that if there could only be one basis of liability then a very general limiting clause must be read so as to exclude that cause of action; this view, attributed to Lord Greene in *Alderslade* v. *Hendon Laundry* (1945) has been rejected by members of the Court of Appeal in *Hollier* v. *Rambler Motors* (1972) and *Gillespie* v. *Roy Bowles* (1973). These recent cases are in sympathy with the objective of protecting the consumer.

(3) *The main purpose rule*

This important rule of construction is designed to cut down the effect of a limiting clause which would produce undesirable consequences if the clause was read literally. The courts look to circumstances surrounding the transaction and, aided by the sometimes dubious premise that both parties are acting as reasonable men, the judges cut down general words in a contract. So in *Glynn* v. *Margotson* (1893) a general clause that gave the carrier of a cargo of oranges the liberty to stay at any port in the Mediterranean, Black Sea or Adriatic was held not to exclude liability for damage to the cargo as a result of delay in proceeding directly from Malaga to Liverpool. The House of Lords presumed the main purpose of the contract was the safe transport of the goods. Lord Halsbury said; "looking at the whole instrument and seeing what one must regard as its main purpose one must reject words, indeed whole provisions, if they are inconsistent with what one assumes to be the main purpose of the contract." If the parties do intend to prevent the judges from imputing a main purpose they may do so but very clear evidence of intention and consent to such a term must be disclosed; *Connolly Shaw Ltd.* v. *Nosdenfjeldske S.S. Co.* (1934).

The Core Obligation and Exclusion Clauses

Can a limiting clause be so widely drafted as to permit the proferens to avoid liability in cases which amount to non perform- ance of the promissory part of the contract? This proposition has troubled the English courts for the past 50 years. The problem was identified in *L'Estrange* v. *Graucob* (1934) when the plaintiff was held bound by her signature to a contract for the purchase of a cigarette vending machine. The exempting provisions of the contract protected the seller in the event of any breach of contract short of non delivery of the machine and outright refusal to service it.

The problem raised by "catch-all" exemption clauses may be one of definition; can a contract exist if the limiting provisions are so sweeping as to empty the contract of all promissory content? An airline that promises, we will fly you from A to B and then conditions this promise by adding, we will not be liable if we cancel all flights from A to B is creating an illusory contract; (see Chap. 1). The difficulty here stems from the fact that the passenger will generally not be aware of this qualifying term or in a position to negotiate an improved contract—he will be told to take it or leave it. (*c.f. Shea* v. *Gt. S. Ry.* (1944), per Davitt J.)

It may be that both parties are prepared to agree that the risk of non performance is to be taken by the purchaser. If each is free to agree to such a contract then the courts should enforce the contract because the core obligation of the contract must be taken to involve this allocation of risk. The point is well illustrated by two Irish cases decided in the 1940s. In *O'Connor* v. *McCowen & Sons Ltd.* (1943) the defendants sold turnip seeds to the plaintiff. Prior to the sale the defendants stated that they had not obtained the seeds from their usual source and could not guarantee them. The seeds produced a plant that bore little resemblance to a turnip and was commercially worthless. The defendant argued that he was not liable because of his statement negativing a guarantee. Overend J. indicated that these words were not such as to amount to an agreement exempting the defendants from liability, following the leading English case of *Wallis* v. *Pratt & Haynes* (1910). Overend J. characterised this case as one where the purchaser was buying goods by description, the goods supplied not answering the description at all. If liability is to be excluded "the very clearest words must be used by the seller, such as: 'you may be purchasing seeds that are not turnip seeds at all.' " Overend J. continued by observing that the obligation in this case did not arise under the Sale of Goods Act: "the buyer, however, got something that was not turnip seed, and *quite apart from the Sale of Goods Act* he had a cause of action." In other words, the fact that a seller tries to exclude the terms implied under statute will not protect him in cases where he delivers goods different from those he contracted to sell. If, to use the facts of *O'Connor* the purchaser is to take the risk of seeds not producing turnip plants at all he must be aware that this forms the basis of the contract. If the seeds sown had merely produced a poor crop of turnips then the seller may be protected, for this would not be the core obligation but a condition of warranty, then amendable to exclusion under section 55 of the 1893 Act. In *Wicklow Corn Co. Ltd.* v. *Edward Fitzgerald Ltd.* (1942), a Circuit Court case, Judge Davitt held a corn factor to be protected by a clause excluding section 14 of the 1893 Act when seed wheat sold produced a poor crop. Here the defect was held to be one of quality only rather than an extreme case where another substance is supplied. In cases where a different substance is supplied it is better to treat this as a case of non-performance, to which the exempting clause is inapplicable except where the evidence suggests that the core obligation was speculative; a *spes*. A contract to sell peas is not performed by supplying beans. A contract to sell a tractor is not performed by supplying three horses. The same point was made by Dodd J., in *Fogarty* v. *Dickson* (1913) when he said "if a man orders a golf cloth cap, the order is not fulfilled by sending him a stylish silk hat". See also the case of *American Can Co.* v. *Stewart* (1915).

The response of the English courts to the problem of the draconian exemption clause was to develop a rule of substantive law expressed by Denning L.J. (as he then was), in the following terms: "exempting clauses of this kind, no matter how widely they are expressed only avail the party when he is carrying out his contract in its essential respects." So the supply of a car that was totally incapable of propulsion could not be excused by a sweeping clause: *Karsales (Harrow)* v. *Wallis* (1956). This is the doctrine of fundamental breach of contract. The difficulty with this rule of law (as many critics have pointed out) is that it treats all exemption clauses and all parties as if they were alike; in fact there are cases where it may be reasonable to permit a limiting clause to operate so as to "shrink" the core obligation, thereby re-allocating risk. The House of Lords in the *Suisse Atlantique* (1966) rejected *obiter* the view that this rule of substantive law or doctrine of fundamental breach was other than a rule of construction. In the later case of *Harbutt's Plasticine* v. *Wayne Tank Corp.* (1970) the unsatisfactory nature of the fundamental breach doctrine was illustrated. The plaintiffs contracted with the defendants who were to install pipes into the plaintiff's factory where plasticine would be manufactured. Molten plasticine was to pass along the plastic pipes installed by the defendants as per specification. Unfortunately the pipes were not strong enough for the task and the molten plasticine caused the pipes to melt, resulting in the total loss of the factory. The parties had agreed that for any loss caused by the defendants damages payable would be limited to £15,000. Now this agreement was struck between two commercial concerns both of whom had the right to consult lawyers. The agreement was obviously drafted by lawyers and the clause clearly covered the case. Insurance was arranged on the basis of this agreement but because of the "fundamental breach" doctrine reliance on the clause was denied to the defendants. The House of Lords *in Photo Production Ltd. v. Securicor Transport Ltd.* (1980) have overruled *Harbutt's Plasticine* as being a doctrine of law of doubtful parentage.

This will no doubt cause the Supreme Court to reconsider its own approach in the leading Irish case of *Clayton Love* v. *B.I. Steampacket* (1966). The parties contracted to transport deep frozen scampi from Dublin to Liverpool. The loading was conducted at atmospheric temperature and this led to the scampi deteriorating to the extent that it was condemned when it arrived in Liverpool. The plaintiffs sued but were met by two exemption clauses, one of which was drafted widely enough to protect the defendants from liability. The second clause obliged the plaintiffs to claim within three days, otherwise the claim would be absolutely barred. Davitt P. at first instance relied on the substantive rule of law and (now discredited) dicta in two English cases, *Spurling Ltd.* v. *Bradshaw* (1956) and *Smeaton Hanscomb & Co. Ltd.* v. *Sassoon I. Setty* (1953) and refused to apply the first limiting clause. It is symptomatic of both the confusion and complexity of this doctrine that Davitt P. then shifted ground, applying the second clause, holding that "it was intended to, and does in face (sic) cover the case of a clause arising from the breach of a fundamental term of the contract." This reasoning seems to be unsatisfactory because Davitt P. applied a rule of law to the first clause and a rule of interpretation to the other limiting clause. The Supreme Court eliminated this inconsistency by holding that the rule of law must apply to the second limiting clause, regardless of the intention of the proferens.

A better approach to the problem in *Clayton Love* would have been to ask if the contract had been freely negotiated; did the shipper have a choice of terms upon which he could ship his goods (as in *Slattery* v. *C.I.E.* (1970))? Most importantly, did the shipper know and consent to loading of such delicate frozen goods at atmospheric temperatures and did he know of the existence of this sweeping clause? It is probable that the Supreme Court would have still found in favour of the plaintiffs but they would have addressed the issues of freedom of contract and consent, factors that were not always considered by pro-fundamental breach judges.

To summarise; the exemption clause which attacks the core obligation does not attack mere conditions or warranties but the foundation of the contract. If this is the case then the courts should consider whether the parties are contracting in circumstances which show that risk is being freely and voluntarily redistributed by the contract. The courts will lean against enforcement of unconscionable bargains and illusory promises by using the rules and principles specifically developed to deal with such agreements.

Refusal to Apply Exemption Clauses

An exemption clause will not be allowed to operate if someone assents to a clause, the terms of which are misrepresented by the proferens or his ostensible agent. It seems immaterial whether the misrepresentation is fraudulent or innocent. For an example where such an argument was raised see *Bolland* v. *Waterford, Limerick & Western Railway* (1897).

If an oral undertaking is given by the proferens the courts will regard the oral undertaking as taking priority over the printed terms in a standard form agreement; see *Evans* v. *Merzario* (1976). If however the oral undertaking is inconsistent with a document that was specifically drafted to record the agreement then it may be that the courts will feel compelled by the last vestiges of the parol evidence rule to give effect to the written terms.

An exemption clause which excludes "all warranties" may not be held applicable to "collateral warranties" unless "collateral warranties" are expressly negatived: *Andrews* v. *Hopkinson* (1957).

The doctrine of privity of contract also raises acute problems in relation to exemption clauses. At one time the view was that only a part to a contract could obtain the protection of an exempting clause but two recent Privy Council decisions suggest that if the parties envisaged that third parties were to be protected, commercial expectations must be respected, even at the cost of doctrinal or legal niceties: we will examine these two cases, *The Eurymedon* (1974) and *The New York Star* (1980) in the Chapter on privity of contract.

Statutory Intervention

In the Republic the Oireachtas has intervened in order to regulate the extent to which a limiting clause may be relied upon in many everyday transactions.

In cases of bailment specific rules apply under the Hotel Proprietors Act 1963. If a hotel proprietor displays a notice informing persons who book sleeping accommodation that liability for loss of guests' property is to be regulated by the Act, the proprietor will, under section 7 of the Act, only be liable to compensate up to a maximum sum of £100. If the loss of property is the result of an act of God, act of war or is due to the actions of the guest or a person accompanying him, the proprietor is exempt from liability. The £100 ceiling does not operate if a notice is not conspicuously displayed at the reception desk, or if the loss results from the wrongful act, default or omission of the proprietor or his employees. If goods are left for safekeeping with the proprietor and they are destroyed, damaged or lost the proprietor cannot rely on the £100 ceiling. Nor will the £100 limit apply if the guest's motor car is lost, damaged or stolen when the vehicle is brought onto hotel property. While the Act in some cases limits the proprietor's liability and this is of benefit to him, a balance is struck by s.9 which provides that a term excluding or varying liability is void. Similar legislation is in force in Northern Ireland: see the Hotel Proprietors Act (N.I.) 1958.

In contracts for the transport of goods and passengers the Transport Act 1958 permits C.I.E. a wide discretion as to the terms upon which it wishes to contract. Section 8(3) provides that C.I.E. "may attach to any service provided by it such terms and conditions as the Board thinks fit." The Railway and Canal Traffic Act 1854 attempted to limit the content of contracts of carriage to conditions which were judged by the court to be "just and reasonable." The Act, as amended by the Transport Act 1958 prevents a court from ruling on whether the terms imposed are "just and reasonable" for sections 8(4) & (5) of the 1958 Act provides that all contracts for the carriage of merchandise which are deemed to comply with Statutory Rule and Order 13 of 1930 "shall be deemed to be carriage of that commodity under terms and conditions which are just and reasonable." This statutory presumption does not operate if a passenger is injured but it remains open to C.I.E. to limit liability for such injuries too. Section 40(*b*) of the 1980 Act prevents section 39 of the Act (which imposes implied undertakings as to the quality of a service) from applying until such time and on such terms as the Minister for Transport sees proper. Contrast section 3 of the Unfair Contract Terms Act 1977, a British Statute in force in Northern Ireland.

The Sale of Goods and Supply of Services Act 1980 now makes it impossible in consumer contracts for the sale of goods and hire purchase to contract out of the implied obligations as to title, merchantability and fitness for purpose. Even before the 1980 Act the owner of goods bailed under a hire purchase contract had little freedom to "contract out." This topic is also considered in O'Malley, *Commercial Law*.

Contracts Governed by Foreign Law

It may be possible for a limiting clause to be invalid if the contract is governed by foreign law, the clause in question infringing the domestic law rules of that jurisdiction. This point is illustrated by *McNamara* v. *S.S. Hatteras* (1931) where a provision in a bill of lading was struck down because it infringed United States legislation: see now the Sale of Goods and Supply of Services Act 1980, s.42.

8 Importance and Relative Effects of Contractual Terms

Not all contractual terms are of the same weight and importance. At one time the common law position was different. All promises were independent in the sense that if one party failed to perform his contractual obligations the contractual obligations of the innocent party subsisted; the innocent party could not use the other's breach as an excuse for non performance. He was obliged to perform and sue the other for all loss occasioned by the breach of contract. If both parties broke the agreement and one party sued, the defendant could not plead that the plaintiff's own breach of contract excused the defendant. The defendant's remedy was a cross action for damages. So a promise by A to pay £1,000 for a piece of land owned by B was described in the language of the day as an independent promise. Should B fail to convey land he could not excuse non performance by asserting that A had broken his own covenant to pay £1,000 at a date prior to the agreed date for completion; B's remedy was an action for the £1,000.

Lord Mansfield identified this as a source of some injustice; should A be unable to pay £1,000 this would oblige B to convey without giving him any realistic hope of obtaining the consideration promised by A. In *Kingston* v. *Preston* (1773) Lord Mansfield laid down that contract terms could be broken down into three types of obligation. First of all, promises could be dependent; A's failure to perform an obligation was a condition precedent preventing B's obligation from accruing at all. Secondly, promises designed to be performed simultaneously with those of the other contracting party were described as concurrent obligations; this concurrent obligation was dependent in the sense that if the plaintiff alleged breach by the defendant he could not recover damages unless he pleaded performance of his own obligation or at least willingness to perform; thirdly, obligations could be independent. These promises were actionable without reference to the obligations of the plaintiff.

The problem that bedevils this classification is who is to decide which category the obligation falls into? If the parties have taken the trouble to "label" each obligation then the courts will respect this but, in the real world, commercial men are not so fastidious. As a result, obligations and their importance came to be an area for the exercise of judicial discretion. So, in *Ritchie* v. *Atkinson* (1808) a vessel left the Port of St. Peterburgh with a short cargo. Loading was broken off because of the danger of hostilities breaking out between Britain and Russia. On its arrival in Britain the merchant refused to pay the shipowners their freight, claiming that the obligation to deliver a full cargo was a condition precedent to the merchants obligation. To uphold such a plea would have permitted the merchant to obtain free transportation of his goods. The Court of Kings Bench held the breach of contract had minor consequences for the merchant. The obligation to deliver a full cargo was independent and the merchant was obliged to pay freight on a *pro rata* basis; any loss suffered by the defendant as a result of the short cargo was to be actionable in damages.

In the Irish case of *Knox* v. *Mayne* (1873) the Court of Exchequer upheld a plea of condition precedent. The vendors of a cargo of maize sued the defendant purchasers for non-acceptance. The purchaser was to have "privilege of having shipment to direct port" to be nominated by him. The vendors shipped the final cargo without requesting a port of discharge, whereupon the defendants took delivery but refused to pay for the cargo. The plaintiffs argued that it was for the defendants to show loss resulted from the breach. It was held that the right of selection had to be given to the defendants. The failure here was failure of a condition precedent, not a collateral or independent covenant.

It is established that if a farmer acquiring land under an agistment or conacre agreement fails to pay the contract price this constitutes breach of a dependent covenant; the landowner may treat this failure as terminating his own obligation to permit user of the land.

On the other hand, the agistment case (*Carson* v. *Jeffers* (1961)) must be contrasted with obligations under a lease. In *Athol* v. *Midland Gt. W. Ry. Co.* (1867) the lessor covenanted to permit the plaintiff lessees user of a conduit for draining excess water from the land leased to them. The defendant lessor diverted the conduit. An action by the plaintiffs was met with the plea that they had not paid rent and that payment was a condition precedent to the defendant's obligation to permit user of the conduit. The plea failed; each obligation was held to be independent.

The identification of the dependent covenant is an almost mystical process. It may be that the parties do stipulate that A's failure to perform such and such an obligation will prevent B's own obligations from coming into play but this is unlikely. The courts then operate without clear guidance from the parties in many of these cases. The process of construction or interpretation has at its root three important principles; (1) statutory guidance; (2) precedent or commercial practice; (3) the desire to do justice and award the most appropriate remedy, given the loss suffered. Again we should be aware that Lord Mansfield's views are enjoying something of a renaissance, the principles that produced *Kingston* v. *Preston* (1773) can be closely identified with guiding principle (3).

Before we turn to this however it is necessary to mention the effects of the Sale of Goods Act 1893 on the common law rules outlined above. Although this Act should not have influenced the courts in non sale of goods cases the Act had a "spill over" effect which is only now being expunged from the common law.

Conditions and Warranties

The 1893 Act was not designed to be a radical measure of reform; it was primarily designed to codify the rules that had evolved at common law. But the difficulties surrounding the question of discharge of contractual obligations were met by invoking a new theoretical framework which, while it relied heavily on the dependent/independent covenant dichotomy, led to the temporary obliteration of the old common rules, even in non sale of goods transactions.

The 1893 Act divided obligations into conditions and warranties. Unfortunately the draftsman did not define such obligations but contented himself with setting out the consequences of breach of each obligation. A condition is a term, breach of which entitles the innocent party to elect to rescind the contract and sue for damages or affirm the contract and sue for damages: see *White Sewing Machine Co.* v. *Fitzgerald* (1894). Under section 11(1)(c) the right to rescind was lost once delivery of goods had taken place and the contract executed. (The revised section 11 in the 1980 Act abandons this restriction on the right to rescind). If the term is a warranty the innocent party has a remedy in damages only. A warranty is defined in section 62(1) as something "collateral to the main purpose of such contract." This technical use of the word "warranty," which connoted at common law a contractual representation has been a source of some confusion and students should bear in mind that "warranty" may mean different things according to context.

The effect of this dichotomy was to provide a right of rescission if the obligation was a condition but a right to damages only if the obligation was a warranty. This is graphically illustrated by *Re Moore & Landauer* (1912). The contract was for the sale of 3,100 cases of Australian canned fruit packed 30 tins to a case. Some cases were delivered with less than 30 tins to a case, some with more. The total number of tins delivered met the contract requirement. No loss resulted for failure to meet the contract description yet the buyer was held entitled to rescind simply because section 13 (requiring goods to answer their description) was broken by defective packing of goods.

This rigid and inflexible result could be avoided by an exemption clause but in the absence of such a clause the courts could not overturn the 1893 Statute because (so it was thought prior to 1975) *all* contract terms in sale of goods cases were either conditions or warranties. After 1893 there was no room for the old approach in which the courts asked, has the breach gone to the root of the contract? Has the innocent party been substantially deprived of the fruits of the contract?

The first indication that the condition/warranty dichotomy was not all embracing was given by the English Court of Appeal in the *Hong Kong Firs* case (1962). A contract for the charter of a cargo ship for a period of two years was broken because the vessel was unseaworthy. Repairs were necessary and the vessel was out of service for 20 weeks. The charterers sought to rescind the contract claiming the obligation to provide a seaworthy vessel was a condition. (The charterers wanted to repudiate because a lowering of freight charges would permit the charterers to acquire another vessel at a lower cost). The Court of Appeal rejected this view of the bargain. The Court looked to the pre-1893 case law and held that a seaworthiness obligation was not a condition in the sense that failure to supply a seaworthy vessel discharged the charterers obligation to take the vessel and pay freight or the cost of hire. Upjohn L.J. observed that to hold a seaworthiness obligation as a condition would lead to absurdities; "if a nail is missing from one of the timbers of a wooden vessel or if proper medical supplies or two anchors are not on board at the time of sailing, the owners are in breach of the seaworthiness stipulation. It is contrary to common sense to suppose that in such circumstances the parties contemplated that the charterer should at once be entitled to treat the contract as at an end for such trifling breaches."

So, in non sale of goods cases the condition/warranty dichotomy was challenged; unless there was conclusive evidence that the parties intended breach of such a term to lead to a right to rescission or damages only the courts will now ask, "does the breach of the stipulation go so much to the root of the contract that it makes further commercial performance of the contract impossible, or in other words is the whole contract frustrated: If yes, the innocent party may treat the contract as at an end. If nay his claim sounds in damages only;" per Upjohn L.J. (*supra*).

The problem with this approach is that it is very litigation oriented. It has been attacked as inconsistent with the 1893 Act and undesirable because it leads to uncertainty and unpredictability of result. The *Hong Kong Firs* case was thought to be applicable only in contracts where the 1893 Act could not apply. Since the decision in *Cehave N.V.* v. *Bremer Handesgesellschaft* (1975) it is established that even in sale of goods cases the courts should not give the extreme remedy of rescission unless the parties have clearly so agreed or unless a precedent binds the court so to hold. In *Cehave* the Court of Appeal set out a series of questions that should be asked:

(1) Does the contract *expressly* confer a right of termination for such a breach? If so the courts must respect this and allow rescission even if loss resulting is minimal or non existent.

(2) If no to question 1, does the contract impliedly give a right to rescission or only a right to damages? Again an affirmative answer will be conclusive but as *Schuler A.G.* v. *Wickman Tools* (1973) shows, the absence of loss will point towards the next question coming into play.

(3) Does a statute or *stare decisis* point towards the obligation being a condition or warranty? The *implied* obligations under the 1893 Act (as amended by the 1980 Act) remain conditions or warranties so *Re Moore & Landauer* (*supra*) would still be decided in the same way; similarly, case law determines that a statement that a ship will be ready to load is a condition: *Behn* v. *Burness* (1863); so too is an expected date of arrival stipulation: *The Mihalis Angelos* (1971); the recent decision in *Toepfer (Hamburg)* v. *Verheijdens Veervoeder Commissiehandel (Rotterdam)* (1978) in which the Court of Appeal held an obligation to make prompt payment to be a condition illustrates that if the court feels that commercial practice requires the obligation to be a condition the contract term will be so construed. On the whole the courts take the view that it is best if the courts, acquainted with all the facts, have the power to decide which remedy is to be the most appropriate. If we have another look at the facts of *Knox* v. *Mayne* (1873) it is likely that a modern Irish court, influenced by these English authorities, would not be so ready to hold the destination clause to be a condition and would now test the case by asking the fourth question posed in *Cehave N.V.*;

(4) Has the breach gone to the root of the contract so as to deprive the injured party of that which he contracted for? Unless this central or core obligation can no longer be obtained—several English judges and commentators call this *the* fundamental term—damages will be deemed to be the most appropriate remedy. This trend is only part of a movement towards conferring wide discretionary powers on the courts.

The facts of *Laird Brothers* v. *Dublin Steampacket* (1900) the leading Irish authority on this question, are instructive. The plaintiffs agreed to build a ship to be delivered by August 1, 1897. Payment was to be made by instalments. The contract provided that the sixth and final instalment of £5,000 was not be payable unless the vessel were completed on the agreed date. The vessel was not completed until September 1897. The defendants had not suffered loss but they argued that under the terms of the contract completion on the due date was a condition precedent to the payment of the last instalment. Andrews J. regarded the matter as one of construction and posed the following question: "are the words of the clause, . . . so precise, express and strong, when taken in connection with the entire contract, that the intention prima facie so unreasonable, is the only one compatible with the terms employed?"

It would appear that the court was reluctant to give the contract term its plain and ordinary meaning—which would have favoured the defendants—because, as Andrews J. said, "it is impossible to hold that this delay went to the root of the matter so as to render the performance of the rest of the contract by the plaintiffs a thing different in substance from what the defendants stipulated for" yet as we have seen, such a question can only be asked *after* the court has ascertained what the parties have agreed upon; a clear statement of intention must be given effect even if the result is unreasonable. It appears to this writer that Andrews J. went some way towards modifying the terms of this agreement by ruling that an unreasonable contract provision can only be given effect if an unreasonable result is the only possible interpretation that can be placed on the term.

Part 3
Invalidity

9 Mistake

Introduction

There are insuperable difficulties for any writer faced with the task of producing a neat and intelligible exposition of the law of mistake in contract. The current law is beset with jurisdictional problems that can only be resolved by future decisions or legislation. Effective analysis of the law is hampered by the fact that judges do not use terms consistently: this is particularly true of the expressions "common," "mutual" and "unilateral." Cheshire and Fifoot use this threefold classification as the basis of their analysis, whilst conceding that the courts do not use these terms precisely. Several judges have used the terms "common" and "mutual" as synonyms; Dixon J., in *Nolan* v. *Nolan* (1954) even used the terms "mutual" and "unilateral" interchangeably, regarding any distinction as "largely one of phraseology." As a result I do not intend to use the Cheshire and Fifoot classification which, even in an ideal world, would be unsatisfactory.

Instead, it is proposed that we look to what the courts do rather than what they say they do. We will first of all examine the case law in order to discover when a mistake will be operative, either at common law or in equity. As a second step we will consider the rules that have emerged in relation to the remedies of damages, rescission, rectification and specific performance. Students must bear in mind the fact that if a mistake is operative it does not follow that the party pleading mistake will be entitled to any or all of these remedies. An operative mistake may give rise to the remedy of rescission without allowing the court to change or rectify the contract. Further, even if a mistake is held not to prevent a contract coming into existence the court may decline to award specific performance on the ground that the party labouring under the mistake should not be obliged to perform the contract.

Operative Mistake

(1) *Mistake of law*

One, or indeed both, of the contracting parties may mistakenly believe that a statute or an agreement has certain consequences; this may in turn produce an agreement based upon a misunderstanding of law. Once the true legal position is established an attempt may be made to avoid the contract by pleading its invalidity because of mistake. The legal maxim, *ignorantia juris haud excusat* may come into effect here. It would be inconvenient to allow persons to avoid contractual obligations because of a misunderstanding of the law, particularly in cases where the correct legal position could have been discovered quite easily. Thus it is often said that a mistake of law cannot be operative, either at common law or equity. In *O'Loghlen* v. *O'Callaghan* (1874) the plaintiff leased property to the defendant under an arrangement which permitted the defendant to deduct the rates and pay them to the local authority. *Both* plaintiff and defendant calculated the rate by reference to a section of the relevant Act which was later found to be inapplicable. As a result, a lower rate than that calculated had been payable and the plaintiff sued for £100, being the difference between the rent actually paid and the rent payable had the rates been calculated correctly. It was held that at common law the defendant was not obliged to pay the difference; the mistake as a mistake of law was not operative: contrast *Rogers* v. *Louth C.C.* (1981) discussed in Chapter 11.

In equity a distinction has been drawn between a mistake as to the general law, that is, the ordinary law of the country as found in Public Statutes for example, and private law, the law as found in agreements, wills and Private Acts of Parliament. In *Cooper* v. *Phibbs* (1867) the plaintiff and defendant contracted to permit the plaintiff to lease a salmon fishery in Sligo. Both parties assumed that the defendant's father had earlier owned the Sligo fishery which had descended to them by will. In fact, a Private Act of Parliament made the plaintiff tenant for life. He sought to avoid the contract because in point of law he was already the owner. Lord Westbury, in giving judgment in the House of Lords declared "private right of ownership is a matter of fact; it may be the result also of matter of law; but if parties contract under a mutual mistake and mis-apprehension as to their relative and respective rights, the result is that the agreement is liable to be set aside as having proceeded upon a common mistake". In *Leonard* v. *Leonard* (1812), discussed in Chapter 2, Manners L.C. indicated that equity would not hold the plaintiff bound by an agreement to settle a dispute as to private ownership of land where the other party knew facts, unknown to the plaintiff, which influenced the plaintiff's decision to compromise an action.

In a recent case the English Court of Appeal have ruled that a mistake or misrepresentation as to a foreign law may be a mistake of fact; *Andre* v. *C.I.E., S.A.* v. *Ets Michel Blan & Fils* (1979). If this distinction is valid an Irish businessman contracting in the mistaken belief that a foreign statute or law bears a certain meaning this mistake will be operative.

A mistake made by a legal adviser when executing a document will still be operative and may be avoided by the client; *Monaghan C.C.* v. *Vaughan* (1948). English cases suggest that a solicitor who misinterprets the effect of a statute makes a mistake of law which will not be operative.

(2) *Mistake of fact*

Not all mistakes of fact will justify rescinding a contract concluded under such a misapprehension, whether it be shared by both parties or not. The common law took a very restrictive view of such cases and the conventional wisdom holds that only if the mistake relates to the existence of the subject-matter of the contract or to a person or relationship essential to the whole transaction will it be fundamental enough to operate at common law. If parties contract to buy and sell corn which, unknown to both parties has perished, the transaction will be void; if people who are not married enter into a separation agreement in the belief that they are married, the separation agreement will be void. A life insurance policy or annuity, taken out in the mistaken belief that the person in question is still alive, will be void; see *Strickland* v. *Turner* (1852). The position is different if one party warrants the existence of the person or goods as in *McRae* v. *Commonwealth Disposals Commission* (1951) or is prepared to assume the risk that circumstances are otherwise; *March* v. *Pigot* (1771).

In the leading English case of *Bell* v. *Lever Bros.* (1932) Bell and another former employee of the defendants had negotiated "golden handshake" payments in the belief that Lever Bros. could not terminate the contract of employment in any other way, a belief also held by Lever Bros. In fact, Bell was guilty of misconduct which would have justified summary dismissal. Lever Bros. claimed that this mistake was operative and that they could recoup the £50,000 paid. The House of Lords ruled that the mistake was not fundamental enough to justify rescission. Professor Waddams has argued in his *Law of Contracts* that on the facts the conclusion may be correct; a large part of the payment was reward for services rendered rather than being attributable to "buying out" the contract of employment. Nevertheless dicta in the Lords, particularly the speech of Lord Atkin suggests that a shared mistake as to the quality of goods will never be operative; if two parties contract to transfer a painting which they believe to be an old master and it turns out to be a modern copy, mistake will not be operative unless there is an express warranty or a misrepresentation. There is oblique Irish authority supporting this view of the position at common law. In *Megaw* v. *Molloy* (1878) a mistake was held operative but in so concluding Ball L.C. said that this "is not the case of a seller and purchaser intending to sell and buy the same horse with a misapprehension as to his soundness," thereby implying that such a mistake would not be fundamental enough to induce the common law courts to declare the transaction void.

The equitable rule in relation to shared or common mistake seems to have been wider and more flexible. The leading case of *Cooper* v. *Phibbs* (1867), decided before the fusion of the common law and equity, is often said to be authority for the view that a common mistake can be relieved against on such terms as the court sees fit. In *Cooper* v. *Phibbs* the House of Lords set aside the lease, declared the appellant the owner while ordering that the respondents were entitled to a lien on the property in respect of money paid improving it. The only difficulty that *Cooper* v. *Phibbs* presents rests on the fact that the mistake in that case would probably have been operative, even at common law, by analogy with *Couturier* v. *Hastie* (1856). This weakens the case if it is the primary support for the modern doctrine of equitable mistake. Nevertheless a series of English Court of Appeal decisions establish that while the common law doctrine of mistake may not operate, equity can set aside a transaction on such terms as the court sees fit. In *Solle* v. *Butcher* (1950) a lease entered into when both parties believed the property not subject to Rent Restriction Legislation was declared voidable and the contract was set aside on terms, the decree giving the tenant the option of leaving the flat or staying on at a rent that in the view of the Court of Appeal accurately reflected the value of the property. In *Grist* v. *Bailey* (1967) a contract to sell a house under the mistaken belief that a tenant was protected under the Rent Acts was also declared voidable, the purchaser being entitled to repudiate or take at a fair market value of £2,250 rather than the agreed price of £850. These cases have prompted Lord Denning M.R. to summarise the law as follows; "common mistake even on a most fundamental matter does not make a contract void at law but voidable in equity." Although the modern English case law has not been ruled on by the Irish Courts the Irish ancestry of the leading case of *Cooper* v. *Phibbs* suggests that the Irish Courts would decline to follow the narrower doctrine of mistake as expounded in *Bell* v. *Lever Bros.*, preferring instead of *Solle* v. *Butcher* line of authority.

The recent English Court of Appeal case of *Amalgamated Investments* v. *John Walker* (1977) indicates that if two parties are mistaken as to the likelihood of a building being declared a "listed building," which has the effect of reducing its value as a commercial property, the courts may view it as desirable that the buyer take the risk that this event may occur. The need for certainty and security of commercial transactions will be viewed as more important than the interests of one distressed litigant. In such cases the buyer should include a term that if at a later date the building is listed the buyer can rescind the contract.

(3) *Mistake as to the terms of the agreement*

In these cases, which are often described as instances of mutual mistake, the parties are negotiating about different things. A wants to buy wheat; B wants to sell barley. At first sight there can be no contract. Indeed, Ball L.C. said in *Megaw* v. *Molloy* (1878) that a "dealing where the parties are not intending the same subject matter, evidently cannot be an agreement." This is not correct. The essential factor to be noted is whether the party pleading mistake has a reasonable expectation that the contract would include the terms contended for. In *Stapleton* v. *Prudential Assurance* (1928) the plaintiff entered a life insurance contract believing that by paying 2s. a month for 11 years she would be paid £25 at the end of the period. In fact the contract provided that such a sum would be payable on her death; at the end of 11 years the policy was convertible into a free paid policy after 25 years. The plaintiff, when she learnt of the mistake sought to get back the premiums paid. Sullivan P. held that while Stapleton laboured under a *bona fide* mistake this would not justify rescinding the contract: see *Jameson* v. *National Benefit Trust Ltd.* (1902) which also illustrates that self induced mistakes as to the terms of a bargain will not ground relief for the mistaken party. The courts are concerned to discover what the parties said and did during negotiations. If the intention of one party, objectively ascertained, indicates assent to a particular term, that term will be included in the bargain. The courts will not permit the reasonable expectations of one party to be defeated if they exist because of the conduct of the other party. This is often described as the rule in *Smith* v. *Hughes* (1871); "if whatever a man's real intention may be, he so conducts himself that a reasonable man would believe he was assenting to the terms proposed by the other and that other party upon that belief enters into a contract with him, the man thus conducting himself would be equally bound as if he had intended to agree to the other parties terms."

Two modern Irish cases provide clear illustrations of the operation of this rule. In *Clayton Love* v. *B + I Steampacket* (1966) the appellants contracted with the respondents for the transport of frozen scampi. The appellants intended the scampi would be loaded at sub-atmospheric temperatures. The respondents intended loading would take place at atmospheric temperature. Applying *Smith* v. *Hughes*, the Supreme Court held that because of the way the respondents had conducted themselves during negotiations they were bound to load the cargo on the terms anticipated by the appellants. They were therefore liable for the deterioration of the goods. In the important case of *Lucy* v. *Laurel Construction* (1970) Mr. Lucy agreed to purchase a house to be built by Laurel Construction. The site plan indicated the plot would be 170 feet long. The plan was in error; the builders only intended to sell a plot 120 feet long. At no time was Mr. Lucy ever told this and all he knew of the builder's intention was disclosed on the faulty site plan. When the builders discovered the mistake they sought to have the plan altered to reflect their intention. Mr. Lucy was held entitled to retain the bargain as initially struck. The site plan was the only objective manifestation of the other parties' intentions; Mr. Lucy had done nothing irregular or dishonest and Kenny J. declined to rectify the contract.

There are cases in which the courts have held that no contract exists because of mistake. In *Megaw* v. *Molloy* (1878) the plaintiff employed a broker to sell maize for him. The maize he intended to sell had been imported on board the "Emma Peasant." The plaintiff had imported another cargo of maize on the "Jessie Parker," which was of a superior quality than that on board the "Emma Peasant." On the morning of the sale a sample purporting to be from the "Emma Peasant" was displayed but this sample was accidently taken from the "Jessie Parker." The defendant purchased the cargo after inspecting the sample but later refused to take delivery when he discovered the true quality of the cargo. The plaintiff sued for non acceptance. The defendant did not plead that the quality of the goods sold did not meet the sample for there was an express disclaimer of a warranty as to quality; he instead successfully argued that there was no contract at all. The vendor intended to sell the cargo on the "Emma Peasant"; the purchaser intended to purchase the bulk out of which the sample had been taken, that is the corn on the "Jessie Parker." Ball L.C. said there was "a misapprehension as to the very substance of the thing in contract, not as to any quality or incident or merit or demerit of it—*error in corpore*." This distinction between a mistake as to quality as against identity is often difficult to draw, as *Gill* v. *McDowell* (1903) shows, and it has been criticised as unsatisfactory in practice.

(4) *Mistake in executing a deed or contract*
Three situations must be kept apart.

(i) Where one party at the time of the agreement assents to a term but notices that the other party has misstated the term when executing the contract document or memorandum of agreement. Here the error may favour the party who notices the slip of the pen. In *Nolan* v. *Graves & Hamilton* (1946) the plaintiff agreed to buy a row of houses sold by auction. Evidence showed that the plaintiff had agreed to pay £5,550; the auctioneer erroneously wrote the price to be £4,550. The plaintiff was not entitled to take at the lower price. The contract was rectified to reflect the bargain actually struck. Similarly, a separation agreement that gave income tax advantages to the wife when it was intended that these would accrue to the husband was rectified upon proof that the wife was aware that the agreement did not carry into effect the intent of both parties; *Nolan* v. *Nolan* (1954).

(ii) Where the contract is executed and one party later comes into court claiming that, as worded, the document does not accurately reflect the bargain struck. Here the party seeking relief will not always claim sharp practice on the part of the other. *Fallon* v. *Robins* (1865) provides a good illustration of this problem. Fallon agreed to take a lease from Robins. The lease, drafted by Fallon's solicitor, was to run for 31 years and it was intended that Fallon would have a right to terminate the lease after three years. The lease was ambiguously worded and Robins purported to take advantage of the termination clause. Smith M.R. held that unless the lease failed to accurately set out the intention of both parties it could not be *rectified;* as we shall see however an Irish court can order rescission on the authority of *Mortimer* v. *Shortall* (1842) in such cases. Nevertheless, in *Fallon* v. *Robins* Smith M.R. interpreted the ambiguous clause to permit Fallon a right of termination only. *Lucy* v. *Laurel Construction* (1970) illustrates this point too; unless the conduct and words of one party indicate assent on the terms now sought, a mistake which is not communicated to the other party will not be operative and the document will not be rectified.

(iii) Where the party pleading mistake shows that, despite the apparent assent of both parties to the written terms of the agreement, the document does not carry into effect what may be described as "the contract formula." Authority for this proposition stems from the unusual case of *Collen Bros.* v. *Dublin County Council* (1908). The council agreed to grant a construction contract to the plaintiffs, the price to be calculated on the defendant's bills of quantities minus a list or bill of reductions designed to lower costs. By a clerical oversight the contract price was £357 less than it should have been. The plaintiffs sought rectification. Ross J. was prepared to permit rectification, dismissing the claim of the council that the plaintiffs were to bear the cost of the mistake; the intention of the parties, when analysed, was that the tender for the original amount of the priced section, less the amount of the priced bill of reductions, should be accepted. The sum of £167,000 was erroneously taken to be that figure, and erroneously embodied in the contract. "In what way does this differ from an error in adding the figures? In no way."

(5) *Mistake as to title and the nature of an interest in real property*

Cooper v. *Phibbs* (1867) establishes that equity will set aside on terms any leasing contract where both parties mistakenly believe that title to the land is vested in someone other than the prospective lessor. In *Gardiner* v. *Tate* (1876) a contract was held unenforceable at common law against a defendant who had been misled by the plaintiff's agent into believing that an interest purchased at an auction was a legal estate in land when in fact it was an equitable leasehold interest.

(6) *Mistake as to identity*

The Irish courts have not considered this problem to any great extent. For the sake of completeness the following propositions, based largely on English case law can be advanced.

If one party contracts face to face with another, believing that other person to be someone else the contract is voidable. In *Lewis* v. *Averay* (1972) a rogue obtained possession of a motor car by falsely representing that he was the television actor, Richard Greene, of the "Robin Hood" series. He showed a false pass from Pinewood Studios and bore a strong resemblance to the actor. Convinced that he was dealing with the actor the owner took a cheque signed "R.A. Green." The cheque bounced. The car turned up with the defendant who had purchased it from the rogue. The Court of Appeal held that the initial owner could not successfully recover the vehicle on the ground of mistake. The contract between himself and the rogue conferred a voidable title upon the rogue which had been transferred to the defendant. This conclusion reached is a proposition of law. Denning M.R., citing Corbin was prepared to follow American practice where "the courts hold that if A appeared in person before B impersonating C an innocent purchaser from A gets the property in the goods against C." The fraudulently induced mistake does not operate to make the transaction a nullity; a similar rule has been advanced and applied in the Irish cases of *Re French's Estate* (1887) and *In Re Ambrose's Estate* (1913), per Ross J.

The rule is otherwise if the contract is concluded by post. The decision of the House of Lords in *Cundy* v. *Lindsay* (1878) was to hold the transaction void, thus preventing the purchaser from the rogue from obtaining a good title. Lord Cairns, in giving judgment seemed persuaded by the view that if "minds do not meet" no "consensus" or contract can result but this is not strictly true—see *Lucy* v. *Laurel Construction* (1970) above. Denning L.J. (as he then was) said in *Solle* v. *Butcher* (1950) that *Cundy* v. *Lindsay* would now be held to be voidable on terms; this seems a preferable solution given that the court could adjust the rights of the parties under the terms of the decree. Legislation on this point is necessary. If it were possible for the original owner to recover the property and be liable damages in the tort of negligence in such a case, section 34 of the Republic's Civil Liability Act 1961 would permit damages payable to the purchaser from the rogue to be reduced "by such amount as the court thinks just and equitable having regard to the degrees of fault of the plaintiff and defendant." Devlin L.J. in *Ingram* v. *Little* (1961) suggested a similar reform be initiated in England. It would be necessary to recognise this situation as one where the negligence of the initial owner should render him liable for economic loss caused to a third party.

Not all mistaken identity cases are instances where one party knows of the others mistaken belief. For this reason the mistaken identity cases are not always instances of "unilateral mistake" to use Cheshire and Fifoot's classification. In *Smallman* v. *O'Moore & Newman* (1959) the two defendants carried on a partnership until 1954 when they converted the firm into a Limited Company. The plaintiff had dealt with the defendants as a partnership and although the defendants circularised their suppliers informing them of their change in legal status the plaintiffs failed to note the new position, even though the second defendant signed cheques in favour of the plaintiffs in the company name. The plaintiff sued the defendants personally for the price of goods supplied, claiming that they were individually liable as if they remained partners in an unincorporated firm. The defendants successfully pleaded that the

only contracts struck were between the company and the plaintiff
even though the plaintiff thought he was contracting with someone
else. Davitt J. held that the plaintiff could not rely on his own
mistake in order to render the defendants personally liable. This
decision should be contrasted with *Boulton* v. *Jones* (1857).

Remedies available for an operative mistake

A mistake operative at common law leads to the contract being
declared void ab initio; *Cundy* v. *Lindsay*. Technically the party
arguing mistake may seek a decree in the courts in cases where the
other party is pressing for performance, or title to goods or chattels
transferred is in question. Equitable remedies in mistake cases prior
to the Irish Union of Judicature Act 1877 were (and are) a good deal
more sophisticated. Despite the fact that we no longer have separate
courts of common law and equity students should bear in mind that
the remedies available have evolved from these distinct streams of
law. At the risk of repetition we shall now turn to consider those
remedies.

(1) *Rescission—both at law and in equity*

At law, a mistake which is common to both parties and which
relates to a fundamental matter of fact such as the continued
existence of goods, (see section 6 of the Sale of Goods Act 1893) or a
person in insurance cases, will prevent a contract coming into being.
The contract price paid will be returnable. Parties contracting at
cross purposes, that is, where both persons contract to buy and sell
different things may be invalid if the party pleading mistake
reasonably but erroneously believes that a certain state of affairs
exists; See *Megaw* v. *Molloy* (1878) and *Leonard* v. *Leonard* (1812).

Rescission in equity is a much more fluid doctrine. The Sligo
fishery case of *Cooper* v. *Phibbs* illustrates that mistakes that are
operative at common law can be treated differently in equity. Brady
L.C., in the Court of Appeal in Ireland said that as a precondition to
equitable relief "there must be something unconscientious on either
one side or the other in order that the aid of this court should be
called for." The modern English cases suggest that unconscientious
dealing is not a precondition for relief, but rather, that ethical factors
may help set the terms upon which rescission will be ordered; see
Solle v. *Butcher* (1950).

A decree of rescission may be given in cases where one party has
sought rectification of the contract, the court refusing this relief. In
Mortimer v. *Shortall* (1842) Sugden L.C. (later Lord St. Leonards)

said, "a mistake on one side may be a ground for rescinding a contract but it is not a ground for taking from a man part of a property demised to him." So in *Gun* v. *McCarthy* (1884) Gun offered to let property to McCarthy for £33.10s. The offer was accepted but as Flanagan J. later found, the figure was inserted by mistake. Gun intended the rent to be £55.10s. McCarthy knew the figure was so low that an error had been made. McCarthy did not know the intended figure. Flanagan J. refused to grant rectification and increase the rent. This would have obliged McCarthy to be bound by a contract he had not assented to; instead Flanagan J. ordered rescission. In *Webster* v. *Cecil* (1861), a similar English case, the court instead rectified the bargain, giving the purchaser the option of taking the property under the terms of the amended contract or rescinding the contract.

The remedy of rescission can be lost for a variety of reasons. If the parties cannot be returned to their pre-contractual position the now superseded common law rule was that rescission would not be ordered. Equity would permit the rights of the parties to be adjusted by the decree. In *Cooper* v. *Phibbs* (1867) the House of Lords ruled the defendants, who mistakenly believed they owned the fishery, possessed a lien against the land for improvements made; the plaintiff was also ordered to pay rent for property he had enjoyed.

Rescission may be refused if there is a delay in seeking equitable relief: The facts of *Stapleton* v. *Prudential Assurance* (1928) illustrate this point graphically. Rescission will also be refused if the mistake renders the contract voidable but before the contract is repudiated a bona fide purchaser acquires an interest in the goods. The Irish case of *Anderson* v. *Ryan* (1967), discussed on pp.112–3, is authority for this proposition.

(2) *Rectification*

Before the Judicature Act a court of common law, faced with a bargain that was not accurately recorded in a written instrument, was obliged to refer the case to a court of equity to enable rectification. Since 1877 the process is simpler. In *Borrowes* v. *Delaney* (1889) the Court of Exchequer, on discovering that a contract document contained a mistake simply treated the contract as if it had been rectified. Dowse B. indicated that this remedy is available even though no express request for rectification had been made by either party. Once the true facts became known the courts will respond accordingly.

The burden of proof resting on the party seeking rectification will be a heavy one. Although parol evidence is admissible Sugden L.C. in *Mortimer* v. *Shortall* (1842) suggested that parol evidence alone will not show conclusively that the written document is inaccurate; "there is no objection in law to rectify an instrument by parol evidence, when you have anything written to go by; but where you depend upon the recollection of witnesses, and the defendant denies the case set up by the plaintiff, to be the true one, there appears to be no remedy." This onus demands rather too much of the plaintiff. The modern case of *Nolan* v. *Graves & Hamilton* (1948) suggests that if oral evidence shows *conclusively* that the instrument is defective rectification will be ordered.

The jurisdiction of a court to order rectification was succinctly stated by Kenny J. in *Lucy* v. *Laurel Construction* (1970) to exist;

    (i)   where there is a shared or common mistake made by the two parties in the drafting of a written instrument which is to give effect to a prior oral agreement;

   (ii) When one party sees a mistake in a written agreement and, aware that the other party has not seen it, he signs knowing it contains a mistake.

A good example of case (ii) is provided by the facts of *Nolan* v. *Graves & Hamilton*, which are related above on p.93. This case also decides that if the instrument as it stood was sufficient to satisfy the Statute of Frauds the rectified instrument will also be deemed within the Statute. The actual decision in *Nolan* v. *Graves & Hamilton* has been doubted by Professor Dowrick. Instead of ordering specific performance of the rectified agreement Mrs. Nolan, who had tried to take advantage of the auctioneer's slip of the pen, was given the option of either taking the property under the terms of the amended instrument or rescinding. Professor Dowrick has pointed out that under section 27(7) of the Union of Judicature Act 1877 specific performance of a rectified agreement can be ordered. Mrs. Nolan should have been ordered to take the property; after all she had agreed to purchase on the terms of the rectified agreement, unlike the tenant in *Gun* v. *McCarthy, supra.*

The remedy of rectification is not dispensed liberally to litigants. In *McAlpine* v. *Swift* (1810) Manners L.C. pointed out that equity will not rectify for mistake unless the court is sure that rectification will not work an injury. For this reason the courts will not rectify a contract document if it appears that the parties have failed to reach a prior agreement on the terms to be inserted into the rectified instrument. As the contrasting cases of *Webster* v. *Cecil* and *Gun* v. *McCarthy* show, compulsory rectification in such a case compels one party to labour under a bargain he did not assent to and in this context the judiciary view this as unacceptable. It is clear that this solution is often reached when the courts strike down exemption clauses, unconscionable bargains and insert implied terms into contracts. It may be that legislation which would permit the courts to vary or cancel contracts concluded by way of a mistake would provide a sensible solution to many mistake cases. The New Zealand Contractual Mistakes Act, s.7 contains just such a provision as part of its discretionary remedy system.

The recent Northern Ireland case of *Rooney & McPartland* v. *Carlin* (1980) illustrates how limited the present remedy of rectification is. Carlin commenced nuisance proceedings against the plaintiffs who operated a quarry in Co. Armagh. The action was compromised by counsel for both parties. Counsel for the plaintiffs purchased land from Carlin believing that the land purchased was all the property Carlin owned in the vicinity. This belief was also shared by Carlin's counsel.

The folio number and the map annexed to the agreement correctly identified and set out the property sold. In fact Carlin owned another field worth some £800 which was not included in the sale. The plaintiffs sought rectification so as to include this field, arguing that they were not obliged to pay further sums of money for this additional property. Kelly J. at trial permitted rectification. This decision was reversed by the Court of Appeal. Lord Lowry in his speech said that there was no mistake as to terms; neither counsel knew of the existence of the field and to talk of a mistaken common intention here was to confuse motive, object and belief with intention. Rectification was refused.

Were the courts able to (1) reduce the price payable to reflect the lower value of the property purchased or (2) to order rectification upon condition a higher price is paid, a fairer result would ensue in such a case.

The most important difference between the English and the Irish Republic's case law on rectification for mistake is to be found in Kenny J.'s judgment in *Lucy* v. *Laurel Construction* (1970) on the question whether a prior concluded oral contract need exist before an instrument setting out contract terms can be rectified. Kenny J., following *Rose* v. *Pim* (1953) and other English cases held that a concluded oral contract must exist. The English Court of Appeal in *Joscelyne* v. *Nissen* (1970) have relaxed this requirement. It is sufficient for the party seeking rectification to show "a continuing common intention" to contract on particular terms, falling short of a concluded contract, and that the parties have outwardly expressed this. It is doubtful whether important practical differences result from these different tests, given the obvious difficulties of proof. The Northern Ireland Court of Appeal in *Rooney & McPartland* v. *Carlin* (1980) have discussed and approved *Joscelyne* v. *Nissen*.

(3) *Damages*

If one party contracts under a mistaken belief as to the terms of the bargain a remedy in damages is not available unless the court can also find that a warranty or fraudulent or negligent misrepresentation was made. A right to damages may also arise under the 1980 Sale of Goods and Supply of Services Act in limited cases. In exceptional cases a court may be prepared to hold that the seller of goods who fails to disabuse a buyer of some mistaken belief may hold that seller liable in damages for fraud. In *Gill* v. *McDowell* (1903) the seller of a hermaphrodite member of the oxen family— "when looked at from the back [it] appeared to be a heifer, but when looked at from certain other directions appeared to be a bullock"— was held liable in damages to the purchaser of the beast. The seller had taken the oxen to a market and sold it without informing the buyer of its unusual characteristics. This is something of a "rogue" decision because the Court denied that a misrepresentation has been made; fraudulent intent seems to have provided the basis of the decision. The precedent value of *Gill* v. *McDowell* is not high.

It is possible for the parties to stipulate that any mistake in the contract is to be actionable in damages only and in *Phelps* v. *White* (1881) such a clause was upheld.

Submissions for statutory reform of the law of mistake have included suggestions that the courts be given a discretionary power to award damages in lieu of rescission or rectification. Again, the recent New Zealand Statute permits a court to grant relief by way of restitution or compensation.

It should be noted that both the Misrepresentation Act (Northern Ireland) 1967, and the 1980 Sale of Goods and Supply of Services Act, reforming aspects of the law of misrepresentation in the Republic permits the courts to grant damages in lieu of rescission. To extend this discretionary power into cases of mistake would seem a natural progression, one which would improve the remedial powers of a court faced with operative mistake.

(4) *Specific performance*

The fact that the defendant has made a mistake cannot, of itself, give him a defence to an action for specific performance. If there has been a misrepresentation or an ambiguity in the contract the court may decline to award specific performance: see *Tamplin* v. *James* (1880).

(5) *Non Est Factum "it is not my deed."*

This plea was initially confined to cases where a blind or illiterate person signed a contract or deed after its effect had been misrepresented to him. The plea expanded so as to become available to all persons who signed an instrument which turned out to be a different document to that which they had assumed or been told they were signing. The plea is useful to the signor because if it is successful the contract is void and not merely voidable. Third parties cannot acquire title to goods where *non est factum* is successfully pleaded by the initial owner. Cherry C.J. in *Bank of Ireland* v. *McManamy* (1916) explained that "the principle of the cases is not, however, that fraud vitiates consent, but rather that there is an entire absence of consent. That the mind of the party who signs under a fundamental error does not go with the act of signing, and that there is consequently no contract at all in fact." *Bank of Ireland* v. *McManamy* establishes that fraud need not be shown although this will exist in most cases: see also *Siebel & Seum* v. *Kent* (1976).

The facts of *McManamy* are worth recounting. The respondents, all 23 of them, were members of a cooperative creamery in Co. Roscommon. They were approached by the creamery manager who, so the defendants said, wanted them to sign forms to order manure and other creamery requirements. The documents were in fact bank guarantee forms. The jury found the defendants were not negligent. An action for a new trial was refused on the ground that it was not necessary for the jury to find fraud; the jury had declined to answer this question.

Although the rationale for the plea is somewhat metaphysical— the mind of the signor did not accompany his hand—there are practical considerations here. As a matter of policy the plea is to be kept within narrow bounds. A party signing must show that the error was "fundamental" in nature. Signing a bank guarantee when one thinks the document is an application for a load of manure is a fundamental misconception; a guarantee of a debt for £100,000 when one thinks the sum was only £100 is also a fundamental error. *Saunders* v. *Anglia Building Society* (1971), the leading English case holds that to assign a house to X for £3,000 when the document is thought to be an assignment of the same house to Y by way of gift is not a fundamental enough error to ground *non est factum*. If the signor shows a fundamental error he must show he has not been careless at the date of signing the contract. To sign a document without reading it is carelessness which will prevent the signor from relying on *non est factum*. In *UDT* v. *Western* (1975) the English Court of Appeal held that someone who signs a loan proposal form in blank, leaving another person to fill in the details, acts carelessly. There is one important exception to this rule. In the case of *Petelin* v. *Cullen* (1975) the High Court of Australia ruled that if A misrepresents a document's effect to B and B signs without reading it, then the document will not be valid if A tries to rely on it. Should A transfer his interest to C, an innocent third party, carelessness or negligence will be material here. *Saunders* v. *Anglia Building Society* (1971) illustrates this point well. The Building Society, an innocent third party was not to bear the loss resulting from Mrs. Gallie's negligence in signing a document unread.

10 Misrepresentation

A misrepresentation is made when one contracting party has uttered a statement of fact which is untrue. We have discussed in Chapter 5 the extent to which the Irish courts are prepared to go in holding a precontractual statement to be a part of the contract. In such cases the injured party can sue for breach of a contractual term. The remedy available will depend on whether the promise takes effect as a warranty, condition or intermediate term (see Chap. 8).

The misrepresentation may also produce a remedy in tort. Should a court refuse to hold the statement to be a contractual term the injured party may still be able to recover damages or repudiate the contract if the misrepresentation can be deemed fraudulent, negligent or innocent. As we shall see, the remedy available depends largely on which category the statement falls into. As in the law of mistake equitable principles and remedies differ from those developed by the common law courts. Limited measures of statutory reform have recently come into operation in both parts of Ireland. As a result it is possible for a misleading statement to take effect in one of three ways; it can produce a remedy in contract; alternatively, the statement can produce a remedy in tort; thirdly, it could produce a remedy under Part V of the Sale of Goods and Supply of Services Act 1980 or The Misrepresentation Act (Northern Ireland) 1967. Notwithstanding this bewildering array of remedies there is substantial scope for further legislative reform.

In this chapter we will confine our attention to the tortious and statutory remedies available to someone who has entered a contract as a result of a misrepresentation. The contractual position has been considered earlier in the book. Readers should refer back to Chapters 5 and 8.

The Statement

For a statement to take effect as a misrepresentation several citeria have to be met. The statement must not be a statement of law. We have discussed this problem in the context of the law of mistake and it is suggested that the exception drawn in *Cooper* v. *Phibbs* (1867) is operative in misrepresentation cases also.

A statement of opinion will, in certain cases, be outside the law of misrepresentation. If the person uttering the statement knows it is false or had the opportunity to check its accuracy he will be bound, particularly if the representee was unable to investigate the facts for himself. If I say, "in my opinion, the car is sound" and I know the vehicle is fit only for the scrapheap I have misstated my true opinion; this constitutes a misrepresentation. In *Esso Petroleum* v. *Mardon* (1976) the appellants were held to have made a misrepresentation when they told a prospective tenant that, in their opinion, a filling station would sell 200,000 gallons per annum at the end of a two year period. This opinion was held; the English Court of Appeal said Esso were liable for a misrepresentation nonetheless. The appellants were said to have misrepresented that they had exercised care and skill in calculating this figure. It should be noted that Esso were in the best position to estimate "throughput."

If neither party is in a position to verify the statement an opinion that turns out to be wrong will not always be actionable. In *Smith* v. *Lynn* (1954) the plaintiff and defendants were both interested in buying the same house. The plaintiff outbid the defendant at auction. Both parties had read an advertisement stating that the property was "in excellent structural and decorative repair." Six weeks after the plaintiff bought the property he put it back on the market. The plaintiff used the same advertisement and, when asked by the defendant why the property was being resold the plaintiff replied that the sale was due to personal reasons. The defendant purchased; after the sale it was discovered that the house was infested with woodworm! The defendant refused to proceed with the purchase pleading that the plaintiff has misrepresented that the house was sound. The defence failed. The advertisement was held to be a statement of opinion, an advertising "puff" not intended to have legal consequences. Both parties had inspected the premises and, in the view of the court, the defendant could not avoid the bargain.

In *Smith* v. *Lynn* the court also formed the view that the defendant had not relied on the statements made. He purchased on the strength of his own examination of the building. A statement will not constitute a misrepresentation if it is not read or heard by the other party or if it is not relied upon. In *Grafton Court Ltd.* v. *Wadson Sales Ltd.* (1975) the defendants took a lease in a shopping complex. They pleaded that the plaintiff developer had represented that the other tenants would be high quality commercial concerns. The defendants pleaded that the other tenants did not meet this standard. Finlay P. held that if this statement had been made the defendant had not relied on it. When the lease was signed the other units were occupied. The true facts were known to the defendant when the contract was entered into.

In *Sargent* v. *Irish Multiwheel* (1955) it was held that the representee does not have to inform the representor that he has seen the misleading statement; it is enough to show the fact of reliance. Sargent was therefore able to sue on an advertisement which represented that a van which he later purchased was English assembled. A statement will also be actionable even if it is only one reason why the representee entered the contract.

A very curious result occurred in *Cody* v. *Connolly* (1940). The plaintiff inspected a mare and was told that it would do all kinds of work. The plaintiff, before buying, had the mare inspected by a vet, despite the defendants saying "what do you want to do that for? Didn't I tell you she was all right." The sale was concluded. The mare was badly winded. The vet did not discover this during the examination. The plaintiff sued for misrepresentation. O'Byrne J. held that the inspection could not affect the plaintiffs rights against the defendant because it was not part of the contract that the animal be inspected. This seems beside the point. If the plaintiff purchased only after the inspection he would be placing his faith on the vet, not the seller's representation. It is submitted that the defendant should not have been liable. The proper action would have been to sue the vet for his negligent inspection.

It is not unusual for the contract to attempt to place an obligation on the representee to verify all statements made to him. In *Pearson* v. *Dublin Corporation* (1907) the plaintiff was about to tender to the corporation for a construction contract. He was told by the defendant's agent that a wall had been built on the construction site and that the foundations of the wall were nine feet deep. This statement was untrue and it adversely affected the price contained in the tender, which the defendants accepted. The contract provided that the plaintiff had to verify all representations for himself and not rely on their accuracy. Palles C.B. held that this provision was effective and he refused to leave an issue to the jury, dismissing the action. The House of Lords granted a new trial. The statement was made by the agent fraudulently; several members of the House of Lords said that, in general, a person cannot avoid the effect of his or her agent's fraudulent statements by inserting a clause in the contract that the other party shall not rely on them. Any other rule would encourage fraudulent practices. Section 46 of the Sale of Goods and Supply of Services Act 1980 limits the effectiveness of such clauses to cases where a clause is "fair and reasonable in the circumstances of the case."

A representee who becomes aware of the untruth of a statement before he enters into the contract has no remedy; he has not relied upon the statement because he has notice of its falsity. Notice means actual and not constructive notice. In *Phelps* v. *White* (1881) the plaintiff was told that timber on land he intended to lease would be part of the property transferred. This was untrue. The plaintiff was furnished with documentation which would have revealed the misrepresentation. The Court of Appeal in Ireland refused to hold the plaintiff had notice of the misrepresentation.

On the effects of a fraudulent agent who sets up a deal on behalf of a principal and whether the agent's knowledge binds the principal see *Sankey* v. *Alexander* (1874).

(1) *Fraudulent misrepresentation*

A fraudulent misrepresentation is actionable in the tort of deceit. In the leading English case of *Derry* v. *Peek* (1889) Lord Herschell said "without proof of fraud no action of deceit is maintainable." In that case the House of Lords held that fraud is proved when it is shown that a false representation has been made knowingly, or without belief in its truth, or recklessly, without caring whether it is true or false.

In *Fenton* v. *Schofield* (1966) the vendor of land represented that over the last four years a river running over the land had yielded 300–350 salmon a year and that he had spent £15,000 renovating the property. Both statements were untrue as the vendor well knew. A purchaser paid £17,000 for the land. The value of the property was calculated by assuming each statement to be true. When the purchaser learnt of their untruth he sued in deceit, recovering damages based on the difference between what the land was worth and what it was represented to be worth. In *Carbin* v. *Somerville* (1933) the vendor of a house in Clontarf misrepresented that the house was dry. The Supreme Court held the plaintiff, who purchased the house on the strength of this assurance, entitled to rescind the contract.

The facts of *Pearson* v. *Dublin Corporation* (1907) show that fraud can exist even when the representor does not necessarily know that his statement is false. When the agent told the plaintiff that the foundations of a wall stood on the site the agent did not know if this was true or false: the statement was nevertheless fraudulent.

An action in deceit may lie even if the representor has no intention to cause loss to the representee. In *Delany* v. *Keogh* (1905) Keogh, an auctioneer was employed by Bradley, a solicitor to sell Bradley's interest in a leasehold property. The conditions of sale stated that while the rent was £25 per annum the landlord had accepted £18. Before the sale Keogh was told by the landlord that the full rent of £25 would be charged to the purchaser of the lease. Bradley advised Keogh that in his view the landlord would be estopped from charging the full rent. Keogh was advised not to change the conditions of sale. The plaintiff purchased the lease. The Kings Bench Division refused to find Keogh liable in deceit because it could not be shown that Keogh intended to mislead. The Court of Appeal reversed this decision. Holmes L.J. found that the misrepresentation stemmed from a failure to make known that he had reason to believe that the landlord would charge the higher rent. While Keogh believed what Bradley had told him this would not absolve him. Keogh should have mentioned, after reading out the conditions, that while he had been informed by the landlord that a higher rent would be charged it was Keogh's solicitor's opinion that the landlord was legally estopped.

Holmes L.J. also distinguished the leading case of *Derry* v. *Peek*. "The directors of a Tramway Co. that had authority to use steam power with the consent of the Board of Trade, believing that this consent would be given as a matter of course issued a prospectus in which it was stated that they had the right to use steam power without reference to any condition. It was held that this was not actionable, inasmuch as the statement was made in the honest belief that it was true. This is, I think old law; but if the directors had known, before they issued the prospectus that the Board of Trade had refused to consent or had announced its intention to refuse, the case would have been like this, and the directors would have no defence; nor in such a case would their position have been improved if their solicitor had assured them that there would be no difficulty in obtaining from Parliament an amending Act removing the condition."

(2) *Negligent misstatement*

In *Derry* v. *Peek* the House of Lords ruled that there is no liability in deceit for a false statement made carelessly and without reasonable grounds for believing it to be true. In the absence of a contract, negligently made statements could be the subject of an award of damages only if a fiduciary relationship existed between the parties, such as solicitor and client. In 1963 the House of Lords declared that liability in the tort of negligence could arise from a negligent misstatement. In *Hedley Byrne* v. *Heller* a bank negligently represented a company to be on a sound financial footing. This caused the appellant to invest in the company which later collapsed.

The Law Lords stated *obiter* that where a "special relationship" exists, a duty of care will arise between the parties. *Esso Petroleum* v. *Mardon* (1976) establishes that liability will arise under this cause of action where the misstatement results in a contract between the parties.

The *Hedley Byrne* principle has been considered by the courts in Ireland. In *Bank of Ireland* v. *Smith* (1966) Kenny J. cited *Hedley Byrne* although the learned judge found the misrepresentation in that case would ground liability in contract. In *Stafford* v. *Keane Mahony Smith* (1980) Doyle J. discussed the *Hedley Byrne* principle, as extended in *Esso Petroleum* v. *Mardon*. Doyle J. noted that *Hedley Byrne* had been approved by Davitt P. in *Securities Trust Ltd.* v. *Hugh Moore & Alexander Ltd.* (1964). Doyle J. declared that "in order to establish the liability for negligent or non-fraudulent misrepresentation giving rise to action there must first of all be a person conveying the information or the representation relied upon; secondly, that there must be a person to whom that information is intended to be conveyed or to whom it might reasonably be expected that the information would be conveyed; thirdly, that the person must act upon such information or representation to his detriment so as to show that he is entitled to damages." The action in *Stafford* v. *Keane Mahony Smith* was brought against an estate agent who had represented that a certain property would be a good investment. The plaintiff purchased the house but later had to resell it at a loss. The action failed because Doyle J. found that any representations made were not made to the plaintiff but to his brother.

(3) *Innocent misrepresentation*

Prior to the *Hedley Byrne* decision it followed that all misrepresentations that were not fraudulent were classified as an innocent misrepresentation. The fact that a misrepresentation was negligently made could not (in the absence of a fiduciary relationship) avail the injured party. While *Hedley Byrne* has qualified this proposition it is still true to say that an innocent, non fraudulent misrepresentation secures limited redress to the representee. It is at this point that jurisdictional factors become important. At common law the victim of an innocent misrepresentation could only repudiate the agreement if there was a total failure of consideration, that is, if the thing contracted for was not supplied at all or it was a totally different item from that envisaged at the time of agreement. The courts of equity permitted rescission upon proof that the misrepresentation was material in that it induced the contract. It was unnecessary to show a failure of consideration. This essential difference was overlooked in *Carbin* v. *Somerville* (1933) when Fitzgibbon J. in the

Supreme Court held the vendor entitled to repudiate only if the statement was fraudulent or a total failure of consideration resulted. This proposition overlooks the equitable jurisdiction in which rescission could be ordered if an innocent misrepresentation were made.

Equity ordered the drastic remedy of rescission because historically an award of damages in lieu of rescission was not part of an equity court's array of remedies. Because the common law courts took a restrictive view of the cases in which an innocent misrepresentation would be operative, many victims of an innocent misrepresentation, were denied a remedy in damages unless the statement could be elevated into a contractual term or a collateral warranty. In *Connor* v. *Potts* (1897) the plaintiff agreed to purchase two farms, innocently misrepresented to be 443 acres in all. The price was calculated at £12.10s. an acre. The farms fell 67 acres short of the figure represented. The plaintiff was held entitled to specific performance of the contract; the price payable by the plaintiff was reduced by calculating £12.10s. x 67. In certain cases the representee may decide that it is better not to rescind the contract.

(4) *Statutory right to damages*

While pre-contractual statements are increasingly likely to be characterised as contractual terms (see Kenny J. in *Bank of Ireland* v. *Smith* (1966), the Oireachtas has recently created a right to damages in cases of innocent misrepresentation. Section 45(1) of the Sale of Goods and Supply of Services Act 1980 provides:

> "Where a person has entered into a contract after a misrepresentation has been made to him by another party thereto and as a result thereof he has suffered loss, then, if the person making the representation would be liable to damages in respect thereof had the misrepresentation been made fraudulently, that person shall be so liable notwithstanding that the misrepresentation was not made fraudulently, unless he proves that he had reasonable ground to believe and did believe up to the time the contract was made that the facts represented were true."

This section is based upon section 2(1) of the English and N.I. Misrepresentation Acts 1967. In England the Act has been most useful as a means of avoiding the rule in *Bain* v. *Fothergill*, (see Chap. 17, pp. 230–1). The Irish Republic's provision cannot apply so as to negative *Bain* v. *Fothergill* because section 43 limits "contract" to contracts for the sale of goods, hire purchase agreements, contracts for the letting of goods and the supply of services. The 1967 Northern Ireland Statute like the English counterpart, is not so limited.

The statutory action in the Republic under section 45(1) does not create a right to damages where a representor fails to make an accurate statement. The proviso to section 45(1) will permit a misrepresentor to avoid the obligation to pay damages if he can point to some objectively reasonable ground for believing the accuracy of his statement. Like *Hedley Byrne*, negligence will ground liability under this section. The right of action under section 45(1) is wider than that under *Hedley Byrne*; no "special relationship" need exist. *Hedley Byrne* on the other hand will apply to contracts for the sale of land which, because of section 43, section 45(1) is excluded from; see *Stafford* v. *Keane Mahony Smith* (1980). It is suggested that section 43 be repealed.

The statutory action for damages for innocent misrepresentation poses problems on assessment of damages. This will be discussed in Chapter 17.

The Equitable Right of Indemnity

Although an action for damages is not permitted for an innocent misrepresentation some limited pecuniary remedy is available to a representee where the terms of the contract have required the representee to make this expenditure. The courts have been careful to limit the right of indemnity for it is often difficult to distinguish expenditure *required* by the contract from expenditure *envisaged* by the contract. In the New Zealand case of *Power* v. *Atkins* (1921) the plaintiff agreed to purchase a hotel after an innocent misrepresentation had been made to him. The plaintiff repudiated the contract when he discovered the true facts. The plaintiff sued for the return of the deposit paid and expenses such as board and lodging, advertising, train fares, preliminary expenses, an accountants fee for investigating the account, a valuer's fee, the cost of investigating legal title. Salmon J. permitted recovery of the deposit as well as legal fees incurred in researching title. The accountants fee was irrecoverable but a fee paid to a valuer of stock in trade was allowable on proof that the contract required this valuation be made. All other expenses were rejected as being appropriate to a claim in damages. The difficulty and uncertainty surrounding this doctrine is illustrated by the fact that another New Zealand judge in the case of *Duncan* v. *Rothery*, also decided in 1921, held legal fees to be irrecoverable in the equitable action for an indemnity.

These cases will be of interest in the Republic of Ireland, again because the 1980 Act, s.43 does not permit an action for damages when real property forms the subject matter of a contract.

When will the right to rescind be lost?

(i) **When the contract is executed.** In *Legge* v. *Croker* (1811) the defendant innocently misrepresented that a leasehold interest he was about to sell to the plaintiff was not subject to any public right of way. The transfer was executed. Manners L.C. held that an executed lease could not be set aside, even under the wider equitable jurisdiction to rescind, unless there is a fraudulent misprepresentation. This statement was taken up by later courts and forged into a doctrine commonly known as the doctrine in *Seddon* v. *North Eastern Salt;* this rule provides that were a contract has been executed a contract will only be set aside in equity where there has been equitable fraud. The rule was not confined to cases where land formed the subject matter of the contract. In *Lecky* v. *Walter* (1914) the plaintiff purchased bonds issued by a Dutch company. The plaintiff had been told that in the event of liquidation his claim would take priority as a security. The bonds were not so secured and were in fact virtually worthless. The plaintiff's action for rescission failed. It was held that an executed contract can only be repudiated if the representation is fraudulent or if the plaintiff has suffered a total failure of consideration. In *Lecky* v. *Walter* the plaintiff could not make out a case under either of these exceptions.

The rule has been attacked; see in particular the English Court of Appeal's decision in *Leaf* v. *International Galleries* (1951). Section 1(*b*) of the English Misrepresentation Act 1967, giving effect to the Law Reform Committees recommendation for reform provides that no matter what the subject matter of the contract may be, the fact that a contract has been executed should not impede rescission. Section 44(*b*) of the Sale of Goods and Supply of Services Act 1980 is based on the desire to sweep away the rule but, again, section 43 of the Act prevents this. Most of the cases that arise under *Seddon* are cases involving land and such contracts are outside the 1980 Act. Even the decision in *Lecky* v. *Walter* would not be different; shares are choses in action and cannot be goods—see *Lee & Co. (Dublin) Ltd.* v. *Egan (Wholesale) Ltd.* (1979)—so further reforms are necessary here too.

(ii) **Delay in seeking relief or "laches."** Because rescission will generally be sought in equity the equitable doctrine that litigants should seek equitable relief promptly may operate here. The doctrine of laches, as well as the Limitation Act, 1957 may prevent equitable relief. The courts have shown a willingness to hold that the victim of a fraudulent misrepresentation need not be as prompt as someone who has contracted on the strength of an innocent misrepresentation. In *O'Kelly* v. *Glenny* (1846) the plaintiff, in ignorance of the full value of her interest in her deceased fathers estate, sold the interest to her solicitor who fraudulently misrepresented her position. Ten years later an action setting the transfer aside was brought. Laches was held not to prevent rescission. See also *Murphy* v. *O'Shea* (1845). If the defrauded party, on learning of the fraud, fails to rescind within a reasonable time however acquiescence will be imputed; delay of 27 and 54 years would be fatal to a claim of rescission; see *Hovenden* v. *Lord Annesley* (1806).

The victim of an innocent misrepresentation is not treated so indulgently. In *Leaf* v. *International Galleries* (1951) an innocent misrepresentation that a picture, "Salisbury Cathedral" was painted by *the* John Constable was made at the time of sale. Five years later the purchaser learnt this was untrue. He claimed rescission based upon the innocent misrepresentation. The Court of Appeal held the action must fail. By analogy with other sale of goods cases the right to rescind is lost if it is not sought within a reasonable time after the sale. Five years was not a reasonable time. Jenkins L.J. noted that the proper claim was for breach of warranty and not rescission; it may be that the plaintiff sued for rescission to avoid a finding that the statement as to the identity of the painter was not a contractual term.

It should also be noted that in Ireland a second ground for refusing rescission would have been the rule in *Seddon's* case; the Republic's 1980 statute would now remove such an objection if *Leaf* v. *International Galleries* were an Irish case occurring after 1980: s.44(*b*).

(iii) Third party rights. Although one early Irish case holds a fraudulent conveyance by A to B to be void and not merely voidable (*O'Connor* v. *Bernard* (1838)) it is now established that fraud renders a contract voidable and not void unless the party seeking to invalidate the transfer of property can show that the misrepresentation had the further effect of rendering the contract void at common law, as in *Cundy* v. *Lindsay* (1878).

Rescission will not be available if a third party acquires an interest in the property and the third party can show he is a bona fide purchaser for valuable consideration. The leading Irish case is *Anderson* v. *Ryan* (1967). Davis owned a Mini. He answered a newspaper advertisement offering a Sprite motor car for sale. The parties agreed to swap vehicles, no money changing hands. The Sprite was a stolen vehicle. Davis was dispossessed of the Sprite but the Gardai eventually returned his Mini to Mr. Davis. The Mini had been the subject of two subsequent deals. The defendant purchased the vehicle from a person representing himself to be Mr. Davis. This person was, in all probability, the person who had misrepresented that he owned the Sprite. The defendant in turn sold the Mini to the plaintiff Anderson who was dispossessed by the Gardai. Anderson sued Ryan claiming that under sections 12(1) and 21(1) of the Sale of Goods Act 1893 Ryan lacked title to the goods at the time of the transfer of the property to him, Anderson. The Circuit Court judge found for Anderson. The decision was reversed on appeal to the High Court. Henchy J. found the essential issue to be whether Ryan had a good title to the car when he sold it to Anderson. Davis, the original owner had parted with the vehicle as a result of a fraudulent misrepresentation but this rendered the contract voidable. Because the contract between Davis and the rogue not been avoided before the sale between Anderson and Ryan had been concluded Ryan, had, under the terms of section 23(1) of the 1893 Act a valid, if voidable title. This title was transferred to Anderson. As Henchy J. observed, the seizure of the Mini by the Gardai was a wrongful act and redress should be sought from that direction.

If property is transferred to a person who subsequently cannot be traced rescission can be effected by informing the Police of the fraud in the hope that property can be recovered; this will prevent further transactions involving the property from passing a good title to the transferee, even if he is an innocent third party; *Car and Universal Finance Co.* v. *Caldwell* (1965).

Specific Performance

Should the plaintiff be responsible for making a misrepresentation the defendant may avoid an action for specific performance by pleading the plaintiff's misrepresentation. This is discussed by Delaney in (1951) *Irish Jurist* 51. The representee may be permitted to obtain an injunction preventing the representor from continuing an action. Such an injunction was awarded a misrepresentee in *Costello* v. *Martin* (1867).

Power to Award Damages in Lieu of Rescission

The Sale of Goods and Supply of Services Act 1980, s.45(2) permits a court to declare a contract subsisting and award damages in lieu of rescission if the court is "of opinion that it would be equitable to do so." This statutory restriction on the right to rescind seems sensible given the restrictions developed by the courts on the right to rescind; see *Cehave* v. *Bremer Handesgesellschaft mbH* (1975) discussed in Chapter 8. If should be noted that the court may award damages in lieu of rescission only if the remedy of rescission was still available to the representee. If rescission has been lost because of lapse of time, affirmation or waiver it is not possible to award damages under section 42(2). This is unfortunate; the discretion should not be so limited, particularly in cases where the doctrine of laches applies.

The Duty to Disclose and Silence as a Misrepresentation—Uberrima Fides

In the early part of this Chapter we talked of a misrepresentation in terms of being a false "statement." Can silence constitute a statement? It is generally held that silence or failure to disclose a material fact may constitute a misrepresentation in exceptional cases. If I have made a statement which, while true at the time it was uttered, is subsequently rendered false by subsequent events, my failure to advise of the change of circumstance will constitute a misrepresentation. On the other hand, if I agree to sell goods there is no obligation on me, the seller to advise the buyer of material facts which may influence his decision to purchase. The case of *Gill* v. *McDowell* (1903) conditions this proposition somewhat. The purchaser of the hermaphrodite animal thought he was buying a cow or a bull. The seller failed to disclose the true facts. Because the animal was sold in a market where cows or bulls were sold, the seller was held to be under a duty of disclosure. The decision may have been different had the buyer purchased the animal while visiting the sellers property. The fact that the Irish courts have developed a duty of disclosure in the context of contracts to sell animals, a not unreasonable development in a primarily agricultural society, is further illustrated in *Kennedy* v. *Hennessy* (1906). Gibson J. there declared that to sell a yearling heifer in calf without disclosing this fact—such an animal being less valuable because of the dangers of such an early pregnancy—may be actionable if the seller has knowledge of this.

The obligation to disclose has been considered in the context of sale of leasehold property which is subject to restrictive covenants. In *Power* v. *Barrett* (1887) the plaintiff, lessee of premises in Abbey St. Dublin, wanted to sell his lease, which was to his knowledge subject to a covenant that the lessee would not carry on any dangerous, noxious or offensive trade. He sold his interest to a chandler, who wanted to store oil on the premises. This would breach the restrictive covenant. The defendant pulled out of the contract when he learnt of the covenant. Chatterton V.C. refused to order specific performance against the chandler; "if a purchaser state the object which he has in purchasing and the seller is silent as to a covenant in a lease prohibiting or interfering with that object, his silence would be equivalent to a representation that there was no such prohibitory covenant." This rule applies to sales of leasehold interests only. The duty of disclosure applies even to clauses the "representor" is unaware of; *Flight* v. *Barton* (1832).

A general duty to disclose does apply to fiduciary relationships. A failure to disclose material facts was held fatal in *Dunbar* v. *Tredennick* (1813) where the transfer was between agents and trustees on the one hand, and principal and beneficiary on the other. Members of a family are also under an obligation to disclose all material facts; *Leonard* v. *Leonard* (1812).

The most common instances of actionable non-disclosure concern insurance contracts. It is often said that when the prospective insured makes an application for insurance he is in the best position to know the circumstances surrounding the application. This is certainly true in cases of life assurance and health insurance. The applicant is in the best position to know his age, health, and plans for the future. A failure to answer truthfully *and* disclose all material facts may each invalidate the insurance policy. If the contract is one of marine insurance the Marine Insurance Act (1906) still has effect in Ireland. This Act, sections 17 and 18 require the owner of a vessel to disclose only facts known exclusively to himself; he does no have to disclose matters of common knowledge. In other cases the obligations on the prospective insured are onerous.

In cases of non disclosure the test is not intent to defraud but whether the *insured's silence* related to a material fact. The duty to disclose all facts that a reasonable insurer would think material to the risk requires a lot of the insured; he is required to know what the insurer thinks material. He cannot rely on the fact that he as an insured would not think the fact to be material. Even if the insured answers honestly and he discloses all facts known to him the insurance company invariably inserts what is known as a "basis of contract" clause into the agreement. If a reply turns out to be wrong the contract will be avoided; the clause will have the effect of requiring not only an honest and full disclosure but a totally accurate disclosure. In *Life Association of Scotland* v. *McBlain* (1875) McBlain failed to disclose that other applications had been turned down. It was pointed out that, independent of fraud, the failure to reply accurately to this and other questions would invalidate the contract because of the "basis of contract" clause. So if an insured, is at the time of the contract, suffering from some serious illness that would effect an insurance risk, the contract may be avoided even if the applicant or his medical advisers are unaware of the illness.

This produces very hard cases. In *Farrell* v. *S.E. Lancs Insurance Co. Ltd.* (1933) Farrell purchased a bus. An insurance broker filled in the form on Farrell's behalf, misstating that Farrell had paid £800 for the vehicle when in fact only £140 was paid. The "basis of contract" clause invalidated the application.

In cases where a life assurance contract is taken out, the insured misstating his age, the common law renders the contract void. The courts cannot form an opinion as to the terms upon which the policy would have been effected if there had not been a misrepresentation and permit limited recovery; *Irish National Assurance Co.* v. *O'Callaghan* (1934). The Oireachtas stepped in to pass the Insurance Act 1936 which permits such a calculation in contracts of industrial assurance, defined as life assurance contracts, the premiums being taken by collectors often on a weekly basis. This limited measure of consumer protection is now redundant because section 3 limits "industrial assurance" to policies to obtain £25 or less. It does represent a signicant precedent for updating insurance contract remedies which are currently inadequate. For a case applying the provisions of the Act see *McCarthy* v. *New Ireland Assurance Co.* (1941).

The insurance companies are given other advantages by the courts over the insured, over and above the use of "basis of contract" clauses. In *Farrell* (above), the broker was seen as agent of the insured, not the insurer, thereby fixing the insured with the loss occassioned by the broker's mistake. Knowledge of surrounding circumstances will bind the insurance companies agents only in relation to facts made known while the agent is employed by the insurance company: *Taylor* v. *Yorkshire Insurance* (1913). If the broker acts as agent for the applicant and he fills in the application form incorrectly or fails to disclose a material fact the policy will not bind the insurance company. The applicant will be able to recover in an action against the broker; *Chariot Inn* v. *Assicuragioni General Spa and Coyle Hamilton, Hamilton Phillips* (1981). In general, constructive knowledge of the falsity of a representation made to an insurance company will not bind the company. In *Griffin* v. *Royal Liver Friendly Society* (1942) the applicant for a burial insurance policy falsely stated he was in good health. The insured was examined by a doctor who failed to notice the true medical condition of the applicant. The company were held not to have constructive knowledge so as to estopp them from declaring the policy void.

On the other hand, an applicant is not obliged to do the insurance company's job for it. If the insured informs the company of all the circumstances surrounding an application and the company fail to pursue and inquire further, the policy may still be valid; *Kreglinger and Fernau Ltd.* v. *Irish National Insurance Co. Ltd.* (1954). It should be noted that in this case no false statement was made; Griffin in the preceding case was guilty of a fraudulent misrepresentation. The court was obviously reluctant to permit an estoppel to work in such a case.

In *Re Sweeney & Kennedy's Arbitration* (1950) the High Court used the *contra proferendum* rule to facilitate the insured's claim on a motor vehicle insurance policy. The proposal form asked "are any of your drivers under 21 years of age or with less than 12 months driving experience." The applicant answered no. While this was true at the date of application the insured later hired a driver below 21 years of age who had less than 12 months experience. Kingsmill Moore J. refused to hold that the "basis of contract" clause could operate here; in cases of ambiguity the question in a motor insurance proposal form should be drafted precisely. It was possible for the insured to ask whether the applicant intended to use young inexperienced drivers and in the absence of specific questions the insurer should bear the loss. This case is considered in detail in Ivamy, *Fire and Motor Insurance* (1978) pp. 214–6, 272–3.

Proposals For Reform

The doctrine of *uberrima fides* seems to be unduly favourable to the Insurance Companies. An EEC Draft Directive of June 1977 may produce substantial changes in Irish Insurance Contracts. The Commission of the European Communities in Brussels has produced a fifth draft on the co-ordination of legislative and administrative provisions governing insurance contracts. The draft (which unfortunately does not cover life insurance contracts) in article two limits the duty disclose to "circumstances of which he [the insured] is aware which may influence the insurers assessment of acceptance of the risk."

Facts which subsequently come to light are not to entitle the insurer to terminate as the basis of contract clause now permits; rather, the insurance company can propose new terms which may be rejected by the insured and a repayment of premiums effected. No response to the implications of the draft directive has come from the Irish Law Reform Commission but the English Law Commission in Working Paper No. 73 have considered this question in detail.

11 Duress

This plea has traditionally been kept within narrow limits by the common law judges. It is invoked by a party to a contract who claims that he was forced into entering the contract. This is of course consistent with the restrictive circumstances in which duress will succeed as a defence to a criminal charge. The Privy Council, in the recent case of *Barton* v. *Armstrong* (1975), an appeal from the High Court of Australia, have ruled that duress may render a contract void. In that case threats to the safety of a man or his family were sufficient to vitiate consent to the contract. While it may seem that duress can only operate at common law where the danger apprehended is assault or injury to the person, it is suggested that the Irish Courts have taken a more liberal position on the plea of duress.

In *Lessee of Blackwood* v. *Gregg* (1831) an old man of 92 was abducted by relatives. He executed a deed in favour of one of the captors. The deed was not read over to the old man. The trial judge was held by the Court of Exchequer to have correctly left it for the jury to decide whether the personal restraint imposed on the old man constituted duress. In *Rourke* v. *Mealy* (1870) Palles C.B. indicated that a person threatened with the prosecution of a relative unless he or she undertakes to pay a debt owed by the relative, may, in certain instances, be able to plead duress in equity.

In *Griffith* v. *Griffith* (1944) a young man was threatened with imprisonment and dishonour unless he married a young girl he was alleged to have made pregnant while on a camping holiday on Howth Head. His father and the local priest joined with the girls mother in pressing him into a contract of marriage. When it became known that the plaintiff was not the father of the child he successfully claimed that his contract of marriage was void for duress. The court indicated that if he were the father a petition for a decree of nullity would not have been successful.

The most important Irish decision on duress is *Smelter Corporation of Ireland* v. *O'Driscoll* (1977). The plaintiff company sought specific performance of an option agreement which gave them a right to purchase O'Driscoll's land in County Cork. The option had been

118

given reluctantly, the agent of the plaintiff company believed that if O'Driscoll did not sell to them directly, the County Council intended to make a compulsory purchase order. When the agent communicated this to O'Driscoll he felt he had no alternative but give the option. In fact, the County Council did not intend to purchase the land. O'Higgins C.J. in the Supreme Court said "in these circumstances it appears to me that there was a fundamental unfairness in the transaction." The unfairness stems from O'Driscoll's belief that he was going to lose his land, one way or another. He could not be said to have consented to the agreement. Specific performance was refused.

An action for money had and received is the best way in which a person paying money under protest may recover the sums paid. In *Gt. Southern and Western Railway Co.* v. *Robertson* (1878) a railway company were under statutory obligation to transport soldiers and their equipment at a rate of tuppence per ton per mile. They charged the plaintiff, a carrier who had agreed to act as agent for the military, a higher rate. The plaintiff paid the excess, some £601, under protest. He was held entitled to recover the excess as money had and received to his use.

In these cases the party exercising duress often does so because of some misinterpretation of the legal position. This will not justify the exercise of coercion and, further, restitution will be ordered even though it is generally true to state that a mistake of law will not be operative. The oppressive conduct of the payee will justify an award of restitution even if the mistake of law was shared by both parties. In *O'Loghlen* v. *O'Callaghan* (1874) and *Jackson* v. *Stopford* (1923) this rule against holding money paid under a mistake of law to be recoverable was affirmed. Although this question of payment of money under a mistake of law could most properly be examined in Chap. 9 there can be a considerable overlap with principles of duress.

There seems to be a trend towards widening the circumstances in which recovery of money paid under a mistake of law will be ordered. In *Rogers* v. *Louth County Council* (1981) money was paid to the defendants in order to redeem an annuity. This figure was calculated in good faith according to guidelines distributed by the Department of Local Government. After payment was made a decision of the Supreme Court held this basis of assessment inaccurate. The plaintiff sought to recover £953.53 as an overpayment. On a case stated to the Supreme Court by the Circuit Court it was held that the sum was recoverable. Despite the fact that both parties knew the (albeit erroneous) calculation was the result of advice from an independent source the Supreme Court declared the parties not to be *in pari delicto* (see pp. 145–7).

This, it is submitted is beside the point. The case relied upon in *Rogers* is an authority on illegality not mistake of Law, *viz. Kiriri Cotton Co.* v. *Dewani* (1960). The factors that will justify a court refusing to follow the rule against non-recovery were stated in *O'Loghlen* v. *O'Callaghan* (1874) to be "mala fides, ... fraud or imposition;" *per* Whiteside C.J. It is hoped that when the Supreme Court reconsider *Rogers* they will follow the narrower view advanced in *O'Loghlen* v. *O'Callaghan* (1874) and overrule *Rogers*, even though the cases could be distinguished on their facts.

There are important English developments on the question of economic duress; see *The Atlantic Baron* (1978). The Ontario Court of Appeal case of *Ronald Elwyn Lister Ltd.* v. *Dunlop Canada* (1980) is also instructive.

12 Equitable Intervention

1. The Equitable Doctrine of Undue Influence

The doctrine of undue influence enables a court to set aside contracts, transfers of property *inter vivos* and dispositions by will whenever it appears that one party has not freely consented to the transaction. The doctrine is designed to discourage sharp practice, particularly on the part of persons who are in positions of trust and confidence and who may abuse the power they acquire over other persons.

The presumption of undue influence

Persons who acquire a considerable amount of influence over others often do so because of the very nature of the relationship that exists between them. A patient may place trust and confidence in his physician; *Aherne* v. *Hogan* (1844). A trustee who employs an agent to carry out his obligations places that agent in a fiduciary relationship *vis à vis* the beneficial owner of the property; see *Murphy* v. *O'Shea* (1845) and *King* v. *Anderson* (1874). A solicitor will hold some degree of influence and dominion over a client; *Lawless* v. *Mansfield* (1841). In these cases it goes without saying that the solicitor, trustee, or physician should not misrepresent or trick the other party into conveying property to him. Equity also requires all transactions between these persons to be justified by the party in whom trust and confidence is placed. In certain cases the courts go so far as to say that there is an absolute incapacity to contract. In *Atkins* v. *Delemege* (1847) a purchase of property was set aside when the purchaser turned out to be the legal representative of the estate, the sale being ordered by a court. The solicitor, in such circumstances was declared to be incapable of purchasing. The general rule is that once the purchaser falls into a category of person in whom trust and confidence is reposed he is obliged to show that the sale was fair and freely assented to. In *Molony* v. *Kerman* (1832) it was held that before an agent could take a lease from his principal the agent must show

121

that full information was given to the principal and that the contract was entered into in good faith.

Undue influence will also be presumed where property is transferred to a religious association by a devotee. In *White* v. *Meade* (1840) the plaintiff then aged 18, entered a religious establishment as a lodger. It was envisaged that if the plaintiff decided at a later date to take holy orders she could do so after being allowed to consult with friends. The defendants prevailed on her to take holy orders while actively preventing her from seeking guidance from her brother. The order also managed to get the plaintiff to transfer £1100 and a large amount of realty to the order. The transfer was set aside.

It is not necessary to show that the religious order practised coercion. It is enough to show that the religious devotee was unable to freely consent to the transaction because she was incapable of exercising independent judgment. *Allcard* v. *Skinner* (1887) shows that even if a court does not impute improper motive or unconscionable behaviour to the party taking under the contract or transfer, the transaction will be set aside unless it can be shown to be fair and freely consented to. In *Kirwan* v. *Cullen* (1854) a gift to the Catholic Church was upheld. The executor of the donor's estate alleged that one of the trustees of the property conveyed had been the religious confessor of the donor; the transaction was upheld when it was shown that the trustee in question had ceased to be the donor's confessor two years before the gift was made.

Other relationships the courts view with suspicion include parent and child, guardian and ward. In *Wallace* v. *Wallace* (1842) and *Croker* v. *Croker* (1870) transfers of property by a son in favour of his father were set aside because in both cases the fathers were unable to show that the transfers were freely made. In *McMackin* v. *Hibernian Bank* (1905) a guarantee signed by a young girl living with her mother was set aside because of the undue influence of the mother. This presumption also applies to instances of guardian and ward; *Mulhallen* v. *Marum* (1843).

There are other instances where the courts may eventually hold that the burden of showing the propriety of the transaction rests upon the party seeking to uphold it. The value of the presumption is that it results in the transaction being set aside if the onus is not discharged. This is a reversal of the burden of proof in most civil actions where it normally rests on the person impugning the transaction. This was considered recently by the Northern Ireland Court of Appeal in *Re Founds Estate* (1979). An action was brought by executors of Mrs. Founds estate to set aside legacies on the ground of undue influence having been exerted by a niece of the deceased. Jones L.J. said; "the presumption of undue influence may arise in two sorts of cases. The evidence may show *a particular relationship* for example that of solicitor and client, trustee and cestui que trust, doctor and patient or religious adviser and pupil. Those cases or some of them, depending on the facts, *may of themselves* raise the presumption. Such examples, as regards undue influence, have much in common with the doctrine of *res ipsa loquitur* in relation to negligence. But then there is the other sort of case, the precise range of which is indeterminate, in which *the whole evidence*, when meticulously considered, may disclose *facts* from which *it should be inferred* that a relationship is disclosed which justifies a finding that there is a presumption of undue influence. In other words the presumption enables a party to achieve justice by bridging a gap in the evidence where there is a gap because the evidence is impossible to come by."

This second instance of a presumption operating in favour of the party seeking to invalidate the transaction can be illustrated by peripheral family relationships which may give one person the opportunity to gain dominance over the other. Brother and brother; *Armstrong* v. *Armstrong* (1873); brother and sister and uncle and nephew; *Gregg* v. *Kidd* (1956); brother-in-law and sister-in-law; *Evans* v. *Cook and Elwood* (1874). These are all cases where the presumption may come into effect after evidence has been given to show that a relationship of trust and confidence developed between these persons. English case law suggests the same is true of husband and wife and persons engaged to be married.

Undue influence as of fact

If the presumption does not arise automatically and if the court does not feel that the facts shown raise an inference that the transaction was not freely consented to, it is necessary to convince the court that the transaction should not stand. The courts will not presume that undue influence exists if, at first sight, one person is in no position to hold dominion over another. In a sense the courts presume that the parties deal on an equal footing. In the recent case of *Mathew* v. *Bobbins* (1980) the English Court of Appeal ruled that the relationship of employer/employee does not give rise to the presumption that the employer stands in a dominant position vis-à-vis the employee. The Court of Appeal reasoned that 20th century employment protection legislation has readjusted an imbalance that clearly existed in the last century. Mr. Bobbins was held not to have been prevailed upon by his employer when he "agreed" to sign a document which changed his status from a tenant into a licensee of accommodation provided by his employer. It is open to doubt whether employment legislation, either in Ireland or in Great Britain, has reached the level of sophistication or effectiveness contemplated in this case. For a case of an ordinary sale between persons outside the presumption see *Barry* v. *O'Grady* (1846).

Discharging the onus of proof

Once the presumption operates the party seeking to uphold the transaction must show that consent was freely given and that the party with whom he contracted did so with his eyes open. The cases suggest that this can be done by advising that independent advice be sought from a respectable source. In *McMackin* v. *Hibernian Bank* (1905) a bank was denied enforcement of a bank guarantee because the guarantor, their clients daughter, should have obtained legal advice; the case where the guarantor is also a client of the Bank is considerably *a fortiori; Lloyds Bank* v. *Bundy* (1975). The recent case of *Smyth* v. *Smyth* (1978) holds that it is enough if the party seeking to enforce the bargain shows that it was contemplated that independent legal advice would be given before the contract was completed. This may be a dangerous precedent to rely on. The best advice would be to advise the other person to seek out and obtain independent legal advice. If the advisor turns out to be a trusted friend or respected member of the community this may suffice.

In fact, cases in which no advice was sought or given have been upheld. What the doctrine boils down to is the protection of persons who are not able to freely consent to a transaction. If, after hearing the evidence, the court feels that the bargain should stand, no *a priori* test will stand in the way. This is shown vividly by *Smyth* v. *Smyth* (1978).

In *McCormack* v. *Bennett* (1973) Finlay P. upheld a transfer of farm property made by an elderly couple to a daughter, who in return, agreed to look after them for the rest of their lives. The disposition was challenged on the ground that no independent advice was given. The action was dismissed; "the presence of full and satisfactory independent advice is not the only way of proving that a voluntary deed even though it may be on the face of it improvident resulted from the free exercise of the donor's will . . . I think it is a reasonable inference from the evidence which I have heard that he was a sufficiently astute man to know that no form of bargain or commercial transaction was likely to secure for himself what they really needed and that was personal care and attention granted largely through affection and kindness by a member of their family." See also *Provincial Bank* v. *McKeever* (1941).

As a general rule it is more difficult for administrators of an estate to convince a court that the deceased was unable to freely consent, particularly if the deceased later seems to have approved the consequences of her action; see *Kirwan* v. *Cullen* (1854). This reluctance to "second guess" the deceased, particularly when he or she seems mentally competent, is evident in *McCormack* v. *Bennett* also.

Delay in seeking relief

A party who later approves and seeks to take advantage of a bargain will be bound by it, even if it was suspicious at the time it was entered into; *De Montmorency* v. *Devereux* (1840), affirmed by the House of Lords.

In cases where the presumption operates but there is no evidence of fraud or overbearing conduct, relief must be sought promptly. In *Allcard* v. *Skinner* (1887) relief was refused because of a delay of five years in seeking relief. Where fraud or overbearing conduct exists as of fact a delay of 12 years was held not to be fatal in *O'Kelly* v. *Glenny* (1846). Time begins to run from the date of emancipation from the dominion of the other party.

2. Unconscionable Bargains

The Irish courts of equity have intervened in unconscionable bargains by setting aside the transaction or amending the terms in order to produce what the court sees as a fairer transaction. Historically the courts, both here and in England, have protected persons who mortgaged or sold an interest in family property by obliging the mortgagee or purchaser to show the bargain to be a fair one. This jurisdiction extended into cases where an aged or illiterate person for example sold property, of which they were in possession, for an inadequate consideration. The equitable doctrine relating to expectant heirs and reversioners, as these persons came to be known, has, in part, produced a wider equitable jurisdiction.

In the case of *Slator* v. *Nolan* (1876) Sullivan M.R., after reviewing the early cases declared "I take the law of the Court to be that if two persons—no matter whether a confidential relation exists between them or not—stand in such a relation to each other that one can take an undue advantage of the other, whether by reason of distress or recklessness or wildness or want of care and where the facts show that one party has taken undue advantage of the other, by reason of the circumstances I have mentioned—a transaction resting upon such unconscionable dealing will not be allowed to stand." In *Slator* v. *Nolan* itself, a young man, in want of money because of his youthful excesses, was able to set aside a sale of his inheritance.

These cases proceed on a finding that the parties were not equal at the time the contract was struck, largely as a result of the individual circumstances into which one the parties has fallen. In *Rae* v. *Joyce* (1892) a pregnant woman who mortgaged a reversionary interest in property at undervalue was held entitled to set the transaction aside. The mortgagee, a Dublin moneylender was clearly the more commercially astute; the delicate medical condition of the mort-gagor and her needy circumstances, allied to a rate of interest fixed at 60 per cent., convinced the Irish Court of Appeal that the bargain should be set aside, a rate of interest of 5 per cent. being substituted instead. The mortgagor was unable to show that the bargain was not a hard one.

Although sharp practice, misrepresentation and collusion often appear in these cases, the basis of relief is not fraud in any real sense. If a bargain is harsh in its terms and if one party is clearly in a stronger bargaining position equity will intervene. The hardness of the bargain was stressed to be the foundation of intervention in the English case of *Benyon* v. *Cook* (1875).

The Irish Courts are extremely protective of elderly persons who sell or dispose of farmland outside the family unit. In *Buckley* v. *Irwin* (1960) McVeigh J., in the Northern Ireland Chancery Division refused to grant a decree of specific performance in favour of the plaintiff who had purchased the defendant's farm at undervalue. The parties were not equally competent in business matters; the plaintiff was described as "sharp-eyed and experienced," the defendant characterised as "a person who would require protection and guidance in carrying out business affairs." In *Grealish* v. *Murphy* (1946) a transfer of land made by an elderly, intransigent and illiterate farmer, again at undervalue in favour of a younger man, was set aside by Gavan Duffy J. on the ground that the parties were not on an equal footing.

At this point we should consider whether the basis of invalidity is always a finding that the weaker party has been "overreached." Many cases turn upon the fact that one party, while he or she cannot be said to be insane, is unable, for reasons of idiocy, senility or lack of business acumen, to understand the implications of the contract. *Grealish* v. *Murphy* is such a case. Here the transaction was drafted and explained to the old man by his lawyers. While Gavan Duffy J. held that the lawyers had not done everything they could have done to bring home to *Grealish* the implications of the transaction it is difficult to see how this would be possible if the old man was incapable of grasping the consequences of the contract. In these situations invalidity results from the fact that the bargain is so improvident that no reasonable person would enter into it. Students should examine the old cases of *Garvey* v. *McMinn* (1846) and *Scott* v.

Scott (1847) on this question. The best modern authority is provided by *Lyndon* v. *Coyne* (1946). The aged owner of land transferred his property to his nephew in return for a promise by the nephew to permit the old man and his wife to remain on the property for their lives, and for periodic payments of cash. Given the health and age of the old man the instrument was a foolish or improvident one. There was no revocation clause included in the instrument; payments were likely to end at an early date—the old man died three months later—and the instrument as a whole was curiously drafted, suggesting to the court that it was not understood by the old man. O'Byrne J. set the deed aside.

Upholding the unconscionable bargain

Rae v. *Joyce* (1892) suggests that in cases of the sale of a reversionary interest the purchaser must show that the bargain is, in point of fact, fair, just and reasonable. *Kelly* v. *Morrisroe* (1919) suggests that where an eccentric and elderly owner of property sells to a younger person the onus of showing the bargain was fair rests on the purchaser. As in cases of undue influence the purchaser will discharge this onus by convincing the court that the vendor contracted with his eyes open and was given the market value of the property. The prudent purchaser will advise the vendor to seek independent advice before contracting.

In *Smyth* v. *Smyth* (1978) the trustee of real property purchased part of the land from the beneficial owner, a young man who suffered from a drink problem. The young man had first raised the question of sale. The sale took an "inordinate" length of time to complete, so there was no question of the bargain being concluded without giving the vendor time for reflection. Costello J. refused to find the bargain invalid. He rejected evidence that the consideration paid was inadequate and, despite the fact that no independent solicitor was consulted—one solicitor acting for both parties—the transaction was, in the learned judge's view, neither unconscionable nor improvident.

It is clear that judges will take radically different positions on the implications to be drawn from the evidence—witness the old case of *O'Rorke* v. *Bolingbroke* (1877), an appeal to the House of Lords from the Court of Chancery in Ireland, and the recent English Court of Appeal decision in *Re Brocklehurst* (deceased) (1978)). Many academic commentators are critical of the unconscionability doctrine because of the uncertainty surrounding its application to individual cases, yet it is difficult to see how else the courts could satisfactorily deal with the cases in which unconscionability is pleaded.

The Moneylenders Acts 1900–1933

Although the old moral and legal prohibitions against usurious contracts were swept away by the repeal of the usury laws in 1854, contracts to borrow money at excessive rates of interest were still potentially unconscionable and invalid on that ground; see *Chapple* v. *Mahon* (1870). The Moneylenders Act 1900, s.1 also gives some measure of protection to borrowers who contract for a loan, the cost of which is excessive. If the court feels the cost of the loan is excessive s. 1 requires the court to go further and decide whether the transaction is "harsh and unconscionable." The factors that will be important here are relative bargaining position of the parties; the risk to the lender and the conduct of both parties. In *Thomas* v. *Ashbrook* (1913) a loan at an interest rate of 80% per annum was struck down. There was little risk to the lender so the court decided to substitute a rate of interest of 25 per cent. Excessive interest alone may, in certain circumstances, lead the court into finding the transaction harsh and unconscionable; see *Wells* v. *Kerr* (1912). Section 17(1) of the Moneylenders Act 1933 provides that where interest is in excess of 39 per cent. per annum the courts are to conclusively assume that the interest charged is excessive and that the transaction is harsh and unconscionable.

If the financial institution and the prospective lender are on an equal footing there may be a reluctance to intervene. The Oireachtas, in a desire to facilitate the growth of Credit Unions, have exempted these institutions from the terms of the Moneylenders Acts; see section 28 of the Credit Union Act 1966.

The courts are reluctant to re-open old transactions and it is best to apply promptly for relief under the Moneylenders Acts; witness the decision in *Stone* v. *Hamilton* (1918).

Part IV
Public Policy

13   Illegal Contracts

INTRODUCTION

A contract may be rendered invalid because the transaction runs into conflict with some important value or principle which must be upheld, at the cost of rendering a bargain void or enforceable. These cases are often divided into two categories; the first category is reserved for cases which are illegal in the purest sense; these transactions infringe a statutory or common law rule to the extent that the whole contract is rendered invalid. Cases falling into the second category, often described as void contracts, do not produce the cataclysmic effects that attend illegal contracts. It is possible for the courts to remove or "sever" the unpalatable or void term while enforcing the rest of the transaction. This distinction seems well established, particularly in English law.

Many writers regard the distinction with distrust but, in general, the cases fall into line with the classification. A further consequence of the distinction concerns collateral transactions which may also be invalid if the main contract is illegal Megarry J. observed in *Spector* v. *Ageda* (1973) "a transaction may simply be void, or it may be unenforceable, and in either case other connected transactions may nevertheless be perfectly valid and enforceable. But illegality is another matter; for it may by contagious."

Part One

(1) *Illegal contracts at common law*

(i) Contracts to commit a crime or tort.   Agreements of this nature are obviously contrary to public policy. Problems that arise from related transactions are less easy to resolve. It has been decided that contracts of insurance are invalid if payment under the policy would encourage persons to commit criminal acts like suicide or murder; Furmston, the editor of Cheshire and Fifoot's *Law of Contract* has argued (16 U.T.L.J.) 267 that contracts of insurance which indemnify the insured for his unlawful acts should, in certain

131

instances, be enforceable. Nevertheless, the recent English case of *Gray* v. *Barr* (1971) takes the rule of public policy even further. The plaintiff was acquitted of murder. The widow of the deceased sued the plaintiff in negligence for causing the death of her husband. The Court of Appeal refused to allow the plaintiff to rely on an insurance policy covering "home accidents." This seems to be both undesirable and improper. If the plaintiff had already been acquitted of the offence the Court of Appeal acted irregularly when it imputed improper conduct to him.

(ii) Contracts prejudicial to the administration of justice.

It should be noted that a person who protects or shelters a felon is at common law guilty of a criminal offence. Contracts which serve to subvert the cause of justice, while not of themselves criminal, are illegal and cannot give rise to enforceable contractual obligations. In *Brady* v. *Flood* (1841) the defendant was paid a sum of money to get criminal charges of conspiracy dropped. Brady C.B. refused to hear litigation arising from this transaction because it was clearly illegal.

The courts view it of the utmost importance that criminal proceedings, once commenced, should be completed without interference from persons who may have some personal interest in the case. Although the courts view agreements to compromise civil suits favourably, agreements relating to a criminal offence are viewed differently. The public interest requires persons accused of criminal offences to be prosecuted, particularly if the offence committed is serious. In the leading English case of *Keir* v. *Leeman* (1846) an agreement to compromise criminal proceedings arising from a riot was held to be illegal; Lord Denman indicated that if the criminal proceedings commenced can also be the subject of a civil action it will be possible to execute a valid compromise. In cases of assault, which has the dual characteristic of being a tort and a crime, a compromise of proceedings will be enforceable. The decision in *Nolan* v. *Shiels* (1926) illustrates that this exception will be viewed restrictively. The plaintiff, victim of an *indecent* assault was given a cheque for £50 in return for her promise not to prosecute the defendant's friend who had committed the offence. Judge Pigot refused to allow an action on the cheque; he noted that if the offence committed had been the less serious offence of *common* assault *Keir* v. *Leeman* would have allowed an action to succeed.

If no prosecution has commenced and the promissory note is given in exchange for a promise not to take the matter further, the case of *Rourke* v. *Mealy* (1879) suggests that an action may succeed. The plaintiff held a negotiable instrument which he suspected had been forged by a relative of the defendant. He informed the defendant of his suspicions, whereupon the defendant made himself liable on the instrument in consideration for the plaintiff's promise not to charge the relative with forgery. The plaintiff was held entitled to sue the defendant on the instrument. This was not an agreement to stifle a prosecution for no proceedings were in progress; nor did the public interest require the truth of an allegation of forgery to be ascertained.

A person who fraudulently abuses judicial proceedings to obtain the benefits of bankrupt status should be brought to justice; an agreement between a creditor and the defrauding debtor in which proceedings to set aside a discharge as fraudulently obtained are compromised for a promise to pay the debt is illegal: *Daly* v. *Daly* (1870).

A rather surprising result was reached in *Bagot* v. *Arnott* (1867). The plaintiff had lent large sums of money to S, who, in return for a further advance, gave bills of sale to the plaintiff as security, instructing the plaintiff to sell the property covered by the bills to realise the security. Bagot knew that S had committed forgery and would use the advance to flee abroad and avoid prosecution. The goods were seized by other creditors. The plaintiff successfully sued in tort to recover the goods. The Court of Common Pleas held that, notwithstanding Bagot's knowledge that S intended to use part of the funds to evade prosecution, *the purpose* behind the advance was to obtain security for earlier bona fide debts, not to enable S to leave the country.

The common law judges gave also viewed contracts which encourage speculative litigation as undesirable. If a third party lends assistance to a litigant in circumstances which are viewed as improper he is guilty of the crime of maintenance. If he stands to gain from the litigation—by agreeing to pay legal fees in return for an agreed portion of the damages awarded, if any, the contract is described as champertous. Strictly speaking, lawyers who agree to fund litigation on a contingency fee basis are guilty of champerty. In *Littledale* v. *Thompson* (1878) Whaley was a party to a dispute concerning the right to a clerical living or advowson. Thompson agreed that if Whaley continued to press his claim to the advowson Thompson would pay legal fees if Whaley would in turn convey the advowson to him, if successful. Littledale, Whaley's executor, sued Thompson when he failed to pay the fees. The action was dismissed as being part of a champertous contract.

(iii) Agreements which serve to defraud the Revenue. Attempts are sometimes made to reduce the tax liability of the vendor of real property by misstating the purchase price. In *Starling*

Securities v. *Woods* (1977) the plaintiff purchased real property under an oral contract which would have been enforceable had it not become apparent to McWilliam J. that the consideration had been misstated in order to defraud the Revenue Commissioners.

Collusive arrangements between employers and employees in which the employee is given "expenses" in order to reduce his liability to P.A.Y.E. contributions are also illegal. Indeed, an employee party to such an agreement has been held unable to recover arrears of wages and unable to bring an action for redundancy payments or unfair dismissal; see the English cases of *Napier* v. *N.B.A.* (1951) and *Tomlinson* v. *Dick Evans "U" Drive* (1978). It is doubtful whether any policy objective is served by denying an employee compensation for loss of his job and it is hoped that *Tomlinson* will not be followed in Ireland. In these cases the employee is suing to recover under statutes which do not themselves make an illegal act of this kind a defence to the action; the employer will generally be more culpable than the employee and it seems absurd to allow him to take advantage of his own wrongdoing.

(iv) Agreements which serve to corrupt public officials. In *Lord Mayor of Dublin* v. *Hayes* (1876) the defendant was appointed Marshall of the City of Dublin, a position which also gave him the post of Registrar of Pawnbrokers. This entitled the defendant to collect fees which he agreed to transfer to the City Treasurer. It was clear that the appointment was made in exchange for the defendant's promise. The promise was held unenforceable because such a contract would tend to encourage corrupt practices amongst public officials.

(v) Contracts tending to encourage immorality. Even if the conduct contemplated by the contract is not itself illegal, as would be the case in an arrangement to procure the seduction of a girl below the age of consent, a contract that promotes some illicit sexual behaviour is illegal. Illicit sexual behaviour simply means sexual intercourse which takes place outside the confines of marriage. The older common law cases draw an important distinction; a contract that contemplates an obligation to provide future sexual intercourse is illegal while a contract that is made in consideration for sexual favours already conferred is not illegal; it may be invalid for want of consideration. This can be overcome if the promise is in a deed under seal. In *Reade* v. *Adams* (1855) a deed was executed providing an annuity to any children of the union should the woman marry another man. The annuity was held enforceable; the deed did not require the woman to continue illicit sexual intercourse in order to retain the annuity: contrast the badly reported case of *Quidihy* v. *Kelly* (1788).

The English courts, faced with the trend towards stable relationships being formed outside marriage, have decided to respond by permitting one partner to acquire rights in the other partner's property through the doctrines of estoppel, contractual license, and constructive trust; See in particular *Tanner* v. *Tanner* (1975) and *Pascoe* v. *Turner* (1979). The words of Sable J. in *Andrews* v. *Parker* (1973), a Queensland decision, are instructive;

> "are the actions of people today to be judged in the light of the standards of the last century? As counsel for the plaintiff said, cases discussing what was then by community standards sexual immorality appear to have been decided in the days when for the sake of decency the legs of tables, wore drapes . . . I do not accept that immoral today means precisely what it did in the days of *Pearce* v. *Brooks*. I am, I believe entitled to look at the word under modern social standards."

A prostitute would nevertheless have extreme difficulty in recovering a fee if she performed her part of a bargain on credit terms. Incidental transactions may also be invalid. In *Pearce* v. *Brooks* (1867) a contract for the hire of a carriage to a prostitute who, to the knowledge of the owner intended to use it in furtherance of her "immoral vocation," was breached when the carriage was returned in a damaged condition. The owner's action failed; his knowledge of the immoral purpose behind the contract meant he "participated" in the illegality.

A contract designed to promote unlawful gambling is just as illegal as one aimed at furthering illicit sexual activity. In *Devine* v. *Scott and Johnston* (1931) the plaintiff let premises in Belfast to Johnston who intended to carry on an unlawful bookmaking business. The plaintiff's agent was fixed with knowledge which bound the principal. An action to recover arrears of rent was dismissed.

(vi) A contract to trade with enemies of the State. A contract between nationals and enemy aliens is contrary to public policy. In *Ross* v. *Shaw* (1917) a contract to purchase yarn to be supplied from a mill in Belgium could not be lawfully performed once the mill was occupied by German troops during World War I. The plaintiff's action for non-delivery failed.

(vii) Contracts that breach foreign law. The courts refuse to enforce a contract that is illegal according to the law of the place where it is to be performed. In *Stanhope* v. *Hospitals Trust Ltd.* (1936)

the plaintiff in Natal posted Irish sweepstake tickets to the Dublin office where the draw was to take place. The tickets were not included in the draw. Sweepstakes were illegal in Natal; the contract was illegal according to the law of the place where the contract was formed; it was not illegal under Irish law and could be enforceable in Ireland. A joint enterprise to violate foreign and domestic customs laws will be illegal and unenforceable by both parties; *Whitecross Potatoes* v. *Coyle* (1978)

(2) *Statutory illegality*

Rules of public policy, whether designed to further social or economic objectives, are articulated by the legislature in the Acts of the Oireachtas or Statutory Instruments. Contractual arrangements that fall foul of these policy objectives may be invalidated by legislation, either expressly or impliedly. The distinction drawn by the courts between a void and an illegal contract is not always relied upon by the legislature.

Legislation expressly proscribes contracts in many situations. In the Republic The Moneylenders Acts, 1900–1933, makes contracts entered into by unlicensed moneylenders void; charging of compound interest is also unlawful. The Family Home Protection Act, 1976, s.3(1) provides "[w]here a spouse, without the prior consent in writing of the other spouse, purports to convey an interest in the family home to any person except the other spouse [subject to legislative exceptions] the purported conveyance shall be void." The Hire Purchase Acts 1946–80 require contracts to be evidenced in writing; otherwise the transaction is void. Contrast the Statute of Frauds (Ir.) 1695 where a transaction is simply unenforceable for want of a memorandum. In employment contracts The Holidays (Employees) Act 1973 makes contracts to give up rights to holiday pay void; so too are contracts to give up rights to minimum periods of notice under the Minimum Notice and Terms of Employment Act 1973. An employer cannot contract with his employees to induce them to bargain away redundancy payments and compensation for unfair dismissal; the same provisions to this effect are to be found in employment protection legislation in force in both the Republic and in Northern Ireland. Licensing legislation of various kinds is a fruitful source of examples of statutory invalidity. Section 36(1) of the Road Transport Act 1933 provides that "it shall not be lawful for any person to enter into an agreement for the carriage for reward of merchandise by any other person unless such other person is a licensee under merchandise license." In *O'Shaughnessy* v. *Lyons* (1957) the plaintiff agreed to train as well as transport the defendant's greyhounds to and from race meetings. Justice O'Briain refused to permit an action to recover the agreed fee for this work because such a conduct was in breach of section 36(1).

An Act may go further than rendering an agreement unlawful. In *Gray* v. *Cathcart* (1899) the defendant had taken a lease of an insanitary house in Belfast. The Belfast Corporation Acts made it an offence to occupy insanitary premises. The landlord's action to recover arrears of rent failed; Johnston J. said "Everyone commits a misdemeanor who does any act forbidden by a Statute: accordingly when these parties entered into an agreement to occupy a house which had been condemned it was a contract to do that which the statute says you could not do. It was a contract to do an illegal thing, and though the parties might go through the form yet such a contract is not binding and cannot be sued upon." It does not follow however that simply because conduct is made a criminal offence any contract in which one party acts in breach of a statute will automatically render the contract illegal. Johnston J. was in error if the above reasoning is advanced as the *modus operandi* to be followed by the courts. If the statute expressly makes such contracts void the courts have no option but to follow this provision. If however, the legislature has not spelt out the consequences of entering into a contract it is not to be assumed that a contract will be invalid. The courts must ask; does this statute impliedly prohibit a contract of this nature? The court should inquire into the purpose behind the statute; licensing arrangements are often designed simply to raise revenue for the Government or to regulate an industry. Changing social and religious values may lead to a statutory prohibition being changed or repealed; see the 1695 statute forbidding Sunday trading (*Brady* v. *Grogan* (1842)), repealed by the Statute Law Revision (Pre-Union Irish Statutes) Act 1962.

The leading English decision on statutory illegality is *St. John Shipping Corporation* v. *Joseph Rank* (1957). The plaintiffs sued for freight owed by the defendants who had contracted for the plaintiffs to transport their cargo. The master of the vessel overloaded contrary to statute, calculating that even after paying the maximum fine a profit would still be made by carrying excess cargo. Devlin J. held for the plaintiffs. This contract was lawful at the time it was entered into. The breach of statute, which occurred during performance did not run foul of any express or implied provision invalidating contracts. The matter is one of construction of the statute; Devlin J. said that the test is not, is there an illegal act during performance of the contract but rather, does the illegal performance turn the contract into one prohibited by statute?

This issue, often described as the problem of implied prohibition, is difficult; the courts lean against finding that the Act, on its construction has this effect because it means treating persons who intend to break the law in the same way as persons who do so unwittingly. The possibility that a lawbreaker will not only be fined but lose the fruits of a contract also contributes towards a restrictive approach to the implied prohibition problem; such a conclusion punishes a person twice over.

The Supreme Court's decision in *Gavin Lowe Ltd.* v. *Field* (1942) is instructive. The plaintiffs sued on a dishonoured cheque which had been given to them by the defendants who had purchased a cow from the plaintiff. The beast was bought after it had been put on the market in such a way as to be "exposed for sale"; Public Health legislation made it an offence to "expose for sale" a diseased animal; the cow had later to be destroyed because it was tubercular. The Statute did not in terms make it an offence to sell diseased livestock; it was therefore possible to buy cattle that were diseased as long as the transaction did not involve an act of "exposure for sale". The plaintiff argued that he was entitled to recover on the dishonoured cheque; he argued that the purpose behind the legislation was not to make contracts for the sale of diseased livestock illegal but to protect the public health by making it an offence to expose for sale diseased meat. The majority of the Supreme Court accepted this argument and permitted recovery on the cheque. Sullivan C.J. held that because the Acts did not make it an offence to sell, the defence of illegality would only succeed if the unlawful act of exposure and the sale amounted "to a unity of design." In the Chief Justice's view this was not so. Murnaghan and Geoghegan J.J., concurrred.

A more satisfactory view is advanced by the dissenting members of the Supreme Court. Meredith J. held it to be "an absurdity" to reach such a conclusion; the prohibition of an act preparatory to sale was designed to preclude the sale itself from being legal. "Prohibition of the bud is then prohibition of the blossom." O'Byrne J. agreed: "it seems difficult to justify such a construction as would recognise the validity of a contract arising out of exposure for sale, though the exposure itself is made a criminal offence."

(3) *Gaming and wagering contracts*

The Gaming and Lotteries Acts 1956–1970 are the most important Acts regulating the way in which gambling is carried on within the Republic. While an analysis of this legislation is outside the scope of this book section 36 of the 1956 Act governs the consequences of the contractual relationship created by gaming and wagering. In Northern Ireland the Gaming Acts 1845 and 1892 remain in force.

(i) Wagering. The legislation does not define a wager but case law has produced the following definition, taken here from Cheshire and Fifoot: "staking something of value upon the result of some future uncertain event such as a horse race, or upon the ascertainment of the truth concerning some past or present event, such as the population of London, with regard to which the wagering parties express opposite views."

It is of the essence of a wager that one party is to win and the other to lose upon the determination of the event. For this reason a bet placed with "the Tote," that is, the Racing Board established by the Totaliser Act 1929, is not a wager. This was decided by Pringle J. in *Duff* v. *Racing Board* (1971). Because the Racing Board are legally bound to pay all the money received to successful ticketholders it follows that the Board can neither win nor lose.

English case law establishes that multipartite arrangements are not wagers; *Ellesmere* v. *Wallace* (1929). The Alberta case of *Breitmeier* v. *Batke* (1966) on the other hand suggests that an arrangement between three persons may be a wager. Fridman, author of the leading Canadian text, suggests that the Canadian authority is to be preferred for "the true test surely is whether one person can win and others lose." Irish cases should follow this test in my view. Nevertheless a tripartite wager may often be a lottery.

Many transactions resemble a wager; a contract of insurance is "a bet on the outcome of a future uncertain event." It is not a wager if the assured has an insurable interest in the subject matter; to insure a ship's cargo against destruction during a voyage is a valid contract of insurance if the assured has an interest in the cargo. It is a wager if not.

Stockbroking arrangements often fall into the category of wagers. "Contracts for differences" involve an agreement between two persons who agree that they will ascertain the difference in price of certain shares on one day and their price at a later date. If the parties do not intend that the shares will be purchased the "contract for differences" will be void. Similarly in *Byers* v. *Beattie* (1867) the plaintiffs agreed to purchase and sell shares which were owned by the defendant. The agreement provided that if the price for which the shares were later sold was greater than that paid by the defendants, the defendants would pay the difference plus any charges and commission to the plaintiffs. The plaintiffs sued for sums due under this agreement. The arrangement was held a wager.

(ii) Gaming. At common law gaming was legal if the element of chance was negligible and the outcome of the game turned upon the skill of the players. The present legislation defines "gaming" as "playing a game (whether of skill or chance or partly of skill and partly of chance) for stakes hazarded by the players"; 1956 Act, s.2. Section 4 of the 1956 Act makes gaming unlawful if (1) the chances of all of the players, including the banker, are not equal or, (2) if a portion of the stakes are retained by the banker otherwise than as winnings (3) gaming is conducted by way of slot machines. Later sections make gaming at a circus, travelling show, carnival, public house, amusement hall and funfair lawful gaming in specific instances.

(iii) Lotteries. Section 21(1) of the Gaming and Lotteries Act 1956 provides "[n]o person shall promote or assist in promoting a lottery." Private lotteries, lotteries at dances and concerts, carnivals and other events, as well as lotteries under permitor licence are lawful. Lotteries on football games are outside the terms of the 1956 Act; see Betting Act 1931, s.32. The Irish Hospitals Sweepstakes is a lawful agreement under The Public Hospitals Act 1933 and is enforceable in the Republic's courts; see *Stanhope* v. *Hospitals Trust Ltd. (No. 2)* (1936).

Consequences of a gaming or wagering contract. Section 36 of the Gaming and Lotteries Act 1956 provides:

"(1) Every contract by way of gaming or wagering is void.
 (2) No action shall lie for the recovery of any money or thing which is alleged to be won or have been paid upon a wager or which has been deposited to abide the event on which a wager is made.
 (3) A promise express, or implied, to pay any person any money paid by him under or in respect of a contract to which this section applies or to pay any money by way of commission, fee reward or otherwise in respect of the contract or of any services connected with the contract is void and no action shall lie for the recovery of any such money."

[Subsection 4 allows the winner of a lawful game to sue for the prize provided it is not a stake].

The section is based in part upon the Gaming Act 1845, s.18, which is repealed in Ireland, by the Schedule to the 1956 Act. The following points must be made about the meaning of the 1956 Act, as gathered from litigation on section 18 of the Gaming Act 1845.

By declaring every contract by way of gaming or wagering void the Oireachtas has reaffirmed that, while the transaction is not illegal, no rights can accrue to either party. Thus in *Pujolas* v. *Heaps* (1938) a bookmaker, licensed under Betting Shops legislation, refused to pay out to a punter who had won his bet. The punter was unable to recover his winnings in an action. If the loser pays by cheque and then cancels it, no action will lie. The legislation confers a privilege upon the loser; if he choses to waive this privilege by paying the winner, the loser has no right to recover the money paid.

The opening limb of section 36(2) produces an interesting problem of construction. One view of this subsection holds that it adds nothing to section 36(1); as a result, a subsequent contract to pay the sum due on a wager may be enforceable if given for good consideration. In *O'Donnell* v. *O'Connell* (1923) the defendant owed debts to the plaintiff, a bookmaker. The plaintiff said he would list the defendant as a defaulter, which would have damaged his credit-worthiness at the track. The plaintiff compromised his admittedly hopeless action on the debt and refrained from listing the defendant in return for a promissory note. The plaintiff successfully sued on the promissory note. The trial judge, Molony C.J., following the [now overruled] English Court of Appeal decision in *Hyams* v. *Stuart King* (1908) held that the 1845 Act did not invalidate an action brought on a promise given for some act of forbearance. The better view of the legislation is that subsequent transactions are rendered unenforceable by what is now section 36(2). The House of Lords so ruled in *Hill* v. *William Hill (Park Lane) Ltd.* (1949). It is to be hoped that the flagrant evasion of the policy underlying the Act leads to a future Supreme Court overruling *O'Donnell* v. *O'Connell*. In any event, *O'Donnell* v. *O'Connell* is inconsistent with two earlier Irish cases; *O'Donnell* v. *O'Sullivan*, (discussed in Chap. 2) and *Walker* v. *Brown* (1897).

The second part of section 36(2) has also received a narrow interpretation. At first sight it should mean that where money had been deposited with a stakeholders no action will succeed. In *Graham* v. *Thompson* (1867) money was deposited with a stakeholder. The plaintiff repudiated the agreement before the money was paid but after the result of the event was known. It was not clear whether the plaintiff was the winner or loser. It was held that whenever the loser of an illegal wager repudiates at any time before the wager is paid he can recover his part of the stake in an action for money had and received. The second part of section 36(2) prevents any person, whether he be winner or loser, from recovering the other person's part of the stake; *McElwain* v. *Mercer* (1859). This interpretation of the words of section 18 of the 1845 Act has carried over into the 1956 Act as the case of *Creane* v. *Deane* (1959) shows.

Section 36(3) deals with the case of a contractual arrangement in which a principal engages an agent to place bets on his behalf. If the agent advances his own money to cover the stake and he is promised, expressly or impliedly, recompense, he cannot recover in an action against the principal. Nor is the principal liable to pay a commission, fee or reward to the agent. Section 36(3) substantially recites section 1 of the Gaming Act 1892, which prevents the ordinary rule that an agent is liable to be indemnified for all lawful acts from extending into wagering transactions.

On the other hand, the principal may have the right to recover if the agent places the bet but refuses to pay over the winnings; *Griffith* v. *Young* (1810). If the agent fails to place the bet and the wager would have been successful the principal has no remedy for breach of contract; *Cohen* v. *Kittell* (1889).

If money is paid to a stakeholder the stakeholder becomes an agent for both parties; as we have seen the stake is recoverable if the agent's authority to pay is revoked before payment is made. The agent will be liable if he then pays the stake to the other party. No action will lie for the recovery of sums actually paid to the winner, in breach of the stakeholder's authority. In *Toner* v. *Livingston* (1896) A made a bet with B regarding the weight of a bullock owned by A. A deposited £20 with a stakeholder to abide the result. The bullock was never weighed but the stakeholder paid the £20 to B. A sued B for money had and received; the action failed, being caught by the words of what is now section 36(3) of the 1956 Act.

Money lent for gaming and wagering. In *Anthony* v. *Shea* (1951) Anthony lent Shea £43 knowing Shea was to use it for gaming. Even though it was not proved that the money was so used Anthony was unable to recover from Shea's estate. The gaming transaction in question may have been lawful gaming but this point was not made; the English textbooks state that money lent for lawful gaming is recoverable.

Cheques and other securities. The party who takes a negotiable instrument which has been given for a gambling debt can sue upon it if he can show he is a "holder in due course."

(4) *The consequences of common law and statutory illegality*

The common law rules which circumscribe the remedies available to persons who have entered a contract which is illegal at common law also apply where the contract is illegal under statute. Legislators do not resolve the problems which arise here by stipulating that such-and-such an illegal contract is to give rise to the following consequences. This often leads to unfortunate results as we shall see.

Three situations must be distinguished:

(i) Where the contract is unlawful on its face.

A contract which creates an illegal consideration is unlawful on its face. When the plaintiff in *Littledale* v. *Thompson* promised to convey a

right to an advowson in return for the defendant's promise to pay
the costs of the plaintiff's litigation the contract was champertous on
its face. All parties to such an agreement are prevented from suing to
enforce any promise under that contract. If a contract is illegal on its
face the contract is said to be illegal at its inception. In *Gray* v.
Cathcart (1898) the landlord was held unable to recover arrears of
rent because the unsanitary premises could not be lawfully let. The
leading case is *Murphy & Co. Ltd.* v. *Crean* (1915). The plaintiffs
agreed to lease premises to Crean who was to carry on the business
of publican, taking all the stout needed for this purpose from the
plaintiffs. The licence necessary was transferred, with the consent of
the local justices, to the defendant. The contract however also
contained a provision which later obliged the defendant to transfer
the licence to any person in another public house nominated by the
plaintiffs. Irish licencing legislation does not permit transferability
of a liquor licence to a person not in occupation of the premises. This
rule is designed to prevent someone whom the licensing justices have
deemed a fit person from transferring the licence to someone who
may not be of good character. This illegal covenant rendered the
whole agreement unenforceable. The plaintiffs were unable to
prevent the defendant from selling stout manufactured by another
company. The leading English case of *Re Mahmoud and Hispani*
(1921) shows that in this situation the rule can operate harshly. The
plaintiff agreed to sell linseed oil to the defendant who falsely
represented that he, the defendant, had a licence to purchase the oil.
Such a licence was necessary under statute. The defendant refused
to take delivery and was sued for non-acceptance. The action failed.
The innocent party was held unable to sue on a contract unlawful at
its inception. *Re Mahmoud* was followed in the Queensland case of
Olsen v. *Mikkelsen* (1937). The plaintiff purchased seeds from the
defendant who supplied them without giving an invoice, an offence
under statute. The seeds failed to germinate. The contract was held
illegal at formation so the plaintiff could not sue for breach of
warranty; see also *Anderson* v. *Daniel* (1924).

(ii) Where the contract is lawful on its face but both parties
intend it to be performed illegally.

A contract that can be legally performed may be unenforceable if
both parties intend that it will be performed by an unlawful method.
In fact, such an agreement is illegal at the time of agreement in
much the same way as in situation (i) above.

In the recent English case of *Ashmore* v. *Dawson* (1973) the
plaintiffs owned a piece of heavy engineering equipment which had
to be transported by lorry. The defendant hauliers agreed to

transport the machinery, a perfectly valid agreement. The defendants, to cut costs, intended to use a particular lorry which did not meet the capacity requirements set out in legislation. The plaintiffs transport manager was present when the machinery was loaded onto the vehicle; he was held to know that the statutory restrictions were being broken. In the view of the majority of the Court of Appeal the knowledge and acquiescence of the transport manager meant that he "participated" in the illegal performance. Phillimore L.J. went further; he found that the contract was deliberately given to the defendants knowing that it would be performed in this manner, rendering the agreement unlawful at its inception. The decision in *Devine* v. *Scott and Johnston* (1931) provides an Irish example of this type of illegal contract.

(iii) Where the contract is lawful on its face but one person only intends to perform unlawfully.

Again, *Ashmore* v. *Dawson* (1973) is in point. Had the transport manager not been present or if it had been shown that he did not know of the restrictions on transporting goods by lorry the plaintiffs would have been able to sue on the contract.

The decision of Finlay P. in *Whitecross Potatoes* v. *Coyle* (1978) emphasises the importance of distinguishing contracts which one party only intends to perform illegally. Coyle, a farmer in Meath agreed to sell potatoes to the plaintiffs, a company in England who intended to use the potatoes in their chain of fish and chip shops. Each party suspected that the United Kingdom and Irish governments were about to impose restrictions on the export and import of potatoes. The agreement provided that if this occurred a higher price would be payable. This clause was consistent with two modes of performance; the plaintiffs explained that Coyle was going to purchase potatoes in Northern Ireland and deliver these to them, thereby getting around the problem of import restrictions. This would be perfectly lawful. The defendant however explained that he intended no such thing; he intended to smuggle the potatoes into Northern Ireland, the higher price covering transport costs. Finlay P. held that Coyle alone intended to perform the contract in an illegal manner. The plaintiffs were therefore entitled to recover for non-delivery of the potatoes.

These distinctions are not always drawn. In *Martin* v. *Galbraith* (1942) the Supreme Court had to consider whether an employee could recover for overtime worked in breach of legislation limiting hours worked in excess of 48 hours a week. The majority of the Supreme Court held such an action must fail; statute made it an offence for the employer to require this work to be done, although the employee did not commit an offence. Murnaghan J. stated: "parties to a contract which produces illegality under a statute passed for the benefit of the public cannot sue upon the contract unless the legislature has clearly given a right to sue." This analysis is too simplistic for if the contract is illegal in relation to overtime an employee could not sue to recover unpaid wages earned during the 48 hour period of lawful employment! The correct questions to ask would be, have the parties agreed at formation that unlawful overtime would be worked? If not, has the employer exacted unlawful performance from the employee who knew of the breach of statute? Are the parties equally at fault?

(5) *Judicial attitudes to illegality*

The general attitude of the courts when faced with an illegal transaction was succinctly stated by Lindley L.J. in *Scott* v. *Brown Doering* (1892), an English case followed in several Irish decisions:

> "*Ex turpi causa non oritur actio*. . . . No court ought to enforce an illegal contract or allow itself to be made the instrument of enforcing obligations alleged to arise out of a contract or transaction which is illegal if the illegality is duly brought to the notice of the court and if the person invoking the aid of the court is himself implicated in the illegality."

It is clear that damages will not be awarded for breach of an illegal contract; indeed, in *McDonnell* v. *Grand Canal Co.* (1853) an injunction preventing a company from carrying into effect an intention to enter an illegal contract was issued. It is less clear why the courts go further by preventing restitutionary relief in cases where property has been transferred as part of the illegal transaction; Lindley L.J. said in *Scott* v. *Brown Doering* that any legal rights a party has apart from the illegal contract may be recognised. The case of *Brady* v. *Flood* (1841) suggests that ownership alone may not be enough to permit restitution. Brady sued Flood for the recovery of banknotes which Flood had been given in return for a promise to get criminal charges against Brady's sons dropped. This agreement was illegal as interfering with the administration of justice. Brady C.B. said "I will not try this case. You are parties to an illegal contract and whoever has got the money I will allow him to keep it." See also *Taylor* v. *Chester* (1869).

The judges shelter behind another latin maxim: *In pari delicto potior est conditio possidentis*, which means that where both parties are equally in fault the condition of the possessor is best. Nevertheless, there are signs that if the contract is illegal and the illegality is neither socially or morally reprehensible—as in a case where the contract is illegal because one party fails to get a licence or complete a document—restitution and/or damages may be ordered. See the controversial case of *Bowmaker* v. *Barnet's Instruments* (1945) when the English Court of Appeal allowed an action in conversion when the hirer of goods under an illegal contract refused to give them up.

The *in pari delicto* rule has unfortunate consequences. First of all, the party responsible for the illegality may use it to his advantage in circumstances which are quite unfair. In *Daly* v. *Daly* (1870) the defendant, a discharged insolvent debtor had obtained his discharge through fraud. The plaintiff, one of his creditors, learned of the fraud and upon confronting the defendant obtained a promise that the defendant would pay the initial debt in full, even though the discharge extended to this sum. The plaintiff dropped proceedings to set the discharge aside for fraud. The action on the new promise failed.

The application of the rules on illegality may conflict with other policy considerations, particularly when a statute is the source of the initial prohibition. In *Martin* v. *Galbraith* (1942) (the facts are given on p.144) the statute prohibiting excessive overtime was designed to ensure, *inter alia*, the payment of wages at fair rates to employees. As O'Byrne J., dissenting, pointed out, the interpretation placed on the legislation defeated the intention of the Oireachtas. A similar United States decision has been criticised by Furmston; see *Coules* v. *Pharris* (1933), discussed in Vol. 16, U.T.L.J. at 288. The courts should be given the discretion to depart from the *ex turpi causa* rule where it produces such unfortunate consequences.

Exceptions to ex turpi causa and in pari delicto

(a) *not in pari delicto*. The first "exception" is not really an exception at all. In the Northern Ireland case of *Sumner* v. *Sumner* (1935) Megaw J. accepted that if one party to the illegal contract entered into the bargain because of fraud, duress or undue influence on the part of the other he may have a remedy. The courts will generally permit recovery of money paid. So too, participation in the illegal contract will not be a bar to relief if the participator can show that he was a member of the class which the statute was designed to protect; see the old English case of *Browning* v. *Morris* (1778). In *Martin* v. *Galbraith* (1942) Meredith J., dissenting, was in favour in holding the employee entitled to recover because the employee was not *in pari delicto*; he did not commit an offence. It can also be argued that an employee who refused to work in an illegal manner may fear dismissal so he is not *in pari delicto*: c.f. *Mathew* v. *Bobbins* (1980). In a recent case the English Court of Appeal permitted a person innocently breaking exchange control regulations to recover in an action for deceit if a successful plea of illegality would permit the rogue to retain the benefits of his fraudulent conduct: *Shelley* v. *Paddock* (1980).

(b) *Repentance.* If the transaction is illegal at formation but has yet to be performed repudiation of the illegal transaction may permit the repudiating party to recover property transferred. A person who parts with property in an attempt to defraud creditors may recover those assets if he repents before any creditors are affected. There are no Irish cases on this point.

(c) *Independent cause of action.* Recent case law suggests that property in goods passes when parties to a contract for the sale of goods (the contract being illegal) transfer physical possession to the purchaser; *Singh* v. *Ali* (1960), a decision of the Privy Council. Indeed, property may pass under an illegal contract even if a third party holds the goods according to *Belvoir Finance Co.* v. *Stapleton* (1971), an English Court of Appeal decision. An action in detinue, a tort independent of contract, will be possible if the transferor later interferes with goods. The Privy Council have decided that the registered owner of land who lets property under an illegal landlord and tenant agreement can rely upon his title to recover possession. The tenant would not be able to plead the illegal contract as a defence to an action in trespass based on the plaintiff's ownership; *Amar Singh* v. *Kulyubya* (1964). Contrast *Brady* v. *Flood* (1841) if banknotes are transferred.

(6) *Separate transactions*

In order to permit a limited remedy the courts may view a transaction as divisible into seperate contracts, thereby isolating or limiting the effects of the illegality. In *McIlvenna* v. *Ferris and Green* (1955) the defendants ordered construction of a building. Under Emergency Powers Legislation such work could only be lawfully carried out under licence. No licence was obtained. The plaintiff's action for work performed under the written contract failed; the court permitted the plaintiff to recover for additional work ordered just after the regulation had been rescinded on the basis that this was the subject of a separate contract. Another Irish decision in point is *Sheehy* v. *Sheehy* (1901).

It is common in building contracts for the parties to expressly covenant that all necessary planning permission has been obtained by the owner of the site. In *Strongman (1945) Ltd.* v. *Sincock* (1955) a similar agreement was held to give rise to a remedy in damages when it transpired that the necessary permission had not been obtained. The action here was brought upon a collateral contract, separate and distinct from the illegal construction contract; contrast *Spector* v. *Ageda* (1973).

Contracts of Guarantee. If the main contract between A and B is illegal in circumstances which make it impossible for A to sue B, can a contract of guarantee be enforceable by A the creditor against C, the guarantor? The question was answered in the negative in *Devine* v. *Scott and Johnston* (1931), Devine, landlord under an illegal letting to Johnston was held unable to recover rent from either Johnston or Scott, the guarantor of Johnston's indebtedness.

(7) *Severance*

In *Devine* v. *Scott and Johnston* only a part of the demised premises were used for the illegal purpose. The plaintiff suggested that the court could permit recovery of a portion of the rent, calculated by reference to the proportion of the property used in a lawful manner. The court rejected the view that such a power exists at common law.

Furthermore, if a covenant contained in the contract is illegal this is said to taint the entire contract. The case of *Murphy & Co. Ltd.* v. *Crean* (1915), discussed above, illustrates this. The plaintiffs were not attempting to enforce the illegal covenant requiring Crean to transfer the licence but this illegal clause precluded enforcement of other covenants which, taken alone, were unobjectionable. The weight of authority, both in England and Ireland is against extending the doctrine of severance beyond cases which are in restraint of trade.

There is support for the other view however. In *Carolan* v. *Brabazon* (1846) the plaintiff sought specific performance of a lease which contained a covenant requiring the tenant to pay poor rates. This covenant was illegal by Act of Parliament. Sugden L.C. said *obiter* that it may have been possible to grant specific performance of the lease minus the term as to payment of the poor rate. In *Furnivall* v. *O'Neill* (1902) O'Neill, an arranging debtor entered into a secret arrangement in 1879 with Furnivall, a creditor, under which Furnivall was promised payment in full. This agreement was illegal. In 1880 this promise was repeated and a contract executed reciting the obligation. This contract also recorded other debts due to O'Neill which were legitimate. O'Neill sought to recover on the 1880 instrument. Andrews J. held that the promise to pay the illegal sums formed the main and operative consideration for the 1880 deed, and was thus fatal to the action. Had the illegal promise been incidental or peripheral then, like *Carolan* v. *Brabazon*, severance may have been possible.

One English case decides that severance may be possible in cases of statutory illegality; *Ailion* v. *Spiekermann* (1976). Templeman J. in that case refused to follow the practice of other judges of "washing" his hands of the illegal contract because he observed such a solution was particularly unsatisfactory where one party is an unwilling victim.

This case is to be welcomed; if severance is a legitimate device to do some measure of justice in restraint of trade cases this is no reason why it should not be available in other contracts where public policy is infringed. Indeed, *Ailion* v. *Spiekermann* and the Court of Appeal's decision in *Shelley* v. *Paddock* (1980) are indicative of a new and refreshing trend towards illegality cases; the English courts now seem reluctant to readily brand each party equally at fault, thereby making a restitutionary remedy available to the less culpable party.

(8) *Pleading illegality*

If the illegality appears on the face of the contract document it is not necessary that illegality be pleaded as a defence. The courts will not enforce the agreement; *James L. Murphy* v. *Crean* (1915). If the agreement is not illegal on its face the party seeking to resist the action should plead illegality if he wishes to avoid liability on this basis; *Whitecross Potatoes* v. *Coyle* (1978). A person may be reluctant to do this, for obvious reasons; a confession of illegality often invites a prosecution later. If, however illegality is not pleaded but during the course of the trial it becomes clear to the trial judge that an illegal contract is disclosed he is not obliged to disregard the illegality. In *Starling Securities* v. *Woods* (1977) McWilliam J. refused to enforce a contract formed with an illegal object in mind, even though illegality was not expressly pleaded as a defence.

Part Two

(9) *Contracts void at common law*

(i) Agreements to oust the jurisdiction of the Courts. Persons who seek to become members of a professional or trade association may find that part of the agreement dictates that in the event of a dispute the decision of the association shall be final. Such a provision is invalid; attempts to uphold agreements and at the same time deny recourse to the ordinary courts are invalid; the public interest requires disputes be amenable to the jurisdiction of the courts; *Lee* v. *Showman's Guild of Great Britain* (1952). The unpalatable clause will be held void.

While in the leading decision in *Scott* v. *Avery* (1856) the House of Lords held it lawful to require a dispute to be referred to arbitration before it can be brought before the courts, the Irish courts have been reluctant to extend this decision. In *Mansfield* v. *Doolin* (1868) a clause which provided that if a dispute broke out over a building contract the award of an architect was to be a condition precedent to any proceedings. The arbitrator's award was held not to constitute a condition precedent. Under the Republic's Arbitration Act 1954, s.35(1) the High Court is given a supervisory jurisdiction; in particular, the arbitrator "may, and shall if so directed by the court," state questions of law or the terms of an award for decision by the Court as a special case. This section re-affirms the inability of parties to absolutely prohibit recourse to the courts.

(ii) Contracts which subvert the sanctity of marriage.

(a) It is said to be a matter of public interest that persons enter into contracts of marriage and affiliated transactions for reasons which are likely to produce satisfactory marriages. Marriage brokerage contracts, in which a fee is paid to a marriage bureau in return for an undertaking to find a wife or husband are void; see the English case of *Hermann* v. *Charlesworth* (1905). In the old Irish case of *Williamson* v. *Gihan* (1805) Williamson, an impecunious young man obtained the help of his friend Gihan in spiriting away a young heiress to Scotland where Williamson married the young lady. He promised Gihan £500, payable from his wife's property for services rendered. Williamson was held not entitled to fetter his wife's estate in these circumstances. It seems that the court frowned upon contracts of marriage that resulted from elopement—despite the fact that the then Lord Chancellor Eldon had procured his wife in this manner—fearing that even collateral transactions between the groom and others would lead to fortune-hunting.

These "void contracts" seem amenable to the criticism's voiced above on p.135 about "immoral contracts."

(b) Unilateral contracts in which one person promised not to marry any person other than the promisee are void; *Lowe* v. *Peers* (1768).

(c) Contracts for Future Separation.

Because of the Constitutional prohibition in Article 41 3 2° against divorce in the Republic of Ireland the petition for a decree *a mensa et thoro*, or judicial separation, is an important but expensive way in which the parties to a broken marriage may get the courts to make financial and property adjustments when a marriage has broken down. The parties may instead wish to make their own arrangements.

Nevertheless a contract which provides that one party is to pay a certain sum to support the other in the event of future separation this agreement will be void as weakening the marriage bond; *Marquess of Westmeath* v. *Marquess of Salisbury* (1830).

If however the parties are not living together but they decide to resume cohabitation, agreeing that if the reconciliation thereby effected should later break down then the wife will be paid a certain sum, this will be enforceable. In *McMahon* v. *McMahon* (1913), Holmes L.J. argued that such an agreement, "far from endangering the unity of the family, it restored it." But for this clause the initial separation would have continued. These agreements preclude further action for financial support, even if the defendant who relies upon the agreement is guilty of adultery; see *Ross* v. *Ross* (1908) in which Andrews J. distinguished actions for a decree *a mensa et thoro* from cases where adultery precludes reliance on a provision restraining divorce actions.

Separation agreements which unwittingly tend to encourage immoral practices are not *per se* void; see *Lewis* v. *Lewis* (1940); contrast the old Irish case of *Jackson* v. *Cridland* (1859).

(10) *Contracts in restraint of trade*

This venerable common law doctrine has been succinctly stated by Diplock L.J. in the English Court of Appeal in the following terms;

> "A contract in restraint of trade is one in which a party (the covenantor) agrees with any other party (the covenantee) to restrict his liberty in the future to carry on trade with other persons not parties to the contract in such manner as he chooses."

This definition, given in the case of *Esso Petroleum Co. Ltd.* v. *Harpers Garage (Stourport) Ltd.* (1966) is a workable but not entirely accurate guide as we shall see. The modern doctrine of restraint of trade is designed to strike at commercial and professional practices which unduly restrict the covenator's freedom to carry on a business or profession; not all restrictive covenants operate in such a way as to incur the wrath of the judges.

Historical antecedents. Restrictive commercial practices were not unknown in late medieval times. Commercial arrangements between traders designed to artificially inflate prices—known as badgering, forestalling, regrating and engrossing—were made criminal offences under statute. The Elizabethan desire to control food prices made the prohibition of such transactions necessary. When commercial attitudes charged these offences were repealed in 1844 under 7 & 8 Vict. c. 24, which extended into Ireland. The establishment of Guilds, Craft Associations and Corporations also led to restrictive practices designed to regulate and protect members of those associations. An Act of 1846, 9 & 10 Vict. c. 76 also attempted to bring these older medieval practices into step with the needs of *laissez faire* capitalism by abolishing the privileges held by trading organisations in Ireland, the Act provided that it was lawful for any person to carry on any lawful trade or profession and take apprentices. Fines and penalties could not be extracted by the Guilds.

These isolated pieces of legislation serve the same policy objectives as the common law restraint of trade doctrine. The courts however had to struggle with the problem, often unaided by statute. In the landmark case of *Mitchel* v. *Reynolds* (1711) it was laid down that a general restraint was bad; partial restraints were valid. Thus a covenant not to carry on trade throughout England was invalid; a provision limiting the prohibition to a town or district was valid if good and adequate consideration was provided.

This general/partial distinction began to wear a little thin when commercial and industrial innovations meant that the consequences of carrying on trade in a remote part of England, or indeed the world, could have severe implications for persons some distance away. The *Mitchel* v. *Reynolds* doctrine was revised in a series of decisions handed down between 1893 and 1916, the most important of which is *Nordenfelt* v. *Maxim Nordenfelt* (1893). In that case a world-wide restraint was held valid.

The Modern doctrine. In the leading case of *Esso Petroleum Co. Ltd.* v. *Harpers Garage (Stourport) Ltd.* (1968)—hereafter *Esso*—the House of Lords gave an comprehensive analysis of the existing rules of restraint of trade. Lord Reid in his speech stressed that the following questions are to be asked:

(1) does the restraint go further than to afford adequate protection to the party in whose favour it was granted; if so the convenant is prima facie void;

(2) can it be justified as being in the interests of the party restrained;

(3) is the covenant contrary to the public interest.

The onus of showing the restraint to be in the interests of the party restrained, or to put it another way, that the covenant is reasonable as between the parties, is upon the person seeking to uphold the transaction. If the agreement is alleged to be unenforceable because it is contrary to the public interest, notwithstanding its reasonableness *inter partes*, the burden of proof is upon the party alleging the invalidity of the covenant.

It should be stressed that while public policy is at the heart of this doctrine two separate policy considerations are at issue here; first of all, the courts view it as being a cardinal rule of public policy that a person be held to a contract freely entered into; *Murphy* v. *O'Donovan* (1939). On the other hand, a man is not to be permitted to unduly fetter his freedom to contract and earn a living for himself and his family; *Langan* v. *Cork Operative Bakers T.U.* (1938). The desire of the courts to uphold both of these often conflicting objectives means, as Lord Morris said in *Esso* that "a certain adjustment is necessary."

Restraints outside the doctrine of restraint of trade. Not all contracts that restrain or prevent a contracting party from entering into agreements must be tested by reference to the restraint of trade doctrine.

Exclusive dealing arrangements between commercial men are valid if they are commonplace and incidental to everyday trading activities; a contract by a restaurant owner to take all the beaujolais he may require from one retailer does not fall within the doctrine. The practice, common in the Cork area, of trading in a public house as a tenant, agreeing to take all the stout and beer from the landlord company is no doubt restrictive of the freedom of the tenant to obtain supplies from other companies but it is not an arrangement that must be justified as reasonable as between the parties and the public interest; see *Murphy & Co.* v. *Crean* (1915) discussed earlier in this Chapter and *Murphy* v. *O'Donovan* (1939).

Restrictive covenants in which the purchaser of an interest in land agrees that he will not use the land for a particular commercial or industrial purpose are also *per se* enforceable; see Wylie, *Irish Land Law*, Chap. 19. Although it is difficult to distinguish these cases from other transactions which fall under the restraint of trade doctrine Lord Wilberforce in *Esso* explained these exceptions as due to the fact that they have "passed into the accepted and normal currency of commercial or contractual or conveyancing relations."

Covenants in employment contracts that restrict or deter an employee from working for a rival concern when he leaves employment are within the doctrine; covenants that restrict an employee while in employment are not. In *McArdle* v. *Wilson* (1876) the contracts of workmen employed in a factory in Tyrone obliged them to give two weeks notice if they wished to terminate employment. The contract provided that if more than five employees gave notice then the notice of other employees would not be accepted. The provision was clearly designed to reduce the effectiveness of strike action; failure to observe the covenant was to result in the docking of one week's wages. An action to recover wages retained failed; the Court of Exchequer found the covenant valid; Palles C.B. went further and held the doctrine of restraint of trade inapplicable. So too, a provision obliging an employee to repay training expenses incurred should he terminate his contract of employment has been held outside the doctrine of restraint of trade because no restriction operated once the employee had left work; *Schiesser International (Ireland) Ltd.* v. *Gallagher* (1971).

The recent House of Lords decision in *Schroeder Music Publishing Co. Ltd.* v. *Macauley* (1974) did not involve a contract of employment, but one for exclusive services, the agreement unduly restricting the freedom of one party during the currency of the agreement. This may, by analogy, lead to a decision in which restrictions operating during a contract of employment may be held within the restraint of trade doctrine; see Heydon, 85 L.Q.R. 229, at 235.

Contracts traditionally within the doctrine

(a) Employment contracts. The freedom of an employee to carry on an activity which adversely affects a former employer may be circumscribed by agreement. In fact the common law furnishes some degree of protection to an employer, and in several Irish cases the conduct of the employee breached a common law rather than a contractual duty. The common law, through the implied obligation to serve an employer faithfully, makes it a breach of contract for an employee to prepare a list of customers intending to use this list after the contract of employment has ended. An employee who solicits orders from his employer's customers intending to meet the orders personally rather than *qua* employee, also breaches this implied term. The facts of *Arclex Optical Corporation* v. *McMurray* (1958) and *Stanford Supply Co. Ltd.* v. *O'Toole* (1972), (in which employees solicited orders to be met by their own concerns while still employed by the plaintiff companies), are in point.

In these cases the employer can seek an interlocutory injunction restraining the employee until the merits of the action can be heard. The injunction is the primary remedy here although an account for profits made or payment of damages can also be ordered.

An employer may wish to extract an express covenant from his employees. The advantages for the employer include greater predictability—the employee knows that he cannot solicit—and certainty of remedy. More importantly, the employee may not be able to carry on his trade or profession for a period after leaving employment. It is essential that the employer shows he has a legitimate commercial interest capable of protection; he must also show that the covenant goes no further than is necessary in order to protect that interest.

If the employee has acquired trade or professional secrets which would prejudice the employer's business if upon termination of employment these secrets could be used by the employee, either for his own or another's benefit the employer can prevent the employee from entering future employment in that field or industry. The secret need not be expensive or complex. In *Forster & Sons* v. *Suggett* (1918) the works engineer for the plaintiff company who manufactured glass bottles knew the correct proportion of gas and air to be introduced into the furnaces during the manufacturing process. He was successfully prevented from working in the glass making industry for a period of five years after leaving employment; the restraint covered the whole of the United Kingdom. An industrial chemist who, in the process of training and employment, acquires trade secrets may legitimately be required to abstain from using those secrets for his own or another company's profit; *E.C.I. European Chemical Industries Ltd.* v. *Bell* (1981). An employer cannot prevent an employee from using the skill he ordinarily employs in his trade, even if the employer has contributed towards developing this talent; so in *Arthur Murray Dance Studios of Cleveland Inc.* v. *Witter* (1952) the plaintiffs could not prevent the defendant from working for a rival studio simply because they taught the defendant to become a proficient dance instructor. No "secret" information or skill was conferred upon the defendant.

The most common interest an employer can advance as worthy of protection has been described as his "customer connection." Businessmen, partnerships and corporations view customers and clients as part of their assets and, as such, the former employee who solicits orders may imperil the stability of the venture. If the employee has a close working relationship with members of the public the chances of the customers "following" the employee are substantial. It is legitimate to try and prevent this. Instances where the "customer connection" may be shown to exist include travelling salesmen *(Arclex Optical Corporation* v. *McMurray* (1958)); warehouse manager *(Waterworthy Eaton* (1905)); laundry manageress *(Franklin Steam Laundry Co.* v. *Anderson* (1903)); solicitor *(Mulligan* v. *Corr* (1925)); hairdresser *(Oates* v. *Romano* (1949)); milk roundsman *(Home Counties Dairies* v. *Skilton* (1970)).

If the employee does not have close contact with the public a restraint will not be allowed to operate. The position of a laundry manageress who has close contact with the public can be contrasted with a menial employee who works in the laundry pressing clothes. Even if there is some degree of contact with the public it does not follow that the employee will have sufficient "pull" to entice away former customers; a law firm would not find its business falling away if a receptionist left to work with a rival firm. In *Dosser* v. *Monaghan* (1932) the defendants were musicians who had formerly played in a band owned by the plaintiff. They had agreed not to enter into similar employment within 50 miles of Gt. Yarmouth, Redcar, Southport, New Brighton and Belfast, towns in which the band played regularly. Best L.J. refused to grant an interlocutory injunction preventing the defendants from breaching the covenant; given the fact that the defendants were obscure members of the band the covenant was not reasonable; "it would be different if the musicians were famous."

(*b*) Covenants on the sale of a business. Again, certain obligations are implied upon the sale of a business. The rule which dictates that a man must not derogate from his grant prevents the vendor of a business from directly soliciting his former customers; *Trego* v. *Hunt* (1896), *per* Lord MacNaughton. If the vendor wishes to open up a shop next door to his former business, trading in exactly the same product, he can do so. As a result, the prudent purchaser of a business will include a term in the contract limiting the freedom of the vendor to compete. Again, a covenant must be shown to be reasonable as between the interests of the parties and in the public interest. In *Nordenfelt*, the House of Lords upheld a worldwide convenant preventing the vendor of a munitions firm from trading for a period of 25 years. On the other hand, if the covenant is designed to go further and prevent the vendor from competing with the purchaser it may be rejected. In *British Concrete* v. *Scheiff* (1921) the plaintiffs, manufacturers of road reinforcements used throughout the United Kingdom, purchased a business which made steel road reinforcements. The owner of the business sold covenanted not to act as servant of any person concerned in the business of manufacture or sale of road reinforcements in any part of the United Kingdom. The convenant was held too wide; the defendant dealt only in a particular kind of reinforcement; he manufactured the product and was not responsible for retail activities. Younger L.J. observed that it is only the business *sold* which is the legitimate subject of protection. In Ireland *Trego* v. *Hunt* was extended in *Gargan* v. *Ruttle* (1931) to prevent a former partner soliciting customers of the old "Firm."

Exclusive dealing arrangements. Members of an industry may decide to amalgamate in order to support and protect their common interests. In the agricultural community it is common for producers to form co-operative ventures, the rules of which may have to satisfy the restraint of trade doctrine. The leading case is *McEllistrem* v.

Ballymacelligott Cooperative Agricultural and Dairy Society (1919), a decision of the House of Lords on Appeal from the Court of Appeal in Ireland. The appellant was a member of a co-op in Kerry, the co-op being formed to develop and improve dairy farming in the district. Members of the society were bound by its rules which provided that while the society was bound to take and market all the milk produced by its members the members were precluded from selling milk to any other local creamery. Members could not resign from the creamery unless the committee consented. The Court of Appeal in Ireland felt bound by two earlier decisions and upheld the rules; these cases, *Athlacca Co-operative Creamery* v. *Lynch* (1915) and *Coolmoyne & Fethard Co-operative Creamery* v. *Bulfin* (1917) were overrruled. The House of Lords reasoned that while the respondents were entitled to protect their venture by ensuring stability, both of supply and in the lists of their customers the restraint went further than was necessary to ensure this; it was no answer to say that the restraint operated locally and that the appellant could carry on farming in another part of Ireland; "in a sparsely inhabited agricultural neighbourhood, with scanty means of communication, a prohibition of trade in every township within a radius of ten miles, might have precisely the same effect upon the business of a small trader, as if the preclusion extended to the remotest corners of Donegal;" *per* Birkenhead L.C.

The most frequently litigated exclusive dealing arrangement in recent years involves contracts between petroleum wholesalers and retailers, the arrangement obliging retailers to take all the petrol and motor oils they may require from one particular wholesaler. These contracts, known as "solus" agreements are common, both in the Republic and Northern Ireland. There are important formal differences between the law on each side of the border.

A solus agreement typically involves a promise given by a wholesaler who undertakes to keep retailers supplied with petrol if the retailer in turn agrees to take all the petrol he will require from that wholesaler alone. The retailer may also promise to keep his filling station open at all reasonable hours and to take a minimum gallonage. The retailer may in return be given a rebate on petrol supplied, as well as interest-free loans and help in purchasing petrol pumps. There are substantial advantages to the wholesaler under such agreements. Distribution costs are kept down and the wholesaler can better predict customer demand in the future. The retailer, apart from the financial advantages, is also guaranteed some degree of security of supply.

In the Republic the "solus" agreement was investigated by the Fair Trade Commission, predecessor of the current Restrictive

Practices Commission, who reported in 1961, that while the "solus" system was generally of benefit to the public, the profitability of the retail trade led to an undesirable proliferation of outlets that could not then be controlled under existing planning legislation. A Statutory Instrument, No. 294 of 1961 was passed in order to discourage the expansion of the "solus" system. The maximum period an agreement could run was for five years; nor could retailers obtain price advantages under a solus agreement for the instrument made it unlawful for wholesalers to directly or indirectly, discriminate as between retailers although rebates are paid to retailers who sign solus agreements; (Pr 1.9044 para. 5.2.)

The 1961 Statutory Instrument produced a change in policy on the part of petrol distributors in the Republic. Wholesalers decided not to invest in retailers who could obtain substantial advantages and ride free of the tie after a relatively short time. This led to wholesale distributors purchasing their own retail outlets. Statutory Instrument 294 of 1961 was modified so that in 1972 a solus agreement could run for a maximum period of ten years. A ban on the acquisition of retail outlets by wholesalers, known as company owned outlets, was also imposed. The Commission in its most recent report (Prl.9044) recommended no change be made in the maximum period of 10 years and that restrictions on the acquisition of outlets by Companies remain with some modifications. While the author cannot give here a detailed outline of the effects of the legislation it should be noted that in S.I. 1981 No. 70 the Minister has continued the 10 year maximum period for the duration of "solus" agreements but has altered the terms and conditions a "solus" agreement may contain. While the wholesaler is not entitled to discriminate between "solus" and "non-solus" retailers, wholesalers may provide training facilities for solus retailer staff, advance loans to rebuild repair or extend stations and any similar service or facility, without being obliged to provide these facilities to "non-solus" retailers. S.I. 70 of 1981 also entitles the wholesaler to charge a lower price to solus "retailers" as long as the differential is "reasonable and justifiable" in the circumstances.

Limitations on the acquisition of company owned retail outlets remain in force, with minor amendments although they only apply to companies that own more than 20 outlets—this is designed to encourage increased competition at wholesale level by making it possible for new organisations to enter the market.

These statutory provisions do not mean that the common law rules, as enunciated in *Esso* by the House of Lords, are superfluous in the Republic. The Statutory Instrument does not mean that all solus ties that operate for less than 10 years are valid; it simply makes invalid ties that operate for more than 10 years. If other factors make a tie oppressive it may still be held an unreasonable restraint of trade notwithstanding that it is to last for under 10 years.

Factors that are important here are the duration of the tie, mutuality of obligation and the position of the wholesaler in the industry. There are signs that a court may permit a new wholesaler, attempting to establish himself in the market, to extract slightly better terms for himself. The desire to stimulate new competition explains this factor. While it is possible for the courts to look forward and anticipate future events like inflation and OPEC price increases—see *Amoco Australia Pty.* v. *Rocca Bros.* (1975),—a solus agreement that is fair and reasonable at the time of agreement cannot be unenforceable if subsequent events produce this result; *Shell U.K.* v. *Lostock Garage* (1972).

The leading Irish case is the decision of Kenny J. in *Continental Oil Company of Ireland Ltd.* v. *Moynihan* (1973). Moynihan, a retailer entered into a solus agreement in 1970 agreeing to take petrol at the plaintiff's scheduled prices. The agreement was to run for five years; Moynihan was obliged to buy all his petrol from the plaintiffs and to give 48 hours notice of his requirements. He was to take the largest possible consignments, not less than 800 gallons. The station was to be kept neat and clean and the number of pumps were not to be reduced. Moynihan benefited from the agreement by purchasing pumps on interest — free hire-purchase terms. Moynihan refused to take any further supplies from the plaintiffs when they operated a differential pricing scheme that threatened Moynihan's already slender profit margins. Kenny J. upheld the plaintiffs' claim for an injunction. Viewed at the date of agreement Kenny J. held the agreement reasonable as between the parties and refused to find that enforcement of this agreement was against the public interest.

While this may be correct, a recent decision of the Court of Appeal in England puts a new light on *Moynihan's* case; if the differential pricing scheme operates harshly it is possible to deny an injunction on the grounds that the wholesaler has not acted fairly and should thus be denied an equitable remedy; See *Shell U.K.* v. *Lostock Garage* (1977).

The duration the tie has to run is perhaps the most important factor in determining reasonableness; in *Esso* the House of Lords held a 21 year tie unreasonable but a four year five month tie valid; the Ontario Court of Appeal however upheld a 10 year tie, with an option to renew for a further 10 years, on the particular circumstances of the case before it; *Stephens* v. *Gulf Oil Canada Ltd.* (1975). The common law rules govern solus agreements in Northern Ireland.

Resale price maintenance and restrictive commercial practices. Agreements between producers or retailers which keep the price of goods or services at a certain level are not invalid at common law unless the person challenging the agreement is able to show the price level maintained is unreasonable or is designed to produce a monopoly. In *Cade* v. *Daly* (1910) an agreement between members of "The South of Ireland Mineral Water Manufacturers and Bottlers Trade Protection Association" that no member would sell beer and minerals below a scheduled price was upheld; the agreement operated within one district of Cork and was to run for a short period. This position reflects a reluctance to protect consumers against artificial pricing arrangements. In the Republic prices of many essential goods are controlled by legislation; see the Prices Act 1958 and Statutory Instruments limiting the price payable for milk, flour, bread and other products.

The Restrictive Trade Practices Acts 1953-1959 make it the task of the Commission established by the Acts to establish fair trading rules in relation to the supply and distribution of goods. Restrictive practices in relation to the distribution of motor spirit and sale of alcohol on licensed premises have been the subject of inquiry; the Minister of Industry and Commerce may, under section 9 of the 1953 Act, prohibit and regulate any restrictive practices.

In Northern Ireland section 45(2) of the Restrictive Trade Practices Act 1976 (United Kingdom) extends the provisions of the Act of Northern Ireland. Restrictive commercial practices may also infringe Article 85 of The Treaty of Rome which make void agreements which reduce the element of competition within the EEC. Detailed consideration of Restrictive Trade Practices legislation is outside the scope of this book.

Trade union rules affecting union members. It is established that because the relationship between a trade union and its members is based on contract, the rules of a union which control or restrict the freedom of union members to earn a living are subject to the restraint of trade doctrine; see *Doyle* v. *Trustees of the Irish Glaziers and Decorative Glass Workers Trade Union* (1926). In the leading case of *Langan* v. *Cork Operative Bakers Trade Union* (1938) a trade union gave financial assistance to members who wished to emigrate and find work abroad. The rules provided that a member who returned to the district was bound not to work as a baker in that locality. The plaintiff was held able to repudiate the agreement upon making restitution of the sums advanced, the agreement being an unreasonable restraint of trade.

Recent expansion of the restraint of trade doctrine. While employment and sale of a business contracts are the classical instances in which the restraint of trade doctrine will operate the categories of restraint of trade are never closed; recent English case law has held the rules of the Football Association, Pharmaceutical Society of Great Britain and the Test and County Cricket Board to be subject to review under the doctrine. These cases involve persons who complain about rules to which they did not consent.

In *Eddie Macken* v. *O'Reilly* (1978) the plaintiff, a world famous show jumper, complained that the rules of the Equestrian Federation of Ireland, which obliged Irish competitors to ride only Irish bred horses, constituted an unreasonable restraint of trade. The rules were protective measures designed to promote the Irish horse breeding industry. Hamilton J. held that the rules, because they denied Macken the opportunity to compete on the best available horses, Irish or otherwise, constituted an unreasonable restraint of trade. In the Supreme Court O'Higgins C.J. and Kenny J., the only judges who found it necessary to discuss the restraint of trade doctrine, ruled that even if the rules did prejudice the plaintiff, they were still to be enforced because the wider public interest required that Macken's individual interests be overriden. O'Higgins C.J. said "the trial judge disregarded entirely the undisputed evidence as to the effect a change of policy would have on the horse breeding industry and on equestrian sport in Ireland. This ought to have been considered as a balance to the harm or inconvenience caused to the plaintiff." With respect, the rules on restraint of trade as they stand do not require such a "balancing process"; if the rule is unreasonable *inter partes* it is unnecessary to consider the public interest; indeed most cases are decided entirely on reasonableness *inter partes*. The view that individual interests which are unreasonably prejudiced must be sacrificed if they conflict with wider public interests is a novel doctrine; contrast *Greig* v. *Insole* (1977).

Construction of covenants in restraint of trade. It is often said that employment restraints, because they are "negotiated" between persons who are in unequal bargaining positions, are viewed restrictively; it is clear that an employer and employee restraint is treated with greater suspicion than a restraint imposed on the sale of a business. The restrictive interpretation of employment covenants is perhaps a sound policy. Employers sometimes rely on provisions which exceed protection of their legitimate interests and the courts should not help an employer who has not drafted the covenant with precision. Two Irish cases support this view; the first is *Oates* v. *Romano* (1950) discussed in Chapter 5. The second, *Coleborne* v.

Kearns (1911) concerned an employee who worked in a shop which involved him in close contact with the community. The employer extracted a covenant that prevented him from working in a similar shop within 15 miles of the employer's shop for seven years should he "leave" employment. The court refused to interpret "leave" as also covering dismissal by the employer.

If however the employer can show he has a legitimate interest to be protected the courts often permit the employer to enforce the covenant, even if it, literally construed, would cover less meritorious cases. The employee will often place an extended, quite fantastic and literal interpretation on a covenant hoping that this will lead the court to strike the covenant as invalid. In *Home Counties Dairies* v. *Skilton* (1970) an employer was able to enforce a covenant against a milk roundsman who worked as a roundsman for a rival concern, even though literally construed the covenant against working as a dairy produce salesman would prevent him from selling cheese in a grocer's shop. The Court of Appeal ruled that the covenant must be construed by reference to the commercial background in which the contracting parties operated. A useful exercise is to compare *Oates* v. *Romano* (1950) with *Marion White* v. *Francis* (1972). Not all employees contract at a disadvantage *vis à vis* their employer; it has been said that "a managing director can look after himself." This may help explain the trend in the English cases towards holding quite sweeping restraints valid; see *Littlewoods* v. *Harris* (1978).

Even if the courts place a very liberal interpretation on covenants in restraint of trade the court may well decide to limit the scope of a restraint by a strict application of the doctrine of severance; see Heydon, *The Restraint of Trade Doctrine* (1971) at pp.122–136.

If the restraint is too wide in relation to the *geographical area* to be covered the court may limit the scope of the covenant by cutting down the area, insofar as this can be done by eliminating towns, districts or even counties through a "blue pencil" test. In *Mulligan* v. *Corr* (1925) the defendant, a solicitor's apprentice agreed that when he left the plaintiff's employment he would not practice (a) within 30 miles of Ballina and Charlestown and (b) within 20 miles of Ballaghadreen. The Supreme Court considered reducing the geographical area by severing (b), leaving covenant (a) enforceable. It was held that even if severance were performed the area covered by covenant (a) was still excessive.

In *Skerry, Wynne & Skerry's College Ireland Ltd.* v. *Moles* (1907) a teacher who agreed not to teach within seven miles of Belfast, Dublin and Cork when he left employment with the plaintiffs as a shorthand typing instructor was held bound. The court severed the geographical restraint by deleting Dublin and Cork. It was also argued that the covenant was too wide in terms of *duration*. The "evil" the plaintiffs were entitled to protect themselves against was the possibility that when the teacher left he would take his students with him. The defendant argued that the restraint, which was to apply for three years was insupportable because the courses offered by the plaintiffs ran only for 12–18 months. Barton J. dismissed this argument. It is suggested that the case is wrongly decided on this point. If the employer can show he has a legitimate interest to protect but the covenant is excessively long a court cannot substitute a reasonable period for the unreasonable period. If however, the plaintiff seeks an injunction the same result may follow from the way in which the courts implement this discretionary remedy. In *Cusser* v. *O'Connor* (1893), the plaintiffs employed the defendant as a commercial traveller, obliging him not to work for any rival business for either, (1) *ten* years after commencement of employment in 1889, or (2) two years after termination of employment. The defendant left employment in 1892; the covenant therefore had seven years to run, an unduly long time. Andrews J., instead of striking down the restraint ruled that the court had a discretion to determine how long the injunction was to run; in the view of the learned judge a reasonable period would be two years. So, although the court could not reduce the plaintiff's substantive rights to reasonable proportions it could limit the scope of the primary remedy available. There is a suggestion in the judgment of McWilliam J. in *E.C.I. European Chemical Industries Ltd.* v. *Bell* (1981) that the courts may now be prepared to "tailor" a restraint which is clearly too wide in terms of area and duration, once the employer can show he has a legitimate interest worthy of protection. In that case the plaintiffs had inserted an excessively wide covenant adding that if the covenant was held invalid "the said covenant shall be given effect to in its reduced form as may be decided by any court of competent jurisdiction." After noting the conflict between the English cases of *Commercial Plastics* v. *Vincent* (1966) and *Littlewoods* v. *Harris* (1978) McWilliam J. expressed *obiter* a preference for the later decision. The *Littlewoods* case has been criticised as unduly favourable to the employer; see Phillips (1978) 13 Ir. Jur. 254.

A restraint will not be allowed to operate through the principle of severance if it is used to prevent or discourage persons from competing with a former employer's business in a *sphere of activity* not previously carried on by the covenantor; *Attwood* v. *Lamont* (1920).

The American courts take a more adventurous view of the doctrine of severance and openly admit that they have the jurisdiction to shape and restrict area, duration and activity restraints to reasonable proportions. The judgment in *E.C.I.*

European Chemical Industries Ltd. v. *Bell* (1981) may herald a similar approach in Ireland.

One final point. Most employment restraints are governed by reasonableness *inter partes*, as are covenants for the sale of a business. The question of reasonableness in the public interest does not generally arise. In the recent English case of *Hensman* v. *Traill* (1980) a covenant preventing a doctor from competing was struck down as being unreasonable in the public interest and *inter partes*; had the covenant been reasonable *inter partes* it would still have been defeated, it being contrary to the public interest to prevent a doctor practising in such circumstances. The same point is made in the Alberta case of *Baker* v. *Lintott* (1981).

Part V

Capacity to Contract

14 Status of Living Persons and Corporate Personality

Most systems of law seek to protect persons falling into particular categories by rendering them unable to contract freely. When this occurs the individual bargain is rendered invalid although it may be that some limited remedy may still be available; see for example s. 2 of the Sale of Goods Act 1893, discussed below.

Infants or Minors

The age of majority in the Republic of Ireland remains 21. In the United Kingdom it has been reduced to 18 by the Family Law Reform Act 1969.

Professor Treitel points out that the law relating to an infant's contractual liability attempts to strike a balance between two conflicting objectives; first of all, the courts seek to protect an infant from the consequences of his own inexperience in commercial matters. On the other hand, the judges seek to protect commercial men who unwittingly contract with infants, particularly if the infant has misrepresented that he is of age. It can be said that the present position in England unduly favours the interests of the infant.

The general rule at common law is that an infant's contract is voidable; voidable in this context bears two meanings. First of all, certain contracts are valid unless repudiated by the infant. Other contracts are voidable in the sense that unless the infant affirms the transaction within a reasonable time after coming of age the transaction does not bind him. Certain contracts are valid at common law; these are contracts for necessaries and beneficial contracts of service.

Necessaries

The following statement found in Coke upon Littleton, a seventeenth century English text, is perhaps one of the most enduring propositions in the common law;

"An infant may bind himself to pay for his necessary meat, drink, apparel, necessary physic, and such other necessaries, and likewise for his good teaching or instruction, whereby he may profit himself afterwards, but if he bind himself in an obligation or other writing, with a penalty for the payment of any other, that obligation shall not bind him."

Necessaries are defined in the Sale of Goods Act 1893, s.2, as "goods suitable to the condition in life of infant or minor . . . and to his actual requirements at the time of the sale and delivery." Many of the old cases were decided before juries, who favoured the interests of the trader by giving an extended meaning to necessaries. It is now the role of the judge to say first of all whether an item is capable of being classified as a necessary. Certain items are incapable of being necessaries. In *Skrine* v. *Gordon* (1875) the defendant who represented himself to be a member of the Surrey Staghunt agreed to buy a hunter from the plaintiff for £600. The price was never paid. Lawson J. ruled that the issue of whether this was a necessary or not should never have been left to a jury: "luxuries or amusement are quite different from necessaries." So, in the leading English case of *Ryder* v. *Wombwell* (1867) jewelled cuff-links were held incapable of being classified as necessaries. One Australian case holds that a bicycle may be a necessary if used to convey the infant to and from his place of work 11 miles away: *Scarborough* v. *Sturzaker* (1905). Canadian case law suggests that a motor car cannot be a necessary even if used for business purposes; *Nobles* v. *Bellefleur* (1963), *Pyett* v. *Lampmann* (1923). Perhaps the time has now arrived in which motor vehicles should be recognised as necessaries in appropriate circumstances. A motor boat is not a necessary: *Prokopetz* v. *Richardson's Marina* (1979).

If the goods can be classified as necessaries the supplier must go further and show that the infant was not adequately supplied with such goods; this will be a difficult burden to discharge. In *Nash* v. *Inman* (1908) eleven fancy waistcoats supplied to an Oxford undergraduate were held not to be necessaries, the father of the infant being able to show his son was adequately supplied with clothing.

The words of section 2 of the 1893 Act indicate that an infant can only be liable for necessary goods if they have been supplied; even then, the section provides the infant is only liable to pay a "reasonable price" for such goods. A contract to purchase goods which will be used to carry on a trade are not necessaries as the English case of *Whittingham* v. *Hill* (1619) and the Nova Scotia case of *Jenkins* v. *Way* (1881) show. Contracts for necessary services are also valid. An infant widow will be liable on a contract to obtain funeral services for her deceased husband: *Chapple* v. *Cooper* (1844). A contract to enable an infant to gain instruction and earn his living as a professional billiards player will be enforceable, even if partly executory in nature; *Roberts* v. *Gray* (1913). Legal advice which results in substantial benefit to an infant may also be a necessary service; *Helps* v. *Clayton* (1864).

Beneficial Contracts of Service

This category of enforceable contract has evolved relatively recently. It seems to have originated in the nineteenth century when the courts began to view contracts of apprenticeship and related transactions as enforceable at common law; contrast *Horn* v. *Chandler* (1670) with *De Francesco* v. *Barnum* (1893). Many cases that are treated as beneficial contracts of service are difficult to disentangle from the category of necessary services. A contract of service will bind the infant if, viewed as a whole, the contract is seen as beneficial to the infant. The fact that one or more terms may be to the disadvantage of the infant will not be conclusive. In *Shears* v. *Mendeloff* (1914) an infant boxer appointed the plaintiff to be his manager. The agreement provided that the manager would get 25 per cent. of the infant's earnings. The manager had not expressly covenanted to obtain fights for the infant and the infant had to pay his own expenses. Avory J. in the English High Court held this contract of service not to be beneficial to the infant. It may be different if the infant also receives instruction as a boxer; see the Australian case of *McLaughlin* v. *D'Arcy* (1918).

If the contract in question is incidental to, or the means whereby, an infant earns his living it may be enforceable. In *Doyle* v. *White City Stadium* (1935) Jack Doyle, then an infant, obtained a licence to box from the British Boxing Board of Control. The terms of the licence provided that should the licensee be disqualified in a contest his portion of the purse would be forfeited. Doyle, never the most scientific of pugilists, was disqualified for a low blow during a title fight. He challenged the validity of the rules, alleging that they could not bind him. The English Court of Appeal upheld them. It was generally in Doyle's interests that the rules prohibit or discourage illegal blows, even if on this occasion the rule operated against him.

In *Keays* v. *The Great Southern Railway* (1940) the plaintiff, a child of 12 held a season ticket, issued at a reduced rate which exempted the defendants from liability for injuries caused by their negligence. The season ticket was purchased to enable the plaintiff to travel to and from school. The plaintiff was injured while travelling on the defendant's line, the injuries being the result of negligence. Hanna J.

after construing the contract as a whole, ruled that the terms of the contract were so harsh as to entitle the infant to repudiate it; "the contract in this case is very unfair to the infant because it deprives her of practically every common law right that she has against the railway company in respect of the negligence of themselves or their servants. For that reason, I think it is not for her benefit." Even a contract entered into by an infant which does not enable the infant to obtain schooling, instruction or a living may fall into this category. In *Harnedy* v. *The National Greyhound Racing Association* (1911) a contract containing an exemption clause which purported to prevent an infant greyhound owner from suing in respect of injuries to the dog was held not to be beneficial and could be repudiated.

Voidable Contracts

The common law courts recognised that contracts in which an infant was capable of being subjected to a series of recurring obligations were voidable in the sense that the infant was bound unless he repudiated the contract within a reasonable time.

1. There is Irish support for the proposition that an insurance contract, which involves a periodic obligation to pay premiums is a voidable contract; see *Stapleton* v. *Prudential Assurance* (1928), discussed in Chapter 9.
2. An infant is also liable on contracts to take shares or to meet "calls" made upon shareholders. This obligation was explained by Parke B. in the leading English case of *North Western Railway Co.* v. *McMichael* (1850) as turning upon the fact that the infant acquires an interest in something of a permanant nature rather than a mere chattel. The exception may implicitly rest on the need to facilitate the development of joint stock companies in general and railways in particular. *McMichael's* case was followed in *Midland Railway* v. *Quinn* (1851). If the infant is to avoid liability he must show and plead that he repudiated the contract within his infancy or a reasonable time thereafter; *Dublin and Wicklow Railway Co.* v. *Black* (1852).

   An action to recover money paid by the infant will fail unless the infant can show a total failure of consideration; *Steinberg* v. *Scala (Leeds) Ltd.* (1923) followed in *Stapleton's* case.
3. An infant who agrees to enter a partnership will be bound by that contract unless he repudiates openly within a reasonable time. *Griffiths* v. *Delaney* (1938) however establishes that the

supplier of goods delivered to the partnership cannot recover the price from an infant partner. Should an infant partner sue other partners for specific performance the action will fail for want of mutuality—the courts do not award specific performance against an infant. The infant will be able to sue should he affirm the partnership agreement upon coming of age; *Shannon* v. *Bradstreet* (1803); *Milliken* v. *Milliken* (1845).

4. Family settlements and those made by an infant in contemplation of marriage may be avoided within a reasonable time after coming of age. Indeed, in *Paget* v. *Paget* (1882) the plaintiff agreed with his father upon the terms of resettlement of family property. At the time of the transaction the plaintiff, unknown to himself, was only 20 years of age. Ten years later he learnt that he was an infant at the date of execution of the settlement and repudiated immediately. He was held to have done so in time. Any delay after learning the true facts would have been fatal to the right to repudiate; *Allen* v. *Allen* (1842).

   Contrast the position where an infant spouse signs a consent form permitting the other spouse to sell the family home; under section 10(1) of the Family Law Act 1981 the consent is not voidable on the grounds of infancy alone.

5. A lease taken by an infant is voidable. If the infant repudiates within a reasonable time after coming of age he will not be liable to pay rent due in the future. The case of *Blake* v. *Concannon* (1870) is authority for the view that if the infant has used and enjoyed the property before repudiation he will be liable to pay for the use and enjoyment of the demised property; the desire to prevent unjust enrichment of the infant is evident in *Mahon* v. *Farrell* (1847) which supports the view that an infant assignee is liable in similar circumstances; see also *In Re Fair* (1850).

   There are decisions the other way. In *Kelly* v. *Coote* (1856) a lease which devolved to an infant by operation of law was held to make an infant liable to pay rent even though the infant tenant had not moved into possession.

   Slator v. *Brady* (1863) has been an influential decision. In Canada it has been held to be authority for the proposition that an infant *lessor* cannot repudiate a contract which is for his benefit; see *Lipsett* v. *Perdue* (1889).

Infants Relief Act 1874

This statute, still in force in Northern Ireland and the Irish Republic is a controversial piece of legislation; Treitel calls it "a somewhat mysterious statute. No convincing reason has ever been advanced to explain exactly why it was passed." One may add that few convincing observations have been advanced to conclusively show what it achieves.

Section 1

"All contracts, whether by speciality or by simple contract, henceforth entered into by infants for the repayment of money lent or to be lent, or for goods supplied or to be supplied (other than contracts for necessaries), and all accounts stated with infants shall be absolutely void" . . . .

Several points must be made about section 1.

1. Contracts in which money is lent to an infant and in which goods are supplied to an infant are rendered "absolutely void" by this section; cases in which the infant supplies goods or lends money are outside the section. It is argued by Treitel (in (1957) 73 L.Q.R. 194) that the exception in favour of contracts for necessaries includes moneylending contracts in which the infant borrows money in order to purchase necessaries. In *Bateman* v. *Kingston* (1880) the plaintiff sued upon a promissory note given by the defendant; the money lent upon the note was used to purchase necessaries. Lawson J. refused to allow an action on the notes *which bore interest*. It was suggested by Lawson J. that *if notes were given to a trader* in return for necessaries an action on the note may lie in such a case. The view that section 1 validates a loan to purchase necessaries seems inconsistent with *Bateman* v. *Kingston* and Treitel has since withdrawn this argument.

2. It is doubtful whether an infant can sue upon such a contract. Although the common law rule was otherwise the wording of section 1 on this point—"absolutely void"—seems to be irrefragable. English textbook writers however tend to favour the view that an infant can sue on the "absolutely void" contract.

3. The orthodox view is that an infant cannot recover back property transferred under an "absolutely void" contract. In order to recover the infant must show that there has been a total failure of consideration. In *Pearce* v. *Brain* (1929) the infant plaintiff exchanged a motor cycle for a motor car. The car broke down four days later. The plaintiff sought to recover his motor cycle. The action failed; the plaintiff had used the car and was thus unable to show a total failure of consideration.

4. The English case of *Stocks* v. *Wilson* (1913) is authority for the proposition that property will pass under an "absolutely void" contract. The Supreme Court of British Columbia, on the other hand has ruled that property will not pass under an "absolutely void" contract unless the infant has paid the purchase price; see *Prokopetz* v. *Richardson's Marina* (1979) discussed by the author at 26 McGill L.J. 110. The English view, because it protects the interests of innocent purchasers from the infant, is to be preferred.

Section 2

This obscure section provides:

> "No action shall be brought whereby to charge any person upon any promise made' after full age to pay any debt contracted during infancy, or upon any ratification made after full age of any promise or contract made during infancy, whether there shall or shall not be any new consideration for such promise or ratification after full age."

Most of the reported cases deal with persons who contract to marry whilst an infant, and who make a new contract, not merely a ratification of the old, upon coming of age. Section 2 has been considered in the Irish case of *Belfast Banking Co.* v. *Doherty* (1879). Doherty was sued upon a bill of exchange drawn by Wilson in consideration for a loan made to Doherty while Doherty was an infant. Doherty accepted the bill of exchange when he attained his majority. Wilson endorsed the bill of exchange to the plaintiffs who took without knowledge of the circumstances surrounding acceptance by Doherty. The Queen's Bench Division held that while section 2 would have prevented Wilson from recovering upon a promise to pay for a debt contracted during infancy it was not to be extended so as to prejudice a bona fide holder for value.

An Infant's Liability in Tort

It was held in *O'Brien* v. *McNamee* (1953) that an infant over the age of seven may be liable in tort so long as the tort in question (1) does not require malice to be shown; (2) does not arise out of a breach of contract. As we have seen many incidents can produce liability in tort as well as contract; see Chapter 10.

The test developed to distinguish viable tort actions against an infant from those that are too closely linked to contract has been summarised by Pollock; the minor "cannot be sued for a wrong, when the cause of action is in substance *ex contractu*, or is so directly connected with the contract that the action would be an indirect way of enforcing the contract [but if the act is] independent of the contract in the sense of not being an act of the kind contemplated by it, then the infant is liable."

The test is artificial in the extreme. The cases of *Jennings* v. *Rundall* (1799) and *Burnard* v. *Haggis* (1863), discussed in the leading English texts, illustrate this point. One obvious way in which an infant might be held liable in tort where he has fraudulently misrepresented his age or credit worthiness for example, would be to sue in deceit. It was held in the Irish case of *Bird* v. *Wilson* (1851) that an infant does not "misrepresent" that she is of age simply by signing a contract.

Even if an infant positively asserts that he is of age, thereby inducing an adult to contract with him, the decision in *R. Leslie* v. *Sheill* (1914) suggests that, because the statement is directly linked to the contract, no liability in deceit can arise. Irish case law, such as it is, suggests that the same rule will apply. In *Bateman* v. *Kingston* (1880) the plaintiff pleaded that he had taken promissory notes from an infant, the infant fraudulently misrepresenting that he was of age. Lawson J. following the English case of *Bartlett* v. *Wells* (1862) held that the infant could not be liable in deceit.

The only Irish authority the other way is a dictum of Crompton J. in *McNamara* v. *Browne* (1843) where it was observed that an infant who gave a bond after holding himself out as of age may be liable on the bond.

If the infant retains property transferred the court will order restitution; *R. Leslie* v. *Sheill* (1914).

An Infant's Liability in Quasi-Contract

An action brought for the recovery of money paid or property transferred to an infant will be successful if the infant retains possession of the banknotes or chattel, even if property in the goods has passed to the infant. In cases like this there can be no question of the infant being forced to perform a contract; all the adult seeks is a limited restitutionary remedy. The cause of action however is, in *substance*, contractual.

In *Stocks* v. *Wilson* (1913) Lush J. suggested that if the infant has obtained property by way of fraud then equity will require the infant to account for the proceeds should he part with the goods. This observation was rejected by the Court of Appeal in *R. Leslie* v. *Sheill* a year later. *R. Leslie* v. *Sheill* has been followed in other jurisdictions but the matter has still to be ruled upon by an Irish Court. It is suggested that a fraudulent infant should be liable to account in such situations. There is an Australian case in point. In *Campbell* v. *Ridgely* (1887) an infant fraudulently misrepresented that he was of age, thereby inducing the plaintiff to do work for him and also supply building materials. The plaintiff sued claiming (1) the value of the materials, £382, or in the alternative; (2) return of so much of the materials still in the infant's possession and (3) an inquiry into the value of the goods not in possession. The defendant challenged ground (3) as an impermissible basis of relief. Although the later case of *R. Leslie* v. *Sheill* would suggest the defendant's challenge should have succeeded the Supreme Court of Victoria rejected the view that an account for the value of property fraudulently obtained and disposed of cannot be ordered against an infant.

It is hoped that this wider view of equitable restitution prevails in Ireland.

The Tasmanian case of *Peters* v. *Tuck* (1915) suggests that an infant can be ordered to repay the value of banknotes bailed with him.

Estoppel

Fraud by an infant will not operate an estoppel; *Levene* v. *Brougham* (1909).

1. Suggestions for reform

The Law Reform Commission Working Paper No. 2 (1977) suggested that the age of majority should be reduced to 18. The Commission also suggested an "absolute minimum age for marriage" of 16 and that persons between 16 and 18 should be able to marry with parental consent. "The free age for marriage," should these proposals be accepted, would be 18 years of age. It was also suggested that a person should, upon marriage, attain his or her majority. It is suggested that this later provision is unsatisfactory; the law should protect a 16 year old person from foolish contracts, regardless of whether he or she is married.

The Law Reform Commission did not suggest any specific reform of the rules relating to contractual liability. This is unfortunate given that all commentators are agreed that the current rules are confused and uncertain in scope.

Unfortunately the author does not have the space to consider in detail the legislative reforms canvassed elsewhere. The New Zealand Parliament has decided to intervene by giving the courts a general supervisory power over infants contracts. Several Canadian provinces are considering legislation which would enable an infant to contract if the bargain is fair and to his advantage. In British Columbia proposals focus on improving the powers of the courts to award fair and reasonable remedies to infant and adult alike.

With the modern expansion of the unconscionable bargain jurisdiction it may be that specific rules on infants' contracts are unnecessary and that the power of a court to protect young persons from unconscionable or oppressive bargains may produce more satisfactory solutions. In the recent Ontario case of *Toronto Marlboro Hockey Club* v. *Tonelli* (1979) the majority of the Ontario Court of Appeal, using *Schroeder* v. *Macaulay*, decided an infant's contract dispute on unconscionability grounds.

It should also be mentioned that two old Irish cases, *Aylward* v. *Kearney* (1814) and *Dawson* v. *Massey* (1809) suggest that equity will protect young, (not necessarily infant) persons from oppressive bargains.

2. Convicts

The Forfeiture Act 1870, s.8 makes a convict incapable of making any contract, express of implied. The statute was discussed in *O'Connor* v. *Coleman* (1947) a case in which a solicitor attempted to recover legal fees from a convicted person. This statute is considered by Hogan, Byrne & McDermott, *Prisoners Rights—A Study in Irish Prison Law* p. 97–98.

3. Mental incompetents

The modern authorities in England favour the view that a contract entered into by someone who is insane is voidable. Such a person has contractual capacity and he may be bound by a contract unless he was known to be insane by the other party, who accordingly took advantage of the others infirmity. This rule, requiring knowledge of insanity can be traced to the old common law cases. There is however authority for the view that a contract entered into by a person who, unknown to the other, was insane at that time will be invalid in equity. The insane person must show that at the time he was so insane as to be incapable of understanding the contract. The Australian case of *Gibbons* v. *Wright* (1953) and the British Columbia case of *Moore* v. *Confederation Life Association* (1918) are in point.

If the degree of mental incompetence stops short of insanity the contract may be set aside if it can be shown that the bargain was improvident or unconscionable; *Grealish* v. *Murphy* (1946) illustrates that the court may intervene if it holds one party to be so stupid or senile as to be incapable of understanding the full implications of the transaction. The recent New Zealand case of *Archer* v. *Cutler* (1980) provides an exhaustive analysis of the law on mental incompetency and capacity to contract.

4. Drunkards

Contracts struck with persons who are so drunk as to be incapable of understanding the bargain are voidable. It is also said that the other, sober party must be shown to have known of this condition. It is likely, that this will be far easier to prove than in cases of insanity; *Francis* v. *St. Germain* (1858), an Ontario case. If the degree of intoxication falls short of the required standard the contract will also be viewed as potentially unconscionable according to the recent case of *White* v. *McCooey* (1976).

A drunkard and an insane person are bound to pay a reasonable price for necessaries supplied; Sale of Goods Act 1893, s.2. See *Re Byrne* (1941).

5. Married women

The Married Womens Status Act 1957 swept away in the Republic the rules and concepts that conferred upon married women limited contractual and property rights. Section 2(1) declares that the capacity of a woman to contract is unchanged upon marriage. The Act does give a married woman additional advantages; see sections 7 and 8 discussed on pp. 188–9.

6. Corporations

An incorporated body of persons, unlike unincorporated associations such as a club, is a competent contracting party, the law recognising the corporation as a juristic entity distinct from the natural persons who constitute the corporation. Corporations may be established in a variety of ways.

(1) At common law a corporation could be formed by Royal Charter; *e.g.* Trinity College Dublin and the Queen's University were established by Royal Charters issued by Elizabeth I and Queen Victoria respectively; see the discussions in *Gray & Cathcart* v. *Provost of Trinity College* (1910) and *MacCormack* v. *The Queens University* (1867).

(2) Corporations may also be established under statute; obvious examples of such corporations are "semi-state" bodies such as the Electricity Supply Board; see generally Goulding, The Juristic Basis of the Irish State Enterprise (1978) 13 Ir. Jur. 302.

(3) Thirdly, (and more commonly) a company may be formed by compliance with the provisions of the Companies Act 1963. It is in this manner that the majority of commercial trading companies are established. The company must have articles of association (governing items of internal administration) and a memorandum of association (which states the objects of the company, its scope of operation and the extent of the companies powers).

The extent to which the officers and directors may bind the company by entering into contracts with third persons will, in the first instance depend on whether the transaction falls within (*intra vires*) the objects of the company.

The doctrine of ultra vires

A statutory corporation (*i.e.* (2) & (3) above) can exercise only those powers expressly or impliedly conferred by the statute itself. The doctrine of *ultra vires* declares an act done which is not authorised by the incorporating statute or the objects clause in the memorandum of association to be void at law.

Thus a company that is empowered to manufacture, sell or hire railway carriages, plant and equipment is not able to validly consent to purchase the right to construct a railway: *Ashbury Railway Carriage Co.* v. *Riche* (1875). On the other hand the memorandum at issue in *Martin* v. *Irish Industrial Benefit Society* (1960) was held wide enough to permit advances to non-members of a Building Society.

Attempts to avoid the *ultra vires* doctrine focus on drafting the objects of the company so widely as to empower the directors to carry on any business which in their opinion might be carried on advantageously in connection with the main business, (whatever that may be); *Bell Houses Ltd.* v. *City Wall Properties Ltd.* (1966). Alternatively an extremely detailed memorandum may be drawn so as to include every conceivable activity; as Gower says (*Modern Company Law* (4th ed., 1979) pp.161–180) a gold company may draft its objects so widely as to empower it to operate a fried fish shop.

Statutory modification

The only real result of the *ultra vires* doctrine in the modern context is to prevent a third party, honestly dealing with a company, from being able to sue on a contract. The harshness of this led the Oireachtas in The Companies Act 1963 enacting in s. 8(1)

"Any act or thing done by a company which if the company has been empowered to do the same would have been lawfully and effectively done, shall, notwithstanding that the company had no power to do such act or thing be effective in favour of any person relying on such act or thing who is not shown to have been actually aware at the time when he so relied thereon, that such act or thing was not within the powers of the company . . ."

The United Kingdom European Communities Act 1972, s.9(1) also amends the *ultra vires* rule but the Republic's statute seems narrower in scope.

In *Northern Bank Finance Corporation Ltd.* v. *Quinn & Achates Investment Co.* (1979) the plaintiffs sought to enforce a guarantee signed by an officer of the second defendant. The memorandum of association stressed that the second defendants main objects were to acquire and hold securities, investments and other property; the incidental objects were to "sell, exchange, mortgage assign . . . generally deal in" such securities. Keane J. held that the transaction, namely signature of a guarantee was *ultra vires*. In considering whether section 8(1) applied Keane J. held that an officer of the plaintiffs had inspected the memorandum and had formed the erroneous belief that the transaction was *intra vires;* in Keane J.'s view "where a party is shown to have been actually aware of the contents of the memorandum but failed to appreciate that the company were not empowered thereby to enter into the transaction in issue, section 8(1) has no application." The plaintiffs' action failed.

It should be noted that section 8(1) is not (unlike the United Kingdom provision) a "good faith" provision. Treitel, *The Law of Contract,* (5th ed., 1979) points out that the solution to the problem posed by the facts of *Quinn* is unclear under the United Kingdom provision.

It is submitted that *Quinn* was decided *per incuriam* because Keane J. overlooked the possibility of applying Regulation 6 of the European Communities (Companies) Regulations (S.I. 1973 No. 163) which presents an alternative test; see Ussher (1975) 10 Ir. Jur. 39.

Other remedies

The question whether a company may sue upon an *ultra vires* transaction which they have executed, conferring a valuable benefit upon a third party was considered in *Crone* v. *Dublin C.C.* (1958).

Water rátes were fixed *ultra vires;* the defendants argued that the fact that they had supplied water to the plaintiff entitled them to recover on an implied contract. A majority of the Supreme Court held that no implied contract existed and the action failed.

It may be possible to plead an estoppel *in pais;* this was considered by Keane J. in *Quinn's* case.

Part VI
Privity of Contract

15 Privity of Contract

The doctrine of privity of contract prevents a contract from being enforceable in favour of, or against, someone who is not a party to that contract. The doctrine resembles the rule (already considered in Chapter 2) requiring consideration move from a promisee before a promise can be enforced by that person. Furmston in (1960) 23 M.L.R. 373 has convincingly argued that these two propositions are in fact two different ways of saying the same thing. A "stranger to the consideration," (*i.e.* a person who has not rendered himself liable upon the contract) does not provide consideration for any promise addressed to him. By the same token, the fact that a gratuitous promise is addressed to a person does not make that person a promisee; the test used to identify persons who are privy to a bilateral contract is whether that person is bound to do anything under the contract; *c.f. Coulls* v. *Bagot's Trustee* (1967), criticised by Coote [1978] C.L.J. 301.

Origins

The cases of *McCoubray* v. *Thompson* (1868) and *Barry* v. *Barry* (1891), discussed in Chapter 2, indicate that the doctrine is designed to prevent persons who are simply the objects of a gratuitous promise from suing others in contract. The doctrine is not popular and some writers have argued that it is in fact a common law doctrine of fairly recent origin. The leading English case is the decision of the Court of Queens Bench in *Tweddle* v. *Atkinson* (1861). An action was brought by a son in law to recover a sum of money from the estate of his deceased father in law. The sum had been promised in return for a similar promise given by the plaintiff's own father upon the plaintiff's marriage. The action failed.

Tweddle v. *Atkinson* stands in marked contrast to a series of earlier English cases, particularly *Dutton* v. *Poole* (1677) where similar family arrangements were held to be enforceable by third parties. These older cases are to be regarded as having been overruled by

Tweddle v. *Atkinson* (1861) and the later case of *Dunlop* v. *Selfridge* (1915), a House of Lords decision.

The most important Irish common law decision is probably *Murphy* v. *Bower* (1866). The plaintiffs, railway contractors undertook construction work for a railway company. The company employed Bower as an engineer to supervise the work. The construction contract stipulated that Bower would issue certificates as work was completed, thereupon entitling the plaintiffs to payment. Bower refused to certify the work. The Court of Common Pleas dismissed the plaintiffs' action against Bower. It should be noted that the plaintiffs had not engaged the engineer; nor was Bower's employer, the railway company, plaintiffs in the action. Monahan C.J. observed, "it has been decided that where the foundation of the right of action is rested upon contract, no one can maintain an action who is not a party to the contract."

Other early Irish common law decisions which uphold the doctrine of privity of contract include *Waugh* v. *Denham* (1865) and *Corner* v. *Irwin* (1875), two cases decided prior to the Judicature Act. The significance of this will become apparent in a moment.

Equity's Response to Actions Brought by Third Parties

The courts of equity adopted a characteristically flexible position. In the early case of *Shannon* v. *Bradstreet* (1803) a tenant for life with a power to lease entered into an agreement to execute a lease in favour of Shannon. Shannon entered into possession but no lease was formally executed (which prevented the possibility of the lease binding successors as a covenant running with the land, (*infra*, p.188)). On the death of the tenant for life the remainderman sought ejectment claiming the lease did not bind him. Lord Redesdale gave judgment for Shannon holding that in equity a remainderman is bound by a leasing agreement made by a predecessor in title.

This isolated example of equity recognising that a third party may be bound by a contract pales into insignificance when contrasted with the line of authority commencing with the English case of *Tomlinson* v. *Gill* (1756), a decision of Hardwicke L.C. Gill promised a widow that if she would appoint him administrator of her deceased husband's estate he would personally meet any debts the estate could not discharge. An action brought by a creditor on this promise succeeded; "the plaintiff . . . could not maintain an action at law, for the promise was made to the widow; but he is proper here, for the promise was for the benefit of the creditors and the widow is a trustee for them."

While traditionally the equitable concept of the trust does provide a right of action to a beneficiary who may sue the trustee should he not discharge his duties it has been said that, in this context, the trust is not apparent. In *Tomlinson* v. *Gill* there was no express intention to create a trust; nor was a trust fund established. Corbin, in his exhaustive review of these early cases (1930 L.Q.R 12), observed of this case that "there was merely a contract between two persons in which one promised to pay a debt owed to a third party; the promisee—the widow—was called a trustee of the promise merely to allow the action in equity to succeed against the promisor."

The trust concept has been discussed in several Irish cases. In *Drimmie* v. *Davies* (1899) a father and son agreed to establish a dental practice. The partnership deed obliged the son to pay annuities to his mother and his siblings in the event of the father predeceasing him. The executor of the deceased partner's estate and the beneficiaries sued to enforce the promise. The executor's action succeeded; Chatterton V.C., in a judgment upheld by the Court of Appeal ruled that the defence of privity between promisor and beneficiaries did not prevail in equity and, following the Judicature Act, the equitable rule namely, "the party to whose use or for whose benefit the contract had been entered into has a remedy in equity against the person with whom it was expressed to be made was to be applied." Note also Holmes L.J.'s judgment in the Court of Appeal. The fact that the trustee himself—the executor—was prepared to sue makes this statement *obiter dictum*; see *Beswick* v. *Beswick* (1967). If the executor/promisee is unwilling to bring proceedings such a dictum may be invaluable.

In *Kenney* v. *Employers' Liability Insurance Corporation* (1901) a bank, mortgagees of Kenney's estate appointed B as a receiver to hold and pay over to them rents and profits. B took out insurance with the defendant to cover acts of default. B defaulted and Kenney, who had paid out to cover B's default, sued on the insurance policy. The majority of the Court of Appeal held Kenney entitled to sue on the contract. Holmes L.J. for the majority said the case fell within *Drimmie* v. *Davies*. Walker L.J., dissenting said that B did not intend to confer a beneficial right on the mortgagor, nor did B intend to make himself a trustee for the mortgagor. The trust device was also applied in *Walsh* v. *Walsh* (1900).

There is one nineteenth century Irish case the other way. In *Clitheroe* v. *Simpson* (1879) John Simpson, father of both the defendant and Alice Clitheroe, late wife of the plaintiff, agreed by deed with the defendant that in consideration of the defendant agreeing to pay Alice Clitheroe £100, John Simpson would convey land to the defendant. The sum was not paid; the plaintiff, executor

of his wife's estate sued but the action failed. Morris C.J., observed
that even if a trust had been pleaded, which it was not, he did not
think any circumstances existed which would bring the case within
that exception to the privity rule. Lawson and Harrison J.J.'s
concurred.

This case, (decided by judges from a predominantly common law
background) was described by Corbin as one in which the judges
looked for a trust fund, "and finding none denied the plaintiff a
remedy. The possibility of regarding the promisee as a trustee of the
contract right did not occur to the Court."

While the primacy of the *Drimmie* v. *Davies* line of authority has
not been directly challenged in the Irish courts the practice of
utilising the concept of the trust as a means of avoiding the privity
doctrine has fallen into disfavour. Lord Wright described it as "a
cumbrous fiction" when used in this context; 55 L.Q.R. 189. The
Privy Council in *Vandepitte* v. *Preferred Accident Insurance Corporation of
New York* (1933) refused to allow a third party to sue on an insurance
contract because it could not be shown that the insured intended to
benefit the third party. In fact the position taken in *Vandepitte* closely
resembles that of Walker L.J., dissenting in *Kenney* (*supra*). In the
case of *O'Leary* v. *Irish National Insurance Co. Ltd* (1958) the court left
open the question whether an intention to create a trust must be
shown before a third party can recover but Barrington J. in *Cadbury
Ireland Ltd.* v. *Kerry Co-op Creameries Ltd.* (1981) seems to have held that
such an intention must be present.

The trust concept is out of favour, both in England and Ireland
because it strikes many judges as intellectually dishonest. More
importantly perhaps, the use of this "cumbrous fiction" can unduly
interfere with perfectly sensible arrangements by preventing the
parties from being able to rescind or vary it by agreement. This
occurs because the "beneficiary", as the possessor of an equitable
interest, must consent to a variation; *Re Schebsman* (1944). Nevertheless it is suggested that the case of *McKay* v. *Jones* (1959), (the facts of
which are given in Chapter 3) should be considered as wrongly
decided. The possibility that the boy's parents were trustees of the
contract promise does not seem to have been argued.

Agency

If an agent is appointed and given the authority to contract on
behalf of a principal then any transaction within the scope of such
authority will bind the principal. Before the agency exception can
operate there must normally exist an intention to create the
relationship of principal and agent; *Sheppard* v. *Murphy* (1867).

In *Pattison* v. *Institute for Industrial Research and Standards* (1979) a trade union, negotiating on behalf of its members obtained a promise from the defendant to pay an additional allowance to the plaintiff, an employee of the defendant. McWilliam J. held that the plaintiff could enforce this promise. The decision can only be explained as resting on a finding that the union negotiated as agent for its members.

The agency exception has produced a controversial series of decisions in recent years. In *The Eurymedon* (1974) machinery was to be transported by ship from England to New Zealand. The consignors in England contracted with a carrier, the contract providing that liability of the carriers, their employees, agents and independent contracts would be limited. The carriers employed the defendant stevedores to unload the machinery, which was damaged due to the stevedores' negligence. The majority of the Privy Council held the stevedores entitled to rely on a limitation clause even though it was contained in a contract between consignor and carrier. The Privy Council, following the earlier case of *Scruttons Ltd.* v. *Midland Silicones* (1960) held if the following four conditions can be satisfied the third party will take the benefit of such a clause:

1. the contract must make it clear that the stevedore is intended to be protected.
2. the contract clearly provides that the carrier has the status of agent for the purpose of obtaining the benefit of the contract for a principal.
3. the carrier has the authority to contract on the stevedore's behalf.
4. there are no difficulties in relation to consideration.

The minority in *The Eurymedon* were unable to find that the contract also contained an offer addressed to the stevedore; the dissenting members of the Boad expressed misgivings about using a legal fiction to avoid the privity doctrine (in much the same way as their predecessors had in *Vandepitte* when faced with the trust argument). Nevertheless *The Eurymedon* has been followed in *The New York Star* (1980), also a Privy Council decision.

In *Fox* v. *Higgins* (1912) Gibson J. also encountered difficulties when confronted with a contractual arrangement intended to bind persons outside the original bargain. The plaintiff was employed by Rev. Busby as a teacher in a national school. Rev. Busby resigned; the defendant Higgins replaced him as school manager. Before the defendant was confirmed as manager Fox fell ill and was away from work for several months. Fox, on his return to work was told that his contract of employment ended when Rev. Busby resigned. Gibson J.

found that Higgins was bound by the National Board rules to enter into a contract with all teachers employed at the commencement of his own service as school manager; this was described as "a kind of triangular pact" by which in certain circumstances the new manager is bound "in the same way and to the same effect as if he had signed the contract."

These tripartite contracts are exceptional; it is a matter of construction whether an arrangement binds all parties equally or whether the relationship between contracting parties subsists in a series of separate transactions; the speech of O'Higgins C.J. in *Henley Forklift (Ireland) Ltd.* v. *Lansing Bagnall & Co. Ltd. et al* (1979) is instructive.

Covenants Running with the Land

Conveyancing practice and a wealth of case law establishes that covenants that "touch and concern" real property may be enforced against, and indeed be enforced by, persons who are not parties to the original transaction. Considerations of space do not permit an extensive review of this exception to the privity doctrine. The law is discussed with great clarity in Wylie, *Irish Land Law*, Chapter 19.

There are no Irish cases dealing with the applicability of such covenants to contracts for the sale of chattels.

Statutory Exceptions to the Privity Doctrine

In England the Law Revision Committee recommended in a 1937 Report that legislation be enacted conferring sweeping rights of action upon third party beneficiaries. This Report has been ignored by the United Kingdom Parliament but two recommendations have been adopted by the Oireachtas.

The first recommendation builds upon section 11 of the Married Women's Property Act 1882. By adopting the trust concept discussed above Parliament in 1882 gave widows and children of a deceased man the right to sue upon a policy of life insurance. Section 7 of the Married Women's Status Act 1957 extends this right of action to endowment policies also. This right of action applies to policies whether the policy is "expressed to be for the benefit of" or "by its express terms purporting to confer a benefit upon the wife, husband or child of the insured": Dowrick (1958) 21 M.L.R. 98.

More importantly perhaps, section 8 of the 1957 Act creates a cause of action in all contracts other than those covered by section 7 if the contract is expressed to be for the benefit of a wife, husband or child of one of the contracting parties or if the contract purports to confer a benefit upon such a third party. As a result the contract will be enforceable by the third party in his or her own name.

The facts of *Jackson* v. *Horizon Holidays* (1975) illustrate the usefulness of section 8. Jackson booked a holiday in Ceylon for himself and his family. The accommodation provided was unsatisfactory so on his return to England Mr. Jackson sued to recover damages for the disappointing holiday. He recovered damages to compensate not only himself but all members of the family. *Jackson* makes good sense but the Court of Appeal's reasoning has been attacked as incorrect in law; see P. Wylie 25 N.I.L.Q. 326 and the House of Lords in *Woodar Investment* v. *Wimpey Construction* (1980). Under section 8 the wife and children of a contracting party would, on similar facts, be able to sue in contract in their own name. Section 8 does permit the contract to be rescinded by the contracting parties at any time before the beneficiary adopts it; the third party is also bound by any defences the defendant may have against the other contracting party.

If a tenancy agreement between a male tenant and a landlord envisages that the tenant's wife is to live on the premises it may be that the wife will fall within the scope of section 8, depending of course on the terms of the letting agreement. If the wife of the tenant is injured because the premises turn out to be defective she should in such a case be able to sue the landlord under section 8. This point does not seem to have been argued in either *Chambers* v. *Cork Corporation* (1958) or *Coughlan* v. *Mayor of Limerick* (1977).

Section 76 (1) of the Road Traffic Act 1961 gives a person claiming against an insured motorist certain remedies against the insurer. If judgment is obtained against the insured section 76(1) (*b*) and (*c*) provide that an application to execute judgment against the owner or user may be brought: *Herlihy* v. *Curley* (1950). Should the claimant not recover judgment against that person then section 76(1)(*d*) provides that the claimant may apply to institute proceedings against the insurer or guarantor, in lieu of the owner or user of the vehicle, if:

1. The owner or user is outside the State, or cannot be found or is immune from process or
2. for any other reason it is just and equitable that the application be granted.

Case law indicates a considerable overlap between these two provisions *e.g. Norton* v. *General Accident* (1940) and *Hayes* v. *Legal Insurance Co. Ltd.* (1941). The Sale of Goods and Supply of Services Act 1980 implements two interesting provisions which further limit the privity doctrine.

Section 13 (2) enacts an implied condition in sales by a dealer of a motor vehicle to the effect that the vehicle is, at the time of delivery free from any defect which would render it a danger to the public, including persons travelling in the vehicle. The provision goes further by providing in subsection (7) that a person using the vehicle with the consent of the buyer, who suffers loss as a result of breach of subsection 2 "may maintain an action for damages against the seller in respect of the breach as if he were the buyer."

Section 14 of the Act also makes a finance house liable for breach of contract and a dealer's misrepresentations if goods are sold by a dealer to a consumer, the dealer being paid the purchase price by a finance house, the purchaser repaying the finance house.

Further Reforms?

Apart from piecemeal legislative reforms the doctrine of privity remains intact. The judges are anxious to limit possible injustices; see *Beswick* v. *Beswick* (1967) as applied in *Snelling* v. *John G. Snelling Ltd.* (1973). There are signs that further judicial reforms may be forthcoming; witness Lord Scarman's speech in *Woodar Investment* v. *Wimpey Construction* (1980) where, after noting Parliament's failure to implement the 1937 Report, the learned judge said "[i] hope the House [of Lords] will reconsider *Tweddle* v. *Atkinson* and the other cases which stand guard over this unjust rule."

Part VII
Discharge

16 Discharge of Contractual Obligations

A. Discharge of a contract through performance

(1) *Entire contracts*

Before a contract may be discharged by performance it must be established that performance complies exactly with the terms of the contract. Only the most insignificant deviations imaginable will be excused under the maxim *de minimis non curat lex*.

Two picturesque examples of the general position were given by Jessel M.R. in *Re Hall & Barker* (1878):

> "If a man engages to carry a box of cigars from London to Birmingham, it is an entire contract, and he cannot throw the cigars out of the carriage half-way there, and ask for half the money: or if a shoemaker agrees to make a pair of shoes, he cannot offer you one shoe and ask you to pay half the price."

Re Moore & Landauer, discussed in Chapter 8, illustrates the harsh results that can follow from this rule. In the Irish case of *Nash & Co. v. Hartland* (1840) it was pointed out that whether a contract is entire or not is a matter of construction. If the contract, expressly or impliedly, sets out that precise and exact performance by one party must be rendered before any obligation accrues to the other, the contract is entire.

The leading English case is *Cutter* v. *Powell* (1795). Cutter was engaged as a second mate to serve on a voyage from Jamaica to Liverpool. He was given a promissory note for 30 guineas, payable 10 days after the vessel arrived in Liverpool, should he serve faithfully in that post. Cutter died *en route*. His widow sued, claiming entitlement to a proportionate part of the sum on a *quantum meruit* basis. The action failed. The normal rate of pay for a second mate on such a voyage was £8. The higher rate of pay was explained as being "a kind of insurance"; Kenyon M.R. The bargain here was an exceptional one. If Cutter served and arrived in Liverpool he would be paid nearly four times the normal rate; if not, he would recover nothing.

The case of *Coughlan* v. *Moloney* (1905) takes the test a little further by requiring the plaintiff to show an implied agreement to pay for the work done. The plaintiff there agreed to build a house for the defendant for £200, to be completed by Christmas 1902. No provision for periodic payment was made. The work was left incomplete and in October 1903 the defendants wrote asking for an account to be submitted so that "the matter should be finally wound up." No reply came; the builder sued for the value of work completed, the defendants having engaged another builder to finish the work. The action for work completed failed; if the employer has a half completed structure on his land he has no choice whether to accept or reject the work. It would be absurd to require the employer to leave the structure in that condition, so if he uses materials left on the site he impliedly promises to pay for their value; he does not impliedly pay for work completed. In *Coughlan* v. *Moloney* the letter of October 1903 was also held not to be a new contract for the builder did not provide consideration for this new promise.

The position taken in *Coughlan* v. *Moloney* is a harsh one; after all, the employer gets a substantial benefit which he does not have to pay for. To mitigate the effects of the general rule the courts have developed a doctrine called substantial performance. If the work has been carried out in all its essential respects the party thus rendering substantial performance will be entitled to the contract price, subject to the employer being able to set-off all sums necessary to engage another person to complete the work. Two factors are important here; (1) the nature of the defects (2) the cost of remedying the defects as against the contract price. In *Hoenig* v. *Isaacs* (1952) a builder agreed to redecorate the defendant's flat for £750; work was not completed and the cost of remedying the defects was £55. The English Court of Appeal held that because the defects were insignificant—a bookcase had to be completed—the builder was entitled to total payments of £695.

In contrast to the conclusion reached in *Hoenig* v. *Isaacs* it has been held that where a central heating system was installed improperly, payment being agreed at £560, the system emitting fumes and working inefficiently, these defects, which would cost £174 to put right meant that the deviation fell short of substantial performance; *Bolton* v. *Mahadeva* (1972).

There is authority for the view that substantial performance will not apply if the builder refuses or abandons work he acknowledges to be due; only if the parties genuinely dispute whether the work completed meets the contract standard can the compromise of "substantial performance" operate. In *Kincora Builders* v. *Cronin* (1973), the only Irish case in which "substantial performance" has been considered, Pringle J. held that where a builder knowingly refused to insulate an attic aware that he was obliged to do this under the contract, this would constitute an abandonment, denying him a remedy under substantial performance.

The entire contract, as Beck has pointed out ((1978) 38 M.L.R.), has been confused with a lump sum contract. The courts all too readily presume that if it is agreed that a lump sum will be payable after performance the parties have made an entire contract. This is a *non sequitur*; it is possible that the parties also intend that periodic payments or payment for partial completion can be claimed while work is in progress.

This error is illustrated by the judgment of Whiteside C.J. in *Collen* v. *Marum* (1871), a case in which a builder agreed to construct a house for a fixed sum. Whiteside C.J. said in such a case the contract is entire and indivisible and that "the employer is not bound to pay for half or quarter of a house for the court and jury can have no right to apportion that which the parties themselves have treated as entire."

The courts hold that a lump sum building contract and an entire contract are synonymous; it is understandable that this should be so, otherwise a builder would be encouraged to abandon work in progress should a more lucrative contract come along, safe in the knowledge that he can recover for the work completed. Before the courts will permit this it must be shown that the employer has acquiesced to the deviation from precise performance; *per* Whiteside C.J. (*supra*).

The English Law Commission in Working Paper No. 65 point out that the result of the present law is to create a strong possibility of an employer being unjustly enriched if a builder, through lack of funds, is unable to complete work. Sweeping restitutionary changes are proposed if it can be shown that one party to a lump sum contract has conferred substantial advantages on the other. A similar development would be welcome in the Republic also.

Statutory modifications. The position reached in *Coughlan* v. *Moloney*, a building contract, is echoed by section 30(1) of the Sale of Goods Act 1893 which provides that while the buyer of goods who takes delivery of a quantity of goods which are less than he consented to take may reject them, he is obliged to pay for them at the contract rate should he accept the goods.

If certain services have already been rendered by A to B, A then terminating the contract without having been paid on a *quantum meruit* basis, there can be no question of B electing to accept or reject partial performance. The Apportionment Act 1870 does give some limited redress. Under the combined effect of sections 2 and 5 "rents, annuities, dividends and other periodical payments," including salaries and pensions "shall be considered as accruing from day to day." A lump sum payment for one period of employment is not a periodical payment so *Cutter* v. *Powell* would be outside this Act; see also *Creagh* v. *Sheedy* (1955), which seems to be decided *per incuriam*.

If the claimant *terminates* employment his termination does not prevent him from relying on the Act. In *Treacy* v. *Corcoran* (1874) Treacy was employed as a clerk, the remuneration being payable half yearly. In April 1872 he resigned. Corcoran took over the job and at the end of the half year Corcoran was paid £115, the sum payable for the whole of the period. Treacy was held entitled to a proportion of that sum, based on the 34 day period he was in employment.

If the claimant is in *breach* of contract English cases suggest the Act will not apply; see *Clapham* v. *Draper* (1885).

(2) *Divisible Contracts*

If a contract is held to be made up of a series of separate obligations, the contract providing that payment is to be due during the process of performance, the contract is divisible. In the building industry contracts are generally drafted so as to entitle the builder to payment as certain stages are completed; to ensure performance the contract normally provides that a proportion of the total price—15 to 20 per cent.—will be retained until the work is due.

If work is to be done on part of a building or some other structure a presumption may arise in favour of the contract being divisible rather than entire. A trade custom in favour of a shipwright being entitled to call for repair work to be payable in instalments explains the leading English case of *Roberts* v. *Havelock* (1832).

In the recent case of *Verolme Cork Dockyard Ltd.* v. *Shannon Atlantic Fisheries Ltd.* (1978) the plaintiffs claimed £28,000, alleged to be due for repair work performed on the defendant's fishing boat. The defendant pleaded that the work was not completed and that the contract was entire. Finlay P. on the evidence held that the contract contained a term requiring a substantial payment on account to be made when a reasonably high proportion of the work had been carried out.

Fault of one party preventing performance. While an entire contract must be performed precisely there will be a remedy available in *quantum meruit* should one party fail to perform his obligations because of some act of default on the part of the other. In the case of

Arterial Drainage Co. Ltd. v. *Rathangan River Drainage Board* (1880) contractors agreed to drain land for the defendant Board, the contract being entire. The contract provided that if the contractors failed to carry out work with due diligence the employer could terminate the contract. The defendant purported to exercise this right. It appeared that work was not performed as quickly as envisaged because the defendant had failed to make land and plans available to the contractors. The Court of Common Pleas, distinguishing *Cutter* v. *Powell*, held that the defendant's default prevented the plaintiffs from performing their obligations. The plaintiffs were therefore entitled to treat the contract as rescinded and sue for the value of work completed.

Tender of performance. When one party unsuccessfully attempts to render performance this is known as a tender. The effects of a tender differ according to the nature of the outstanding obligation.

If the obligation is to pay a sum of money, the creditor refusing to accept the sum, this does not discharge the debtor's obligation to pay. Should the debtor pay the sum into court the creditor may recover the sum by way of action but interest will not be payable; the debtor will recover his costs.

The debtor must meet any contractual terms set as to the place, time and manner of payment. The Northern Ireland case of *Morrow* v. *Carty* (1957) establishes that attempted payment of a deposit required in cash by offering a cheque will not be sufficient. In the Republic of Ireland the Decimal Currency Act 1969 defines legal tender within the State as follows; silver coins are legal tender up to the sum of £10 (s.8(1)); a tender of bronze coins and silver coins up to a value of 10p is legal tender for any sum up to £5 (s.8(2)); bronze coins are legal tender up to a sum of 20p. Banknotes are legal tender up to any amount. United Kingdom banknotes and coins are not legal tender in the Republic because they are not issued under the Coinage Acts 1926–1950, or the 1969 Act. United Kingdom currency is commonly used in the Republic of Ireland however.

Legal tender in the North of Ireland is defined in similar terms by the Currency and Bank Notes Act 1954 and the Coinage Act 1971, s.14(3).

If the tender consists of an attempt to perform actions other than payment of money—the delivery of goods for example—non-acceptance may discharge the obligations of the promisor. Thus if goods are due and they are tendered during a reasonable hour a refusal to accept may amount to a repudiation entitling the seller to treat the contract as discharged; Sale of Goods Act 1893, ss.29(4), 31(2), 37.

Time of performance. While at common law any time fixed for the performance of a contract was held to be "of the essence of the contract," failure to perform entitling the other party to terminate and sue for damages, the equitable rule, which now prevails makes it clear that normally time for performance is not of the essence; see the Judicature Act 1877, s.28(7) and *Mayne* v. *Merriman* (1980).

In Ireland time will be of the essence if the contract so provides; this is frequently done in conveyancing transactions. If the contract does not originally make time of the essence one party may serve notice that he intends to make time of the essence; failure to perform within a reasonable period will entitle the person serving notice to terminate the contract. In *Nolan* v. *Driscoll* (1978) the plaintiff in December 1975 agreed to purchase the defendant's house; due to problems relating to registration of title the sale was still incomplete two years later. On March 2nd 1977 the defendant, being of the view that a sufficient title had been shown, served notice that he now wished to make time of the essence, and that completion should take place at the end of the month. McWilliam J. upheld the defendant's view that he was entitled to terminate and refused to order specific performance.

In commercial contracts the courts are reluctant to hold time of the essence unless the contract so requires: section 10(1) Sale of Goods Act 1893. Due to the nature of the commodity sold time will be of the essence in contracts for the sale of a business as a going concern. The general position is clearly stated in *Laird Bros.* v. *Dublin Steam Packet* (1900), discussed on p. 83.

B. Discharge through Agreement

Post-contractual representations which purport to have the effect of abrogating or modifying contractual terms present acute difficulties, due in the main to a failure on the part of judges to use and define terms like "rescission," "variation," and "waiver" with any degree of precision; the term "waiver" for example bears at least six meanings; Dugdale and Yates (1976) 39 M.L.R. 680. Additional difficulties are presented by jurisdictional factors; modern equitable lines of authority provide solutions which differ from those developed by the courts of common law.

Rescission through accord and satisfaction

For a contract to be terminated by mutual agreement (accord), consideration (satisfaction), must be present. No difficulty arises where the transaction is executory on both sides; mutual promises not to sue for non-performance generate consideration from both parties. Even if the agreement is partly executed on both sides the same rule applies.

If one party only has completely performed his part of the contract a promise given by that person will not terminate the contractual obligations of the other. So, if A has delivered wheat to B but B has yet to pay for the goods a promise by A not to sue B is ineffective unless recorded in a deed under seal or B gives consideration for A's promise.

Section 62 of the Bills of Exchange Act 1882, in force in both parts of Ireland, provides that no satisfaction is necessary for the renunciation of a debt owed to the holder of a bill of exchange or promissory note. So a straightforward way of avoiding the general rule would be for the creditor to take a bill or note in satisfaction of the debt and then renounce the debt; Treitel, *The Law of Contract* (5th ed., 1979), p.79.

Variation

Consideration must also be present if a contractual term is deleted or altered, leaving the rest of the contract untouched; *Fenner* v. *Blake* (1900).

The variation, to be effective, may have to overcome certain evidentiary hurdles. Section 2 of the Statute of Frauds 1695 and section 4 of the Sale of Goods Act 1893, discussed in Chapter 4, come into play here. A variation may have to be recorded in writing. The leading Irish case is *McQuaid* v. *Lynam* 1965. Kenny J. there said:

> "it is essential to distinguish between the case in which the parties to an agreement intend that agreement to find expression in a written contract and that in which the parties make an oral contract which is intended to be binding. If in the later case a memorandum or note in writing is required by the Statute of Frauds, that memorandum or note does not become the contract."

After reading section 2 Kenny J. continued,

> "where the parties intend their agreement to find expression in a written document, a subsequent oral variation of the contract is not effective unless it is evidenced by a memorandum or note in writing . . . but in the later type of case, where the oral agreement is intended to be the contract evidence may be given of an agreed variation even if there is a memorandum or note of the contract but not of the variation."

Waiver

If a contractual term is subject to a variation then as a matter of contract the terms of the agreement are altered. If however there is a request for some degree of forbearance, such request being agreed to, no change occurs *vis à vis* the contractual obligation. In this context it is common to describe the conduct of the party granting the concession as "waiver" of a contractual right.

Again the Statute of Frauds becomes material to the discussion. Waiver of a contractual right does not have to be evidenced in writing, unlike a variation, because in strict theory the right continues to exist while it may be unenforceable—a jurisprudential oddity.

The case of *McKillop* v. *McMullen* (1979) illustrates the effect of a waiver on a contractual obligation. The defendant agreed to sell land to the plaintiff subject to the defendant acquiring a right of way over a road to be built upon the land; the acquisition of planning permission was to be a condition precedent to the sale. When the closing date agreed upon arrived the defendant vendor failed to rescind; in fact he later requested performance. Shortly after this he, without notice, rescinded the contract. Planning permission was granted shortly after. Murray J. held that when the defendant allowed the date for completion to pass, insisting that the parties complete at some later date, that this was a waiver of his right to terminate for failure to obtain planning permission at the date of completion; the waiver was not unqualified however. The right to terminate could be exercised upon giving reasonable notice of a new date; failure to give such notice meant that the waiver remained effective.

Waiver may affect the full range of remedies available to the party forbearing to enforce his rights. In *Car & General Insurance Corp.* v. *Munden* (1936) the plaintiffs, insurers of the defendant's motor vehicle, required in clause 2 of the contract that no admission, offer, promise, payment or indemnity would be given by the insured without the consent of the plaintiffs who were also to have a right to sue in respect of an accident involving the insured. The insured's vehicle collided with a bus, injuring the insured and damaging his vehicle. The insured signed a release note issued by the bus company who paid compensation for his personal injuries. The plaintiffs believed that this broke clause 2; the right of subrogation was thereby extinguished. The plaintiffs therefore claimed to be entitled to recover £130 paid in respect of damage to the vehicle. It was held that while clause 2 may have been broken payment of the £130 constituted a waiver of the right to refuse to indemnify the defendant. The waiver only prevented the plaintiffs from terminating the agreement and obtaining restitution; they were entitled to recover damages, which because of difficulties of proof, were nominal in this case.

This result seems a curious one. It is difficult to see how waiver may be possible in cases of this nature where that person is unaware that the right to terminate has come into play; when the insurance company paid out they were unaware of Munden's non-observance of clause 2. Contrast the position on waiver of constitutional freedoms which, to be effective must be done in the clear knowledge that such a right exists: *Murphy* v. *Stewart* (1972).

Estoppel

It may be that the equitable doctrine of promissory estoppel will, in time, present a universal doctrine which will eliminate the distinctions between variation and waiver; Denning L.J. in *Charles Rickards Ltd.* v. *Oppenheim* (1950) described forbearance, waiver and variation as "a kind of estoppel."

Reform

Dugdale & Yates *(supra)* have suggested that post-contractual statements should be analysed in two ways; firstly, consensual agreements altering the terms of a contract should be effective without consideration. Secondly, conduct which the representor knows should induce a change in position should, if the statement is unambiguous, affect the remedies available to the representor. This scheme seems eminently sensible and would eliminate most of the sterile distinctions in this area.

C. Discharge Following from a Breach of Contract

It is generally accepted that a breach of contract does not of itself terminate a contract. Such a result would be unsatisfactory because a person could, by his own act, put an end to his contractual obligations. The innocent party has an option when a breach of contract occurs; he may elect to treat the breach as discharging his contractual duties as well as the primary obligations of the other party to perform. He may also decide to waive the right to repudiate, choosing instead to treat the contract as remaining in existence. In this second situation the innocent party may recover damages for any loss occasioned by the breach.

Of course the right to terminate does not arise in every case. If the term broken is a warranty the remedy of termination is not available; see Chapter 8.

Although academics and judges are at variance on the correct terminology to apply, the right to terminate will arise in three situations:

(1) where the breach amounts to a repudiatory breach of contract;
(2) where the breach is a fundamental breach, that is, it goes to the root of the contract so as to deprive the innocent party of the commercial benefits envisaged;
(3) where the term broken is such as to amount to breach of a condition.

Repudiatory breach

A repudiatory breach involves a decision by one party that he will not perform his contractual obligations. In *Mersey Steel and Iron Co.* v. *Naylor Benzon* (1884) the purchaser of goods refused to pay for goods delivered by a company the subject of winding up proceedings, the purchaser being wrongly advised that effective payment was only possible with leave of a court. The evidence disclosed that the plaintiffs were in fact anxious to discharge the debt. The House of Lords refused to find a repudiatory breach.

A more controversial conclusion was reached in the recent case of *Woodar Investment* v. *Wimpey Construction* (1980). A contract for the sale of land to Wimpey was subject to a condition that should the property *later* become subject to compulsory purchase proceedings the purchaser would have the right to terminate; land prices fell dramatically and Wimpey, who were anxious to renegotiate the price purported to rescind because part of the land was later compulsorily purchased, even though those particular proceedings were in progress when the contract of sale was concluded. Woodar's agent indicated that his company would not accept the rescission, indicating that "we will retire to our battle stations and it goes without saying I am sure that you will abide by the result as I will." All members of the House of Lords held the rescission to be wrongful but by a majority (3:2) it was held that there was no repudiatory breach; while the fall in land prices provided a motive for termination the conduct of Wimpey did not of itself manifest an intent to breach the contract; termination was purportedly effected under the agreement itself. As Lord Wilberforce said in the leading speech for the majority "unless the invocation of that provision were totally abusive, or lacking in good faith, the fact that it has proved to be wrong in law cannot turn it into a repudiation." A similar view applies in Ireland. In *Continental Oil Company* v. *Moynihan* (1973) it was argued that a differential pricing arrangement, introduced by the plaintiff during the currency of a solus agreement was a breach entitling the defendant retailer to treat the contract as discharged.

Kenny J. dismissed this argument by holding that the conduct of the plaintiff did not evince an intention to repudiate the contract. While this may be so, it is clear that there are other grounds upon which termination may be available to the injured party. Kenny J.'s judgment seems incorrect on this point as we shall see.

While a repudiatory breach may occur during performance of the agreement it is less obvious that such a breach may also occur before performance is due. Further, the innocent party may immediately sue and recover damages even though at the date of judgment the agreed time for performance may be months or even years away.

In the famous case of *Hochster* v. *De La Tour* (1853) the defendant engaged the plaintiff to work as a courier. Agreement was struck on April 12, the plaintiff was to start work on June 1. On May 11, the defendant informed the plaintiff that his services would not be required. The plaintiff immediately sued. Counsel for the defendant argued that the announcement was only an offer to rescind and that until the date of performance the offer may be retracted. Further, until that date arrives there can be no breach of contract. The argument failed. The view that the plaintiff was obliged to remain inactive until June 1st and that he could no find alternative employment for that period without sacrificing his right to sue, proved unattractive to the court. The plaintiff should be encouraged to mitigate loss and the best way of doing this is to characterise a statement of intent not to perform as itself a breach of contract; the innocent party loses a right to expect the contract to be kept open for performance; see *Frost* v. *Knight* (1872) *per* Cockburn C.J.

While this may be so, it is difficult to see why the plaintiff should be able to immediately sue, particularly when granting an immediate right of action makes the assessment of damages speculative.

The doctrine in *Hochster* v. *De La Tour* is known as the doctrine of anticipatory breach. It has been accepted in Ireland. In *Leeson* v. *North British Oil and Candle Co.* (1874) the defendant contracted to supply the plaintiff's nominees with up to 300 casks of paraffin over a winter season. In January the plaintiff was told that due to a strike it would not be possible to supply the paraffin for about two months, by which time of course demand would be negligible. The plaintiff refused to take further orders from his own customers, no doubt fearing that if his own supplier could not meet orders the plaintiff would leave himself open to actions for breach of contract. The plaintiff sued recovering for orders already submitted, as well as for loss of orders that he would have accepted but for the defendant's statement that they would not be able to meet future orders. The defendant argued on appeal that the plaintiff's refusal to accept orders was precipitous; he should have placed orders with the defendant on the chance that a supply of paraffin might be obtained elsewhere. The Court of Queens Bench dismissed the appeal, holding that the statement made entitled the plaintiffs to immediately rescind the contract and recover all profits lost.

Fundamental breach

In this context "fundamental breach" is used to describe a breach of contract, sufficiently serious to entitle the injured party to repudiate the contract; this has nothing to do with the vexed question of the applicability of an exception clause after a fundamental breach: see *Clayton Love* v. *B.* + *I.* (1966), discussed in Chapter 7.

Certain breaches of contract are so cataclysmic that the innocent party may regard himself as free to terminate the contract. In *Robb* v. *James* (1881) the plaintiff purchased fabrics at an auction, the conditions of the sale requiring payment of the price and collection within 24 hours. They failed to comply with these terms and the defendants sold the goods to a third party. The plaintiff failed in an action for breach of contract. Their failure to pay the price and collect was described by May C.J. as a breach of "the most essential term of the contract . . . .under such circumstances, the seller may treat the contract as abandoned by the purchaser, and may detain and resell the goods."

In this context, the question of the objectively ascertained intent of the party in breach is irrelevant; hence the present writers reservations about Kenny J.'s *dictum* in *Continental Oil Company* v. *Moynihan*, discussed above, p. 202–3. This is illustrated graphically by the judgment of Finlay P. in *Dundalk Shopping Centre Ltd.* v. *Roof Spray Ltd.* (1979). The plaintiffs engaged the defendant company to spray a waterproof substance over the roof of a shopping centre. Due to various delays, and the defendants' negligence, the work was carried out inefficiently. Water seeped into the building. It was held that failure to make the roof watertight was a breach of a fundamental term of the contract namely "to provide an effective waterproofing of this roof within a reasonable time." This breach entitled the plaintiffs to terminate the contract and obtain damages for consequential loss.

Far from evidencing an intent to break the contract the conduct of Roof Spray Ltd. showed that they intended to perform the contract; their defective performance was sufficiently serious as to entitle the employer to treat the contract as discharged through breach.

The two most important factors in identifying a fundamental breach are (1) the seriousness of the breach, and, (2) the likelihood of this recurring. Students should re-read Chapter 8.

Breach of condition

Any term which the parties or statute has deemed to be sufficiently important to entitle the innocent party to repudiate the contract when that term is broken may conveniently be described as a condition (sometimes it is called a fundamental term). For example, the Sale of Goods Act 1893, s.12(1) classifies the obligation to give a good title as a condition. It may be that the innocent party will lose his right to repudiate the contract for a breach of condition. Section 11(1)(c) of the 1893 Act prevented a purchaser from rescinding the contract, (1) if the contract was non-severable and the buyer accepted the goods or a part thereof, or, (2) if the contract was for the sale of specific goods, property having passed to the seller. In the Irish Republic the 1980 Act has repealed ground (2): s.11(3). In all other cases a breach of condition by the seller may be waived by the buyer or he may elect to treat the breach as a breach of warranty and not as a ground for treating the contract as repudiated: s.11(1).

Employment contracts

While a breach of contract may entitle the innocent party to rescind the contract it does not follow that the contract is discharged by the breach alone. The innocent party may affirm the contract in the hope that precise performance may later be rendered. In contracts of employment the position is somewhat different. Because specific performance of a contract of employment is traditionally unavailable the innocent party has no option but to accept the breach. An employee wrongfully dismissed must take alternative employment should it come along. Not every breach of the contract of employment will entitle the employer to a right of termination. The test advanced in the English case of *Pepper* v. *Webb* (1969) has been accepted by Hamilton J.; "a person repudiates the contract of service if he wilfully disobeys the lawful and reasonable orders of his master." Not all acts of disobedience however justify termination by the other party. In the case of *Brewster* v. *Burke* (1978) an employee's refusal to bury a dead horse was held not to be a sufficient act of misconduct as to justify summary dismissal. A tour bus courier who works for a rival concern in his own time should be disciplined but not dismissed: *Mullen* v. *C.I.E.* (1979).

Certain breaches of contract are sufficiently serious so as to entitle the employer or employee to treat the contract as discharged. Refusal to pay wages would entitle an employee to terminate the contract; the issue of strike notice may entitle the employer to regard this as a breach of contract although Irish law differs from the English authorities on this point. In *Simmons* v. *Hoover Ltd.* (1976) the

English Employment Appeal Tribunal held that participation in a strike was a fundamental breach of contract entitling the employer to dismiss him without notice. On the other hand, the Supreme Court in *Becton Dickinson Ltd.* v. *Lee* (1973) held that issue of a strike notice, if the period of notice was sufficiently long to comply with the notice requirements necessary to terminate the contract, would not entitle the employer to treat the employee as guilty of a fundamental breach. Walsh J. in his speech expressly approved of Lord Denning M.R.'s theory, advanced in *Morgan* v. *Fry* (1968), in which the Master of the Rolls argued that notice and participation in a strike *suspends* a contract of employment.

There is also Irish authority for the view that in certain cases a fundamental breach of an employment contract may automatically terminate the contract. In *Carvill* v. *Irish Industrial Bank* (1968) O'Keefe J. said

> "there can be some breaches of contract so fundamental as to show that the contract is entirely repudiated by the party committing them, and that such an act might be relied upon in an action for wrongful dismissal, not as justifying the dismissal, but as supporting the plea that the dismissed servant had himself put an end to the contract."

Indeed, one English commentator has argued that a serious breach of contract automatically terminates that contract unless the innocent party chooses to waive the breach: Thomson (1975) 38 M.L.R. 346; (1978) 41 M.L.R. 137. This theory must be regarded as unsound given the recent decision of the House of Lords in *Photo Productions Ltd.* v. *Securicor Transport* (1980). Their Lordships expressly overruled *Harbutt's Plasticine* (1970) and Lord Wilberforce observed that the "deviation" case of *Hain Steamship Co. Ltd.* v. *Tate & Lyle Ltd.* (1936) in which a similar rule is enunciated must be regarded as *sui generis*. Thomson's thesis was based on the correctness and general applicability of these two cases.

Consequences of breach

In general, the innocent party must act promptly and decisively. In *Bord Iascaigh Mhara* v. *Scallan* (1973) the plaintiffs supplied the defendant with a fishing boat on hire purchase terms, the agreement specifying that a particular type of winch would be fitted to the vessel. No such winch was provided but in July 1967 the defendant took possession nevertheless. Some attempts were made to bring the winch supplied into a satisfactory state, but these efforts came to nothing; the defendant continued to use the vessel until October 1968 when he abandoned it in Wexford harbour. While the plaintiffs were clearly in breach of section 9(2) of the Hire Purchase Act 1946 (see now s. 28 of the Sale of Goods and Supply of Services Act 1980) Pringle J. held that the defendant should have repudiated the contract shortly after it became clear the winch could not be made to work satisfactorily; the defendant approbated the contract and thus could not rescind.

As we have seen, the right to rescind a contract for the sale of goods may be lost under section 11 of the 1893 Act, as amended by the Sale of Goods and Supply of Services Act 1980.

The consequences of a breach which entitles one party to terminate the contract and its effect upon certain contractual obligations has been recently clarified by the *Photo Production* case. Photo Production engaged Securicor to provide a security service for their factory. Securicor engaged a worker who maliciously burnt down the premises. The contract contained an exculpatory clause absolving Securicor from the actions of their employees unless the conduct could have been foreseen and avoided by the exercise of due diligence on their part. The House of Lords reversed the decision of the Court of Appeal, rejecting the view that because the fire automatically terminated the contract the limiting provision was unavailable to Securicor. Their Lordships explained that a limiting clause may operate so as to qualify or exclude liability for what would otherwise be a breach of contract. Lord Diplock in his speech described each party's obligation to perform as "primary legal obligations." These obligations may be the result of express agreement or arise through implication of law (statutory or otherwise). Upon breach, the innocent party may elect to terminate his own primary obligation to perform and in certain cases he may also terminate those obligations which the party in breach has yet to perform. This does not mean that all obligations are at an end. This is particularly true of an exemption clause. Lord Diplock argued that when primary obligations are discharged they are replaced by secondary obligations, the most obvious of which is the obligation to pay monetary compensation.

While these primary and secondary obligations may be modified they cannot be eliminated or controlled if this would lead to the contract being deprived of all promissory content.

It should be mentioned that some contractual obligations only become effective after an alleged failure to perform a primary obligation; choice of forum clauses and arbitration clauses are examples of these.

The Irish courts have not endorsed the view advanced in *Boston Deep Sea Fishing and Ice Co.* v. *Ansell* (1888) which permits an employer who terminates a contract of employment on inadequate grounds to rely on other sufficient grounds for termination even though those grounds were unknown at the date of termination. The view that an employer would thus be able to successfully defend an action for wrongful dismissal was examined in *Carvill* v. *Irish Industrial Bank* (1968). O'Keefe J. held that only where the wrongful act amounts to a repudiation of the contract of employment will the *Boston* principle hold good in Irish law. In *Glover* v. *BLN* (1973) Kenny J. went further arguing that the *Boston* principle should be expunged from Irish law. This view is to be supported; further the English courts have rejected this rule in cases of *unfair* dismissal; *W. Devis & Sons Ltd.* v. *Atkins* (1977), a decision of the House of Lords. The E.A.T. in the Republic will permit an employer who becomes aware after the dismissal of facts which support the decision to dismiss to use these new facts if they indicate misconduct similar to the grounds relied upon at the date of dismissal; *Loughran* v. *The Rights Commissioner* (1978).

D. Discharge by Operation of Law—The Doctrine of Frustration

This modern doctrine has evolved in order to deal with cases where contractual obligations can no longer be performed as a result of circumstances beyond the control of either party. The common law required a person who had agreed to perform contractual obligations to discharge those obligations; the fact that it was extremely difficult or even impossible to do so did not excuse non-performance. Thus in *Leeson* v. *North British Oil and Candle Ltd.* (1874) the fact that the defendants could not obtain paraffin from their own supplier because of a strike did not excuse their own failure to supply the plaintiff. Similarly, in *Gamble* v. *The Accident Assurance Co.* (1869) the executor of the estate of Gamble sued upon a life insurance policy which provided that if the insured met with an accident he should inform the insurers within seven days. Gamble died in a drowning accident and could not of course meet this obligation. The Court of Exchequer held that the agreement envisaged that Gamble, in his lifetime, was to arrange for a third party to notify the insurers if he met with an accident which caused his immediate demise. Pigot C.B. in his judgment expressly approved the leading English case of *Paradine* v. *Jane* (1647).

The view that contractual obligations were absolute in the sense that supervening events could never provide a lawful excuse for non-performance was questioned in *Taylor* v. *Caldwell* (1863). The defendants agreed to let a music hall to the plaintiffs for four days. Just before the first day arrived the music hall was destroyed by fire, the accident occurring without the fault of either party. The plaintiffs sued to recover money spent in advertising the scheduled performances. Blackburn J. held that the destruction of the music hall discharged the contract, viewing the agreement as subject to an implied condition that the building remained in existence.

In so holding Blackburn J. used the analogy of a contract involving a person who dies after agreeing to write a book. Such a contract is thereby discharged; the executors cannot be liable upon a personal contract of this nature. The same point is illustrated by *Keon* v. *Hart* (1869). The plaintiff and one Lyster were appointed agents. The contract provided for notice of termination of six months. Shortly after the commencement Lyster died. The plaintiff was then given notice that the agency would end six months hence. He claimed the notice was insufficient. The Court of Exchequer Chamber dismissed the action, Whiteside C.J. observing that regardless of notice Lyster's death itself terminated the contract.

Frustration of the business venture

The cases of impossibility of performance (because of the physical destruction of a person, an object or structure) present difficulties when they are invoked so as to excuse non-performance because subsequent events, while they do not make performance impossible, make it impossible to secure the commercial benefits envisaged at the date of agreement. In these cases of unanticipated difficulty, if it threatens to destroy the basis of the contract or make the contract as performed something fundamentally different to that envisaged at the time of agreement, the contract may be treated as discharged.

The English "coronation" cases are the best examples of this situation. When the coronation procession of Edward VII had to be cancelled due to the illness of H.R.H. many arrangements in which persons obtained the right to view the procession from hotels and rooms overlooking the route, came before the English courts. In *Krell* v. *Henry* (1903) the plaintiff let his flat to the defendant in order to enable him to view the procession. A £25 deposit was paid, the defendant owing £50 which was to be paid on the very morning the ceremony was cancelled. The plaintiff sued for the outstanding sum. The rooms were still available; the defendant could have used the rooms but of course because the procession had been cancelled the purpose implicit in the arrangement would not be attained. The Court of Appeal held the contract frustrated; Vaughan-Williams L.J. in his speech observed that the basis of the contract was the position of the rooms in relation to the coronation procession. The cancellation prevented performance and thus discharged the defendant's obligation to pay the outstanding sum of £50.

The courts have emphasised that a contract will not be frustrated simply because increased costs or labour disputes make it impossible for one party to perform the contract without incurring serious financial losses. It would be undesirable for a businessman to agree to perform a contract for a fixed amount and permit him to seek relief through the doctrine of frustration if, during performance, unanticipated difficulties arise. In the old case of *Revell* v. *Hussey* (1813) Manners L.C. expressed the point thus:

> "Suppose a case that very frequently occurs of a colliery, where the company has contracted to supply iron works at a price agreed on, surely it can be no ground to rescind it that subsequent circumstances have occurred to render it very prejudicial; that the coals may have greatly increased; that the expenses working the mine may have been considerably increased."

In the leading English case of *Davis Contractors* v. *Fareham U.D.C.* (1956) contractors agreed to build houses for a sum of £94,000. The work, expected to take eight months to complete took some 22 months, mainly due to materials shortages and labour difficulties. The work cost £115,000. The contractors claimed that these events terminated the contract, entitling them to claim for the value of the work on a *quantum meruit* basis, which was greater than the contract price. The House of Lords dismissed the claim. Lord Radcliffe in his speech remarked that hardship or material loss does not of itself bring the doctrine into play. "There must be as well such a change in the significance of the obligation that the thing undertaken would, if performed, be a different thing from that contracted for." Additionally, it must be pointed out that these ordinary commercial risks may be covered by contract terms; a failure to provide for these contingencies should not readily be rectified by upholding a plea of frustration. In *Amalgamated Investment Property Co. Ltd.* v. *John Walker* (1977) a building which was sold as a warehouse was listed as a historic building. This event, which occurred shortly after contracts were exchanged, prevented commercial development of the building and reduced its value from £1,710,000, the contract price, to £200,000. While it may be possible to explain the Court of Appeal's refusal to hold the contract frustrated as in part due to the purchasers' failure to show that this listing could not be revised, there was a reluctance on the part of the Lords Justices to reallocate ordinary commercial risks when the contract draftsman had failed so to do.

A contract cannot normally be discharged through the doctrine of frustration if a contract term covers the events alleged to constitute frustration. In *Browne* v. *Mulligan* (1977) Dr. Browne was employed as a physician by the trustees of a charity established to provide a hospital in Ballyshannon, Co. Donegal. His contract of employment provided that if there were insufficient funds to allow the hospital to continue in operation then the contract could be discharged by giving three months' notice. The hospital ran into severe difficulties and in 1974 the trustees purported to terminate Dr. Browne's employment. Dr. Browne argued that his employment was permanent in the sense that it could not be terminated except in specific cases which had not occurred. Gannon J. held that the severe difficulties into which the hospital had fallen discharged the plaintiff's contract. The Supreme Court overturned Gannon J. on this point; Kenny J. pointed out "if it is dealt with in the contract then it was within the contemplation of the parties and the doctrine [of frustration] cannot apply."

If however the events are literally within the scope of the provision it remains open for a court to hold that the events that have occurred are so cataclysmic that the parties could not have intended the clause to cover such a profoundly different set of circumstances. In one English case a clause in a charter party obliging the vessel to sail "with all possible despatch, dangers of navigation excepted" was held inapplicable when the vessel ran aground, the ship being under repair for over six months. The delay was held to frustrate the commercial purpose behind the charter: *Jackson* v. *Union Marine Insurance Co. Ltd.* (1874).

Frustration and illegality

Several of the cases can be explained as being decided in this way because any attempted performance would involve a breach of either the civil or the criminal law. Gannon J. used this reasoning to support his view in *Browne* v. *Mulligan*. If the trustees continued to operated the charity this would involve them in a breach of their duties as trustees.

In *O Cruadhlaoich* v. *Minister for Finance* (1934) the plaintiff had been appointed a judge by the first Dail Eireann. The appointment was for life. These courts were later abolished by statute passed by the Government of Saorstat Eireann. O Cruadhlaoich sued for salary due to him under the contract of employment. The action was dismissed. Following the leading case of *Reilly* v. *R.* (1934) it was held that the abolition of the post by statute discharged the contract of employment.

In *Ross* v. *Shaw* (1917) it can be argued that the German occupation of Belgium operated so as to make lawful performance impossible, thereby frustrating the contract; see another explanation on p. 135.

Self-induced frustration

It is essential that the event or events are outside the control of either party. It is not essential that it be conclusively shown that the only explanation for the event does not involve carelessness or fault In *Joseph Constantine Steamship* v. *Imperial Smelting* (1942) a vessel on charter exploded and sank. Three possible causes of the accident were advanced, one of which involved a finding of negligence by the shipowners. The Court of Appeal held that it was on the shipowners to show that the accident occurred without default. The House of Lords rejected the view that such a heavy burden of proof rests on the party pleading frustration. Their Lordships held the contract automatically discharged by the explosion.

The leading Irish authority on the doctrine of frustration is *Herman and Others* v. *Owners of SS. Vicia* (1942). The plaintiffs were engaged for a round-trip voyage from the United States to Britain and back again. Due to war conditions it was necessary for the owners of the vessel to obtain "travel warrants" in order to ensure safe access to British ports. The vessel docked in Dublin on the way to Britain. The owners of the vessel failed to obtain the necessary documentation from the British authorities. The owners pleaded that this frustrated the contracts of employment entered into with the plaintiffs. It is clear that failure to obtain the necessary documentation was due to the neglect of the defendants themselves; this is then a perfect example of "self-induced" frustration. It is possible to view *Gamble* v. *The Accident Assurance Co.* (1869) in a similar light.

In *Byrne* v. *Limerick Steamship Co. Ltd.* (1946) the defendants engaged the plaintiff to serve on board a ship going to England. The British authorities refused to allow Byrne a war permit. The defendants claimed that this frustrated the contract. The submission failed; the party pleading frustration in these circumstances must show that he took reasonable steps to have the decision reversed. There was no evidence that the employer had pointed out additional factors which may have caused the British authorities to reverse the decision. To this extent then, the refusal was "self-induced".

Contracts of employment

Events which have been held to discharge a contract automatically include the sinking of a vessel upon which the employee serves; *Kearney* v. *Saorstat & Continental Shipping* (1943); conscription has also been held to have this effect; *Morgan* v. *Manser* (1948), as may a prison sentence; Denning M.R. in *Hare* v. *Murphy Bros.* (1974). The courts have frequently been troubled by the possibility that an employee's illness may, in all the circumstances, frustrate the contract of employment. In *Flynn* v. *Gt. Northern Railway Co. (Ir.)* (1953) the plaintiff's contract of employment was held to have been frustrated when medical evidence was introduced to show that his medical condition was such as to make it impossible for him ever to return to his job: see also *Donovan* v. *Murphy & Sons* (1977). The position differs if the evidence does not conclusively show a return to work is out of the question. In *Nolan* v. *Brooks Thomas* (1979), a decision of the Employment Appeals Tribunal, Nolan claimed compensation for unfair dismissal and, in the alternative, redundancy or wrongful dismissal. Nolan was employed as a woodcutter/machinist from October 1969, suffering a severe injury at work in July 1973. He was only fit for work after prolonged treatment in March 1978. In August 1977 the employer purported to discharge Nolan. The injury reduced his capacity for normal manual work considerably: the employment in question was potentially dangerous even to a fully fit person; the period of absence from work was considerable—almost five years. Applying the test evolved in the leading English cases of *Marshall* v. *Harland and Woolf* (1972) and *Egg Stores* v. *Leibovici* (1976) the nature of the employee's incapacity viewed at the date of purported dismissal (August 1977) made it appear likely that further performance of Nolan's obligations in the future would be impossible or at least radically different from those undertaken by him.

It has been held that extraneous factors such as an increase in an exployer's insurance premiums due to an employee's disability may lead to the contract being discharged through frustration, even if the worker is able to perform his duties satisfactorily; *Duggan* v. *Thomas J. O'Brien and Co. Ltd* (1978). This case should be regarded as wrongly decided on this point because it is a factor outside the test advanced in *Egg Stores*, as approved in *Nolan* v. *Brooks Thomas* (1979).

In the case of *Mooney & Others* v. *Rowntree Mackintosh Ltd.* (1980) the E.A.T. indicated that the doctrine is inappropriate in cases where an employee is intermittently absent from work due to a series of minor ailments.

Frustration of a lease

The concept of a leasehold interest in land has caused difficulties in relation to the doctrine of frustration. Because a lease creates an estate or interest in land it is argued that while a building situated on the land may perish in a fire or earthquake the *estate* itself

endures. In Ireland the Landlord and Tenant Law Amendment Act
(Ireland) 1860 (Deasy's Act) creates contractual rights to enter onto
an estate in favour of a tenant; the Act does not confer an estate in
land upon the tenant: see the introductory chapter to Wylie, *Irish
Land Law*. The Act provides a statutory solution to many frustration
problems by enacting that in the absence of any express covenants to
repair, a tenant may surrender his tenancy if the premises are
destroyed or rendered uninhabitable by fire or some other inevitable
accident; section 40.

If however, the premises are rendered uninhabitable by some
event which is outside section 40 it is by no means clear that the
theoretical differences between English and Irish leasehold interests
would lead to the doctine of frustration being held more readily
applicable in Ireland. The majority of the House of Lords in the
Cricklewood case (1945) held a lease could not be frustrated, no
matter how cataclysmic the event. In *National Carriers Ltd.* v.
Panalpina (Northern) Ltd. (1981) their Lordships have overruled
Cricklewood. Frustration of a lease will rarely occur however. In
National Carriers the appellants were lessees of a warehouse under a
10 year lease, commencing in Janurary 1974. Due to the danger of
an adjoining building collapsing the local authority closed the main
access road in May 1979, thereby preventing the appellants from
using the building as a warehouse. It was estimated that the street
would be reopened in January 1981. The appellants claimed the
lease was frustrated. While the House of Lords by 4:1 held that
frustration may occur the facts of this case did not disclose a change
of circumstances grave enough to justify holding the lease frustrated.

There is an unreported Irish case in which O'Higgins C.J. held
that a lease may be frustrated. The reasoning of the Chief Justice is
not entirely satisfactory in this case of *Irish Leisure Industries Ltd.* v.
Gaeity Theatre Enterprises Ltd. (1975). The defendant lessors agreed to
let theatre premises to the plaintiffs for three years. The lease to
commence six months from the date of execution of the lease. The
existing tenant however obtained a six year extension of the lease by
making an application under the Landlord & Tenant Act 1927. This
prevented the plaintiffs from obtaining use of the theatre. O'Higgins
C.J. held the plaintiffs lease to be frustrated. Judgment on this
question was given orally; the only report of the case deals with
assessment of damages. This suggests that the case is one in which
the defendant lessor was in fact in breach.

It is suggested that the Oireachtas should declare the doctrine of
frustration applicable to leases generally; the Ontario Landlord and
Tenant Act (R.S.O. 1970) for example holds the doctrine applicable
to residential tenancies in that Province.

Effects of the doctrine of frustration

If a contract is frustrated the common law courts decree that all future obligations are thereby discharged. So in *Kearney* v. *Saorstat and Continental Shipping* (1943) Mr. Kearney's contract of employment ended with the sinking of his ship, thereby preventing his widow from obtaining compensation under the Workmen's Compensation Acts when he later died.

In *Krell* v. *Henry* (1903) the licensee was discharged from an obligation to pay the balance of £50 because that obligation had not fallen due before cancellation of the procession. It should be noted that the licensee's cross-action to recover the sum already paid was discontinued; because that obligation had arisen before cancellation, frustration could not provide a right to restitution on the ground that the licensee would never enjoy the benefits of the contract. Indeed, if the licensee's obligation to pay had occurred before frustration an action to recover this sum would have been successful; see *Chandler* v. *Webster* (1904).

A right that has come into existence before frustration then cannot be discharged by the event itself; frustration is only prospective in its effects. So in *Herman & Others* v. *Owners of SS. Vicia* (1942) the obligation to repatriate the seamen was an "accrued right" that could not be discharged through frustration. In that case Hanna J. observed that a successful plea of frustration would only prevent the employer from being liable in damages for wrongful termination: see also *Flynn* v. *Gt. Northern Railway Co. (Ir.) Ltd.* (1953).

Section 40 of Deasy's Act also makes this clear; the accident which entitles the tenant to surrender the lease serves to discharge the tenant from all *future* obligations.

The common law position is far from satisfactory. The decision in *Chandler* v. *Webster* (1904) obliged the hapless licensee to produce the sum due even though he had no chance of obtaining even a glimpse of the procession. The House of Lords in the *Fibrosa* case, decided in 1942, overruled *Chandler* v. *Webster* and held that if a party to a frustrated contract can show that no tangible benefit has resulted from the contract then restitution of money paid will be ordered. This result is almost as unfair as that reached in *Chandler* v. *Webster* for the payee may have spent a considerable amount of time and/or money in furtherance of the contract—witness *Fibrosa* itself.

The Law Reform (Frustrated Contracts) Act 1943, which is applicable in Northern Ireland permits some degree of apportionment in these cases; the Act has been adopted in several jurisdictions in the Commonwealth and similar legislation is in force within the United States. In Ireland the courts have not as yet been faced with choosing between *Chandler* v. *Webster* and *Fibrosa*; it is desirable that the Law Reform Commission and the Oireachtas provide some legislative guidelines on this question, perhaps by adding an amendment to the Civil Liability Acts 1961–4. The author would suggest that the United States Restatement of Contracts in particular, s. 468, *Rights of Restitution* would provide useful guidelines for the courts; see Kessler and Gilmore, *Contracts* pp. 794–6.

In the Republic of Ireland s. 7 of the Sale of Goods Act 1893 remains in force. The common law rules on contracts of insurance, carriage of goods by sea and voyage charters, (which are excluded from the United Kingdom Law Reform (Frustrated Contracts) Act 1943) remain applicable in the Republic. For a discussion of these rules and the United Kingdom Act see Treitel, *The Law of Contract* (5th ed., 1979), pp. 673–680.

Part VIII

Remedies Following Breach of Contract

17 Damages

We have considered the important remedies of termination, rescission and rectification at earlier points in this book, particularly Chapters 8, 9, and 16. A work that would satisfactorily deal with the full range of remedies available following a breach of contract would be at least as long as this book. The author has decided to confine his attention to the remedy of damages which is by the far the most difficult and controversial remedy in any event.

Purpose behind an award of damages

An award of damages following a breach of contract is designed to compensate the injured party and not necessarily to punish the party in breach. The motive underlying such an award should be contrasted with the measure of compensation; this was explained by Parke B. in *Robinson* v. *Harman* (1848) as being designed to put the plaintiff "so far as money can do it . . . in the same situation . . . as if the contract had been performed." While this maxim will not always explain the precise measure of damages in every case it should be noted that it is designed to secure for the innocent party compensation in excess of money spent in furtherance of the contract. In contrast, damages assessed in tort actions are generally designed to return the injured party to his or her position before the tort occurred; *restitutio in integrum*.

A simple example may make this clear. A purchases a book for £200 from B who misrepresents that it is worth £500. The book is in fact worth £150. The measure of damages in tort will be £50. B's tort has resulted in A parting with £200; A retains a book worth £150; an award of damages of £50 is necessary to return A to the pre-tort position. In contrast an action brought in contract for breach of warranty will produce an award of £350. A has a book worth £150; B warranted the book was worth £350 more than this. A is therefore entitled to be put in this position through an award of £350, the difference between the actual value of the book and the value as warranted.

This distinction is not always kept clear; witness Finlay P.'s observation in *Hickey & Co. Ltd.* v. *Roches Stores (Dublin) Ltd. No.*1. (1976) criticised by the author at 29 N.I.L.Q. 128 at 130. There are of course cases in which the measure of damages will be the same regardless of the cause of action as the recent English Court of Appeal case of *Esso Petroleum* v. *Mardon* (1976) indicates. Nevertheless the rules on remoteness of damage, mitigation of loss and the possibility of an award of punitive damages are not identical in contract and tort, thereby increasing the chances of differing awards being made depending on the cause of action.

Classification of the Measure of Compensation

Fuller & Purdue in an extremely influential article, *"Reliance Interest and Contract Damages"* (1936) 46 Yale L.J. 52, 573 advanced the view that while damages in contract are compensatory three distinct types of loss are commonly involved:

(1) *The expectation loss*

If P purchases goods on a rising market, the seller subsequently deciding not to deliver to P but sell elsewhere, it would be unsatisfactory simply to entitle P to claim back the purchase price for, as the terminology involved here indicates, P's expectation that the contract will be performed is seen as a legitimate area of compensation. If the price of the self same goods has risen P should be able to buy substitute goods. The measure of damages here will be the difference between the contract price and the price of the substitute goods at the later relevant date—normally the date of breach. Compensating the buyer on this basis also has the advantage of discouraging the seller from breaking the contract for if the courts in effect take away the profit to be made from breach of contract there will be little or no reason for the seller (other than malice) to refuse delivery to the buyer.

(2) *The reliance loss*

A purchaser who hires a lorry from a third party in order to collect goods may find that the goods are unavailable; the cost of hiring the vehicle from the third party would also be a legitimate head of loss which the purchaser may seek to recover. It must be said that such loss—reliance loss—will most frequently be recovered in cases where the court cannot estimate expectation loss because of the impossibility of finding that the plaintiff has or was likely to suffer loss. The plaintiff may elect to recover reliance loss in cases where expectation loss has not occurred as a result of the plaintiff making a bad bargain. It may be that where promissory estoppel succeeds as a plea the courts may elect to award reliance loss rather than expectation loss; justice may require the promisee recovering only the value of what he or she has lost rather than that which was promised: see the "car and bicycle" example given on p. 21.

(3) *Restitution loss*

If P has paid £500 to a seller who refuses to deliver the goods as promised P will be entitled to claim the return of the consideration paid to the seller. This is necessary in order to prevent the unjust enrichment of the seller. Restitution loss differs from reliance loss in that reliance loss may result from transactions involving third parties. In general there is a considerable overlap between restitution and reliance loss.

Other Heads of Loss

Other factors may justify an award of damages. Consequential loss may result from the breach of contract. Suppose a case where non-acceptance of goods constitutes a breach of contract by the buyer; the seller is unable to arrange an immediate resale. The seller's loss will be recoverable if it is not too remote. While this illustration may in fact be also an illustration of "expectation loss"—the resale price will provide evidence of value at date of breach—other cases of consequential loss cannot fall into this category. A splendid illustration of this point is provided by the facts of *Stoney* v. *Foley* (1897). Ten ewes, warranted sound were sold by the defendant to the plaintiff. A few days after the sale, scab developed on the sheep and the plaintiff's land was proclaimed unfit from February until June. Besides compensation for the loss of sheep the plaintiff recovered damages for being unable to let the land for that period.

The defendant may be liable to reimburse the plaintiff for "incidental" losses, for example, the expense involved in arranging to buy substitute goods when a defendant vendor refuses to perform the contract.

Punitive Damages

It is often said that there is no scope for an award of damages designed to punish a party who deliberately breaches a contract. Nevertheless if a cause of action arises both in contract and tort it is clear that punitive damages may be awarded by placing stress on the tortious aspect of the defendant's conduct. In *Drane* v. *Evangelou* (1978) the English Court of Appeal awarded punitive damages against a landlord who was held liable in trespass for the unlawful eviction of tenants.

In *Garvey* v. *Ireland* (1979) the plaintiff, a Garda Commissioner was summarily dismissed from his post. Applying the classification advanced by Lord Devlin in *Rookes* v. *Barnard* (1964) this action was held to be an arbitrary and unconstitutional conduct on behalf of the Government which was seen as meriting the award of exemplary damages against the State.

Unjust Enrichment

There is Irish support for the view that persons who deliberately break contracts because they calculate that they will make a profit from so doing, even after calculating damages payable for loss suffered by the victim, are to be deterred from considering this kind of conduct. In *Hickey & Co. Ltd.* v. *Roches Stores (Dublin) Ltd. No.* 1 (1976) the defendant broke a contract to allow the plaintiff to sell fabric in their store, calculating that even after paying agreed damages they would profit from carrying on the business themselves. Finlay P. stated *obiter* that where a wrongdoer calculates that by breach of contract or through tortious conduct he will profit thereby, such *mala fide* conduct should lead the courts to look at both the injury suffered by the victim and the profit or gain unjustly obtained by the wrongdoer. If the wrongdoer would still obtain a profit after quantifying the victim's loss, damages should be increased to deprive the wrongdoer of this profit.

While this case may be out of step with the English rules on assessment of damages—see the author's note in 29 N.I.L.Q. 128—there is Canadian support in the Manitoba Court of Appeal case of *MacIver* v. *American Motors* (1976).

"Speculative" Damages

In many situations the courts are placed in the invidious position of having to calculate damages in relation to events that will happen at some time in the future—as in cases of anticipatory breach—or according to a formula that must depend on a hypothetical set of circumstances. In *Hickey & Co. Ltd.* v. *Roches Stores (Dublin) Ltd. No. 2* (1980) a claim for loss of profits was sustained on the assumption that Hickeys would suffer loss of business even after the contract could have been lawfully terminated and that the repercussions would last (at a diminishing volume) for a further two years. Finlay P. in particular has shown a considerable degree of willingness to estimate loss of profits figures once it can be shown that loss of profits are certain to result; in a memorable passage in *Grafton Court Ltd.* v. *Wadson Sales* (1975) the learned judge observed that a court "should be alert, energetic and if necessary ingenious to assess damages where it is satisfied that a significant inquiry has flowed from breach."

A court may also be persuaded to award damages if it can be shown that a particular event was almost certain to occur. In *McGrath* v. *Kiely* (1965) the plaintiff who had been injured in a motor accident sued her doctor and solicitor, both of whom had negligently failed to bring to Counsel's attention the full extent of her injuries. She claimed that this failure adversely affected the damages recovered. Henchy J. formed the view that this injury would have resulted in additional damages of £100 being awarded. An even more extreme situation arises when a plaintiff claims loss of opportunity to earn a prize in a competition as the English case of *Chaplin* v. *Hicks* (1911) shows. In the remarkable Irish case of *Hawkins* v. *Rogers* (1951) the plaintiff purchased a racehorse "plus engagements," thereby entitling him to run the horse in a series of Irish "classic" races. The defendant however maliciously withdrew the horse from the races after the sale, thereby denying the plaintiff the opportunity to win prize money. Even though it was clearly impossible to determine the likelihood of the horse winning all or any of the races Dixon J. awarded damages "calculated" in part by reference to the horse's performance in later races. In contrast Pringle J. in *Afton* v. *Film Studios of Ireland* (1971) refused to award damages for lost future profits because he was unable to hold that it was probable that a net profit would result from the venture.

The normal practice in cases where the expectation loss is so uncertain that damages cannot be recovered under this head is to award reliance loss; in *Hawkins* v. *Rogers* the court could have awarded the plaintiff the price paid plus any expenses incurred in maintaining the horse had the plaintiff wished to treat the contract as discharged through breach. The plaintiff wished to retain the horse however so Dixon J. seems to have awarded damages simply to punish the defendant rather than compensate the plaintiff for ascertainable loss; as the report of the case observes Dixon J. felt that "the law might justly be accused of futility if the plaintiff were in such circumstances left without any legal remedy."

Date of Assessing Loss

While this is normally the date of breach the courts in exceptional cases award damages calculated by reference to the value of the promised performance at the date of judgment; see *Peebles* v. *Pfiefer* (1918) (a Saskatchewan case), and the recent judgment of McWilliam J. in *Vandeleur & Moore* v. *Dargan* (1981).

Relationship between the Heads of Loss

In principle the plaintiff should not be able to recover both wasted expenditure—reliance loss and lost profits—expectation loss. If P has hired a lorry in order to collect goods which the seller now refuses to sell P should not be able to recover the cost of hiring the lorry and profits lost because a resale of those goods has now fallen through; had the seller not broken the contract the hire charges would have been necessary in order to realise the profits on resale.

Nevertheless the injured party may choose between the various heads of loss; see the English Court of Appeal decision in *Cullinane* v. *British Rema Manufacturing Co.* (1954) followed by the Supreme Court in *Waterford Harbour Commissioners* v. *British Rail Board* (1981).

In *Waterford* the defendants repudiated a statutory obligation to provide a shipping service between Waterford and Fishguard. The plaintiffs, in anticipation of the service continuing, spent £300,000 in building a new wharf, which, at the time of trial did not produce any income because of the termination of the service. Henchy J. giving judgment for the majority on the question of quantum of damages, observed that the plaintiffs in this case could not sell the building because of its unique nature and situation. If this were possible Henchy J. continued, the plaintiffs would have the choice of claiming damages either for their net capital loss after the sale or for loss of profit.

In England the plaintiff who opts for lost expenditure has been held able to recover for expenditure incurred before the contract was struck or before the contract became legally binding; See *Anglia Television* v. *Reed* (1972) and *Lloyd* v. *Stanbury* (1971). The plaintiffs may on occasion seek to recover heads of damages that are mutually exclusive as in *Fitzpatrick* v. *Frank McGivern Ltd.* (1977). The court must be vigilant in guarding against overcompensating the plaintiff in this manner. Thus in the *Waterford* case the Supreme Court by a majority were of the view that Costello J. at trial had in effect permitted recovery for net expenditure and loss of profits, reversing the decision on this point.

Quantification of Damages

Few problems arise where the plaintiff is seeking damages for reliance loss or restitution; money spent or the estimated value of services rendered will be the basis of the award. If the claim is for expectation loss the court may, in certain cases have to consider whether the plaintiff should recover compensation for deterioration in the value of the property or the cost of remedying the defect. For example, a house that is insulated by poor quality cellulose foam may reduce the value by £2,000; it may cost £10,000 to pull down the walls and remove the offending substance. Which measure is to apply? In general the courts award the measure that seems most appropriate; cost of curing the defect applies in building contracts; *Kincora Estates* v. *Cronin* (1973). In the Republic the measure of damages recoverable against a tenant for non repair is the fall in the value of the reversion that results; section 55 of the Landlord and Tenant Act 1931, considered extensively in *Groome* v. *Fodhla Printing Co.* (1943) and *Gilligan* v. *Silke* (1963). For the measure in English law see the Landlord and Tenant Act 1927, s.18.

Sale of Goods

In cases where the seller fails to deliver, the buyer can go into the market to buy identical goods at the market price. Damages will be the amount by which the market price at the date of breach exceeds the contract price: section 51(3) Sale of Goods Act 1893. In *Cullen* v. *Horgan* (1925) a wool merchant in Cahirciveen agreed on October 26th to sell and deliver wool to the plaintiff in Dublin. No date was fixed for delivery. The defendant declined to answer the plaintiff's letters seeking delivery: meanwhile the market price of wool rose steadily until the following March. The plaintiff was held entitled to recover damages based on the difference between contract price and the market price in the following January, the date by which delivery (in the view of the court) should have taken place. It should be noted that no evidence was introduced to show an available market in Cahirciveen at the date of breach. The court instead heard evidence of the market price in Dublin—some £100 more than the contract price, and after deducting transport costs of £50 saved awarded £50 in damages.

In cases of late delivery of goods the measure of loss is the fall in the value of goods from the agreed date until the date of actual delivery; this rule will also apply if an immediate resale was contemplated; *Heron II* (1969)—providing the loss was not too remote of course.

If goods are sold in breach of condition that the seller had a right to sell, section 53(2) provides that the correct measure of damages is the difference between the ordinary retail price and the contract price. In *O'Reilly* v. *Fineman* (1942) the plaintiff buyer was prevented from obtaining a chesterfield which he had purchased in a sale for £21; the sofa had been initially priced at £24. £3 was awarded the plaintiff in damages: see also *Stock* v. *Urey* (1955).

Where there is no available market—for example if the goods sold are unique—damages are awarded on a speculative basis. Students should consult Treitel, *The Law of Contract* (5th ed., 1979) in which the well known "lost volume sales" cases of *W. L. Thompson Ltd.* v. *Robinson (Gunmakers)* (1955) and *Charter* v. *Sullivan* (1957) are considered: p.704.

Remoteness of Damage

A party in breach is not liable to compensate for all loss resulting from the breach of contract. The rules determining the extent to which damages are recoverable are in the main set out in the leading case of *Hadley* v. *Baxendale* (1854). The plaintiffs owned a mill. A shaft broke and had to be despatched for repair, the defendants being employed to carry the shaft. It was returned at a date later than could have been expected, the defendants being less than diligent in transporting it. The plaintiffs' mill was stopped for the entire period because they could not operate without the shaft. They sued the defendant carriers for loss of profits. Alderson B. observed:

> "[W]here two parties have made a contract which one of them has broken, the damages which the other party ought to receive in respect of such breach of contract should be such as may fairly and reasonably be considered either arising naturally, *i.e.* according to the usual course of things, from such breach of contract or such as may reasonably be supposed to have been in the contemplation of both parties, at the time they made the contract, as the probable result of the breach of it."

Although it is not clear whether the rule in *Hadley* v. *Baxendale* consists of one rule with two limbs or is in fact two rules the point is largely irrelevant; see Ogus, *The Law of Damages* p.72–3. What is important is the fact that different factors are material to each of the separate rules or limbs.

Under limb No.1 it is clear that loss will be recoverable if it can be said to flow naturally from certain breaches of contract; a diseased animal may render the land upon which it grazes unsafe for agricultural purposes; *Stoney* v. *Foley* (1897). Animal fodder laced with lead pellets will fail to meet the contract description and, in the ordinary course of things, injure animals that feed upon it: *Wilson* v. *Dunville* (1879). In that case the supplier pleaded that such loss was outside their reasonable contemplation. Palles C.B. pointed out that

under the rule in *Hadley* v. *Baxendale* if the consequences of a breach
of contract "result solely from the act in question, and a usual
state of things, they are the ordinary and usual consequences of that
act." The state of knowledge or expectation of the parties is
irrelevant under the first limb. So, in *Stock* v. *Urey* (1955) the
defendant sold the plaintiff a car registered in the Republic, the sale
taking place in Northern Ireland. The car had in fact been smuggled
into the North. The vehicle was seized by the United Kingdom
customs authorities and the plaintiff was obliged to pay £68 to get it
back. This constituted a breach of the implied condition and
warranties under section 12 of the 1893 Sale of Goods Act. The court
held that payment of this sum to the authorities was loss naturally
resulting from breach of section 12 for which the defendant was
liable.

If however loss does not arise in the ordinary course of things from
the breach it must be shown that the defendant in particular was
possessed of such knowledge that would enable an ordinary man, at
the time of contracting, to foresee that extraordinary loss would
ensue from breach of contract. In *Waller* v. *The Great Western Railway
(Ir.) Co.* (1879) the defendant failed to supply horse boxes to
transport the plaintiff's hunters to a sale in Dublin. The horses had
to be ridden to the sale where they were sold at a lower price due to
their deteriorated condition. The plaintiff indicated that the horses
suffered on the journey because of an earlier change in diet; but for
this change the journey would have been undemanding. Morris C.J.
in his speech indicated that loss arising naturally would be the
deterioration in the condition of the horses that were fit to make the
trip, such loss being nominal. The second limb of *Hadley* v. *Baxendale*
was not satisfied because the defendants were unaware of the
extraordinarily delicate condition of the horses. Fitzgibbon L.J.
observed that the only loss recoverable was the expense of using
riders to transport the horses plus any fatigue and inconvenience
resulting to both riders and horses.

If we return to the facts of *Hadley* v. *Baxendale* we can also see that
the first limb would not be satisfied for it was possible for example
that a spare shaft was available. Nor would the second limb be
satisfied for the law report indicates that the defendants were
unaware that the mill was stopped. The leading English cases
provide very good illustrations of the limits of the "reasonable
contemplation" test which is often said to form the basis of the
second limb. In *Victoria Laundry (Windsor) Ltd.* v. *Newman Industries
Ltd.* (1949) the defendants delivered a boiler five months after the
agreed date had expired. They knew the plaintiffs intended to use it
immediately in their laundry business and were held liable for lost

profits that would ordinarily result from being deprived of its use; the defendants were not liable for profits lost as a result of having to pass up exceptionally profitable government contracts, for in the absence of knowledge of the existence of these specific contracts they could not have reasonably contemplated their existence. In the *Heron II* (1969) a shipowner who was transporting a cargo of sugar to the port of Basrah, aware that a market for sugar existed in that port, arrived in Basrah nine days late. The cargo owner, who, unknown to the shipowner intended to sell immediately on arrival lost £4,000 by having to sell on a falling market. This loss was held recoverable. A reasonable man would, in the view of the House of Lords, have regarded an immediate sale as "not unlikely" or a "serious possibility"; when this very real possibility was prevented by the delay, thereby occasioning loss, the cargo owner was able to recover for loss of bargain.

"Type" of Loss and "Degree" of Loss

Once the species of loss is held to arise naturally it is unnecessary for the defendant to be able to reasonably contemplate the degree of loss that results; *Wilson* v. *Dunville* (1879): *Parsons Ltd.* v. *Uttley Ingham* (1978).

If however the loss arises under the second limb it may be possible to argue that where the degree of loss is outside the reasonable contemplation of the parties this may truncate the defendant's liability. In *Hickey (No.2)* (1980) Finlay P. held that while the defendants could reasonably contemplate that loss as a result of inflation may occur they would not be able to anticipate that the effects and consequences of inflation would be felt for a period of six years; the defendants were therefore not liable to compensate the plaintiffs for this head of damage suffered. *c.f.* Treitel, *The Law of Contract* (5th ed., 1979), p.720–1.

Cases in which *Hadley* v. *Baxendale* does not apply

Where the failure to pay a sum of money involves a breach of contract the measure of damages recoverable is limited to the sum in question plus interest; *Fletcher* v. *Tayleur* (1855). Despite the great inconvenience and consequential loss that may arise from the breach, the rule in *Fletcher* v. *Tayleur* remains generally applicable.

The common law judges departed from this rule in cases of a banker's refusal to honour a cheque drawn by a customer, the account having sufficient funds to meet it. The resulting damage to the reputation and creditworthiness of the customer was thought worthy of compensation; *Rolin* v. *Steward* (1854). This principle was extended by the Court of Exchequer in Ireland against a mercantile agent who failed to pay a money order submitted to him for payment by a customer of the principal; *Boyd* v. *Fitt* (1863). If however the cheque is presented by the customer himself but the bank refuses to meet it this is outside the "commercial trader" exception established in *Rolin* v. *Steward*; even if third parties overhear the conversation between cashier and customer the sole recourse is an action in defamation; see Kennedy C.J. in *Kinlan* v. *Ulster Bank* (1928). These common law rules are unaffected by sections 57 and 89(1) of the Bills of Exchange Act 1882: see section 97(2).

A further exception is provided by *MacKenzie* v. *Corballis* (1905). The plaintiff was engaged as a servant in South Africa by the defendants who brought her back to Ireland, agreeing that upon leaving their employment the plaintiff would be paid her fare to return to South Africa. The defendants refused to pay the fare and the plaintiff was obliged to stay in Dublin pending the outcome of the litigation. She was held entitled to the fare and the cost of lodgings for this period. Andrews J. explained this case as coming within the second limb of *Hadley* v. *Baxendale*; the agreement "may reasonably be supposed to have brought it within the defendants contemplation that the plaintiff might suffer damage through being detained by reason of not having any funds to return to South Africa."

The general rule in *Fletcher* v. *Tayleur* was not framed by reference to *Hadley* v. *Baxendale* however; it was designed to prevent juries from awarding damages on an arbitrary basis; this view of the origins of the rule is supported by observations made in the Irish case of *Parker* v. *Dickie* (1879) per Lawson J.

The same institutional conflict—the judges devising a rule of remoteness that took this head of loss out of the reach of the jury—explains too the old common law rule denying damages for any distress, disappointment, frustration or loss of enjoyment resulting from a breach of contract. While there are old Irish cases that go the other way—in *French* v. *West Clare Railway Co.* (1897) for example, the plaintiff recovered £10 by way of damages for missing a concert because a train was delayed as a result of the defendant's negligence—the rules laid down in *Hobbs* case (1875) were accepted by the Supreme Court in *Kinlan* v. *Ulster Bank* (1928).

In England the older cases have been swept away in recent years. In *Jarvis* v. *Swans Tours* (1973) the Court of Appeal compensated the plaintiff for a disappointing holiday that failed to meet up to the warranties given in the holiday brochure. This case has been followed in Ireland also. MacMahon J. in *Johnson* v. *Longleat Pty.*

(1976) indicated that where a builder fails to provide a house which meets the standards set out in the contract, damages for physical discomfort, loss of enjoyment and inconvenience will result: see also *Murphy* v. *Quality Homes* (1976) and the authors note on *Johnson* at (1978) 13 Ir. Jur. 186.

In cases of wrongful dismissal the older Irish cases hold that damages cannot be recovered for the high handed or arbitrary manner in which a servant (*Breen* v. *Cooper* (1869)) or an apprentice (*Parker* v. *Cathcart* (1866)) is dismissed. While an oblique attack was mounted on this rule in England in *Cox* v. *Phillips Industries* (1976)—a demotion and not a dismissal case—McWilliam J. in *Garvey* v. *Ireland* (1979) accepted that the sole remedy a dismissed employee has (subject to he or she being employed by the State, in which event punitive damages may be awarded) is an action in defamation.

Contracts for the Sale of Land

Three rules of particular importance here are:

(1) *The rule in Bain* v. *Fothergill*
This rule, which developed as a result of the particular difficulties a vendor had in showing title to land, limited damages, in cases where the vendor, without deceit or wilful default was unable to make a good title, to the sums paid by the purchaser including costs of preparing the conveyance. While the rule may have been valid at earlier periods of time it is unnecessary to-day. Nevertheless it has been accepted in *Kelly* v. *Duffy* (1922) and *McDonnell* v. *McGuinness* (1938); see criticisms of *Kelly* v. *Duffy* by O'Driscoll (1975) 10 Ir.Jur. 203. 209–10.

The courts have refused to extend the rule into areas other than real property; *Lee & Co. (Dublin) Ltd.* v. *Egan Wholesale* (1979). Attempts to limit the scope of rule in property transactions are evident; see O'Higgins C.J.'s judgment in *Irish Leisure Industries Ltd.* v. *Gaiety Theatre Enterprises Ltd.* (1975) and the English case of *Wroth* v. *Tyler* (1973). The vendor must show that everything possible was done to make a good title otherwise wilful default will be imputed; *Malhotra* v. *Choudhury* (1978).

In England the Misrepresentation Act 1967 section 2(1) has been held to produce a cause of action which is outside the reach of *Bain* v. *Fothergill*; a purchaser will, according to *Watts* v. *Spence* (1976) be able to recover damages for loss of bargain. This case has been criticised because the measure of damages under section 2(1) of the Act is probably tortious not contractual; *F. & B. Entertainments* v.

Leisure Enterprises (1976). If this is the case the cause of action will in this context be worthless because it will in effect produce the same measure of damages as *Bain* v. *Fothergill*. In the Irish Republic the point is an academic one because the cause of action given in section 45(1) of the Sale of Goods and Supply of Services Act 1980 does not apply to real property transactions; section 43. The courts in Northern Ireland have yet to rule on their legislative provisions creating this cause of action; see pp. 109–10.

(2) *Damages following breach of or an award of an unenforceable decree of specific performance*
English authorities until recently held that a person who had elected to sue for and obtain a writ of specific performance was bound by this election; if the decree was unenforceable the holder could not collect damages in lieu of specific performance. This peculiar state of affairs was established in cases like *Horsler* v. *Zorro* (1975). An excellent summary of the reasoning that produced such a rule is provided by Oakley in (1980) C.L.J. 58–67. The House of Lords have now overruled this line of authority in *Johnson* v. *Agnew* (1978) and it is firmly established in Irish law that damages in such a situation are recoverable: McWilliam J. so held in *Murphy* v. *Quality Homes* (1976) and *Vandeleur & Moore* v. *Dargan* (1981). In the more recent decision McWilliam J. expressly approved and applied rules 4 and 5 in Lord Wilberforce's speech in *Johnson* v. *Agnew*.

(3) *Deposit*
Sums paid to the vendor of property by way of a deposit may serve the dual function of being part payment and providing security against non performance by either party. In general the purchaser who fails to complete is by this default prevented from recovering this sum, the courts holding the deposit to be liquidated damages. Nor will the doctrine of unconscionability and the equitable doctrines granting relief against forfeiture provide relief. The Irish cases are thoroughly discussed by Professor Wylie in *Irish Conveyancing Law* para. 12.29–12.35.

Mitigation of Damage

It is economically desirable that the resources "released" by the breach of contract be used by the innocent party to minimise the damage that results from breach. In *Bord Iascaigh Mhara* v. *Scallan* (1973) the owners of a fishing vessel which had been abandoned by the hirer were held obliged to retake possession when the hirer wrongfully repudiated the contract. They could not sit by while the vessel was deteriorating and recover for physical damage that resulted. Further, had a prospective hirer come along they would have been obliged to hire it out to him if possible; see *M.C.B. (N.I.) Ltd.* v. *Phillips (Coleraine) Ltd.* (1974). Similarly the buyer of goods which the seller refuses to deliver cannot sit by and watch the market rise, choosing to sue when the goods in question reach an optimum price. The court in *Cullen* v. *Horgan* (1925) said that the buyer must at some reasonable point after breach regard the contract as at an end and seek to mitigate his loss by purchasing substitute goods elsewhere.

A similar rule entitles the party in breach to plead that certain benefits which have accrued to the plaintiff should be taken into account in order to reduce the damages payable. Here the object is not to encourage the efficient use of resources but to prevent over-compensation of the plaintiff; a plaintiff should not be in a better position as a result of breach than would have been the case had the contract been performed. In *O'Brien* v. *White Spunner* (1979) the plaintiff was awarded a decree of specific performance entitling him to enforce a contract for the purchase of a house. The defendant vendors who had refused to complete were held liable to pay the rental value of the property from the agreed date for completion and the date of actual entry into possession. The amount of interest that had accrued to the plaintiff as a result of having the unpaid balance of the purchase price on deposit was offset against the plaintiff's damages however.

Where the injured party has received compensation from another source—an insurance policy or a gift from friends or relatives—the common law rules prohibit those advantages from reducing the damages payable to the defendant; *Bradburn* v. *Gt. Western Railway* (1874). In the Irish Republic the E.A.T. deduct employment benefits paid from any award of compensation for unfair dismissal or redundancy but not from wrongful dismissal claims under the Minimum Notices and Terms of Employment Act 1973. In Northern Ireland the leading case of *Hill* v. *Cunningham* (1968) holds unemployment benefit deductable from damages for breach of contract. Statute often provides that certain social welfare benefits are not deductible—see the Civil Liability (Amendment) Act 1964, s.2 which provides that state and other benefits payable upon the occurance of a non-fatal injury are not deductible. However the Social Welfare Consolidation Act 1981, s.68(1) provides that occupational injuries benefits are deductible in part: an employee who recovers damages for breach of contract which has caused an occupational injury will find damages reduced by occupational injuries benefits for a period of 5 years after the cause of action arose.

Taxation

Although the *Gourley* principle was approved and applied by Kenny J. in *Glover* v. *BLN (No.2)* 1973, and considered to be good law by the same judge in *Browne* v. *Mulligan* (1977) and by Pringle J. in *Afton* v. *Film Studios of Ireland* (1971), its general applicability in the Republic remains uncertain outside cases of wrongful dismissal. Finlay P. in *Hickey No.2* (1980) was reluctant to apply *Gourley* in a loss of profits case, preferring instead to find that the damages themselves should in principle be subject to taxation; indeed the learned judge went further by holding "that the rule or principle followed by Mr. Justice Kenny in *Glover* v. *B.L.N. (No.2)* applies only to damages for wrongful dismissal and breach of a contract of service and is so expressly to be confined."

It should be noted that the Supreme Court of Canada refused in *R.* v. *Jennings* (1966) and *Arnold* v. *Teno* (1978) to follow *Gourley*.

Interest

Under the provisions of the Debtors (Ireland) Act 1840, it is possible for the courts to award interest upon judgment debts; section 26 of the Debtors (Ireland) Act 1840, as amended in the Republic by the Courts Act 1981, s.19(1) obliges the debtor to pay interest of 11 per cent. from the time of entering up the judgment until satisfaction of the judgment. Section 20(1) of the 1981 Act gives the Minister for Justice the power to keep this rate in line with current interest rates.

Whether interest can be awarded to cover the period between breach of contract and the date of judgment is controlled by s. 53 of the 1840 Act. The sum in question must be a liquidated or certain amount and the creditor must have served notice in writing of intention to claim interest at the current rate as from the date of demand. It is acknowledged that this provision is unsatisfactory; *London, Chatham & Dover Railway Co.* v. *S.E. Railway Co.* (1892) a decision of the House of Lords discussing comparable English legislation. The Courts Act 1981 seems to have superseded section 53 of the 1840 Act by providing that where money, including damages is payable as a result of the decree of the court, the judge may "if he thinks fit," award the rate of interest in force under section 26 of the 1840 Act as amended by the 1981 Act, "on the whole or any part of the sum in respect of the whole or any part of the period between the date when the cause of action accrued and the date of the judgment." It is possible for the parties, to agree to a higher or lower rate of interest than the "court rate" by making this a term of the agreement; this is particularly common in cases where a sale of land is not completed on time; *Lappen* v. *Purcell* (1965). A stipulated rate of interest of 20 per cent. was upheld in *Treacy* v. *Dwyer Nolan Investments* (1979).

Penalty Clauses and Liquidated Damages Clauses

The parties to a contract may agree that should one or indeed either of the parties fail to meet contractual obligations a fixed sum of money shall be payable as compensation to the injured party. Both the common law courts and the courts of equity viewed these covenants with suspicion, being of the view that a clause which could oblige a party to pay a measure of compensation grossly disproportionate to the injury produced by the breach, should not be enforceable. A fundamental distinction has been drawn in the modern cases. A clause will be valid if it is a genuine pre-estimate of the damage which will probably result from a breach of contract. Such a clause is called a liquidated damages clause. If the clause is designed to deter one party from breaking the contract by stipulating that breach will result in the payment of a fixed amount the courts will refuse to enforce the clause by holding it to be a penalty. The burden of showing that the sum is a penalty rather than liquidated damages is upon the defendant.

The case of *Toomey* v. *Murphy* (1897) presents a simple illustration of a liquidated damages clause. The defendant agreed to complete construction work by an agreed date. If the work was then incomplete he agreed to pay "a penalty as liquidated damages" of £5 per week. The plaintiff sued for £160 being 32 weeks at £5 per week. The Queens Bench Division held the sum to be liquidated damages.

Whether the clause is a penalty or liquidated damages depends on the intention of the parties at the date of agreement; in this context the words used to describe the clause will provide some indication of their intention. In *Toomey* v. *Murphy* the words "penalty" *and* "liquidated damages" were used so the terminology was equivocal; if the parties describe the clause as a penalty this will provide evidence that the clause is to be held *"in terrorem"* over the head of one party. There are many cases in which a clause has been described as a penalty but has been held a valid liquidated damages clause *e.g. Gerrard* v. *O'Reilly* (1843). The converse is also true; *Kemble* v. *Farren* (1829).

It is generally accepted that the best summary of the rules to be applied in testing whether a clause is valid or invalid is to be found in the speech of Lord Dunedin in *Dunlop Pneumatic Tyre Co.* v. *New Garage & Motor Co.* (1915);

> (a) The sum "will be held to be a penalty if the sum stipulated for is extravagant and unconscionable in amount in comparison with the greatest loss that could conceivably be proved to have followed from the breach . . . "

See *Bradshaw* v. *Lemon* (1929) where a sum payable upon non repair of premises was held a penalty because the loss that could result from breach would not in any case match the sum stipulated.

> (b) The sum will be a penalty if the breach consists only in paying a sum of money, the sum stipulated being greater than the sum which ought to have been paid. Thus if the clause obliges a person to pay £200 upon failure to pay rent of £50 the clause will be penal: see the dictum of Lawson J. in *Wright* v. *Tracey* (1873).

An "acceleration clause" has been held not to infringe this rule. These clauses (which operate in contracts where a debtor repays sums of money in instalments) provide that upon failure to pay any of the instalments the whole balance will become immediately due. Even though the obligation to pay the entire sum will generally be more expensive to the party in breach the validity of such a clause was upheld in *Protector Loan Co.* v. *Grice* (1880), a decision of the English Court of Appeal: see a similar clause in *National Telephone Co.* v. *Griffen* (1906).

The acceleration clause will be carefully policed however. In *U.D.T. Ltd.* v. *Patterson* (1973) the plaintiff advanced £900 to the defendant, repayable with interest by 36 equal monthly instalments. It was a term of the agreement that immediately upon default the whole amount would be due and payable. The defendant paid one instalment and then defaulted. The plaintiffs claimed £1,137.50 being the sum lent minus one instalment paid and interest over the period at 10 per cent. per annum. McGonigal J. ruled the clause penal. It was noted that if the loan were repaid at an early date the contract provided that no interest would be payable for the period after repayment; in this instance the default clause did not provide for payment of interest calculated up to the date of repayment of the principal only. McGonigal J. distinguished *Grices* case by holding "the amount to be paid on default is a larger amount than the amount actually due if calculated on the basis of the balance still outstanding and interest to that date and a larger sum than the amount which would have to be paid if the borrower had elected to pay at that point of time during the currency of the loan."

(c) There is a presumption that a clause is penal when a single lump sum is payable on the occurrence of one or more or all of several events, the events occasioning varying degrees of damages.

In Re An Arranging Debtor (1916) presents an illustration of how this rule can be avoided. Patentees installed equipment into premises under a contract which obliged the hirers not to allow others to use, repair or purchase the machinery, £30 being payable if any of these events occurred. The clause was held not to be penal; the covenants were held to import obligations of equal, not varying, importance. This rule seems to best explain the case of *Schiesser International (Ireland)* v. *Gallagher* (1971). The defendant went to Germany to be trained as a textile cutter. He agreed that if he left the employment of the plaintiff within three years of his return to Ireland he would reimburse them for travelling expenses and training expenses incurred. The clause was struck down as a penalty. It was pointed out that if the plaintiff had left employment one day after his return from Germany or one day before expiry of the three year period the same sum would be payable.

(d) If the consequences of breach are difficult to estimate in financial terms this, far from being an obstacle to the validity of the clause, will point in favour of upholding it, the courts taking the view that it is better for the parties themselves to estimate the damages that will result. While the best illustration of this rule is to be gleaned from contrasting the *Dunlop Pneumatic Tyre* case with *Ford Motor Co.* v. *Armstrong* (1915) Irish students should note that this rule was used to "explain" the difficult case of *Smith* v. *Ryan* (1843) by the majority in *Dickson* v. *Lough* (1886).

Penalty Clauses in Agricultural Lettings

It is clear that the modern case law on penalty clauses has produced different results to those that could have been anticipated under the earlier rules; see *McGregor on Damages* (1972) Chapter 12. This is particularly true of clauses in agricultural leases in which a tenant was bound not to plough land or take away meadowing or grass (*Smith* v. *Ryan* (1843)); not to raise a stone weir (*Gerrard* v. *O'Reilly* (1843)); nor sublet premises (*Boyle* v. *McGovern* (1841)) upon pain of having to pay double the rent due. In these early cases the sums were held not to be a penalty, either at common law, (*Huband* v. *Grattan* (1833)) or in equity, *e.g. Smith* v. *Ryan*. Since then the Irish courts have moved towards holding these clauses to be penalties by holding the leading case of *Smith* v. *Ryan* to depend on rule (d) above; see *Dickson* v. *Lough* (1886) and the Northern Ireland case of *Bradshaw* v. *Lemon* (1929).

Sums Payable on Termination not Breach

It should be noted that in the *Schiesser* case the clause was designed to deter the defendant from lawfully terminating his employment rather than from breaking the contract. The clause then could not be an agreed damages clause in the orthodox sense unless the contract there was for a fixed period of at least three years; no such finding appears in the law report however. Nevertheless the rules applicable to penalties upon breach were held applicable.

The applicability of these rules to hire purchase contracts has caused great difficulties for the courts in Northern Ireland and England. It is an essential part of a hire purchase contract that the hirer have a right to terminate the agreement; should the hirer so wish a minimum payment clause may be inserted into the contract obliging the hirer to compensate the owner for depreciation in the value of the goods by bringing payments up to a percentage of (or indeed the whole of) the hire purchase price. In The Republic section 5 of the Hire Purchase Act 1946 obliges the hirer to pay any sum necessary to bring the sums paid up to 50 per cent. of the hire purchase price; any minimum payment clause which seeks to vary or increase this figure would appear to be void.

If however the hirer does not *terminate* but rather *breaks* the contract, typically by defaulting on a payment it is a vexed question whether section 5 of the 1946 Act applies in the Republic so as to invalidate as a penalty any stipulation that the hirer pay a sum in excess of this figure. While the Hire Purchase Act 1965, ss.27 and 28 now provides in the United Kingdom that the 50 per cent. of hire purchase price clause will apply no matter how the agreement is terminated, (see also the Consumer Credit Act 1974, s.100) the position is different in the Irish Republic. While it is clear that section 5 of the 1946 Act makes it impossible to stipulate a "penalty" in excess of 50 per cent. in cases of *termination* by the hirer, it is the author's view that section 15 of the 1946 Act makes it clear that a penalty clause obliging the hirer to pay a fixed percentage of the hire purchase price following *breach* by the hirer remains perfectly valid. It is suggested that section 5 of the 1946 Act be amended to apply to all cases of termination.

Effects of the Penalty Clause

If the clause is held to be a penalty clause it is unenforceable. If the plaintiff can prove actual loss he will be limited to the amounts proved; the *Schiesser* case. If the clause is a penalty, which, because of subsequent events, does not cover the loss suffered it is said that the plaintiff can opt to rely on the clause or sue for the actual loss suffered; see *Wall* v. *Rederiaktiebolaget Lugudde* (1915).

Index